The
Quiet
Revolution
in Email Marketing

The Quiet Revolution in Email Marketing

BILL NUSSEY

iUniverse, Inc.
New York Lincoln Shanghai

The Quiet Revolution in Email Marketing

iUniverse, Inc.

For information address:
iUniverse, Inc.
2021 Pine Lake Road, Suite 100
Lincoln, NE 68512
www.iuniverse.com

This publication is designed to provide accurate and authoritative information in regard to the subject matter covered.

ISBN: 0-595-33060-6 (Pbk)
ISBN: 0-595-66741-4 (Cloth)

Printed in the United States of America

For Melinda, Alex, and Ben

Table of Contents

FOREWORD

Imagine a medium that allows marketers to understand and respond to individual customer behaviors like never before…a medium that helps marketers identify products and services based on customer interests and purchases, craft campaigns based on those interests as well as on past behaviors, then identify the best-performing campaigns—all within a fraction of the time and at a fraction of the cost of any medium that has come before it. This may sound like a marketer's dream, but it is all possible today with email.

Yet as I travel the country interviewing and consulting with executives, I find that the realization of such a dream is still the exception, not the rule. Email marketing has been with us for nearly ten years, but many marketers are still failing to harness the richness of customer profile data. A 2003 executive survey by my company (JupiterResearch) found that just 40 percent of marketers were using customer open and click-through rates to target follow-on campaigns. Marketers who have taken advantage of these data have not only grown revenues, but have deepened their customer relationships.

We're living in an incredible time, when Internet technologies are revolutionizing the marketing industry. However, such advancements have created an interesting paradox: Email has created such efficiency that marketers have lost their incentive to invest enough resources to use the medium properly. Because email is so inexpensive, many marketers are continuing to funnel the bulk of their budget into traditional offline marketing mediums, while passing over many of the capabilities inherent in email.

Even the largest and outwardly most sophisticated companies fall prey to this problem. I recently received an email marketing offer from the DMA (Direct Marketing Association) with the subject heading, "Every Marketer Will be at DMD NY Today…Will You?" trying to compel me to register for an industry event. The message even included a generous discount off the regular DMA member fees. The problem with this email offer is that I had been registered for months not only as an attendee, but also *as a presenter at the event*. I was even listed in the program guide. Even the figurative "grandfather" of the direct marketing industry was failing to use the most basic aspects of my customer profile to send me a more relevant communication.

Although email marketers haven't vastly improved their sophistication over the years, consumers have. Consumer email behavior is changing radically. Overloaded inboxes are challenging the efficiency of the medium. Just as consumers are getting more email messages, they are spending less time reading those messages. The spam onslaught has created an arms race. Blocks and filters are enabling consumers to fight back, but the unintentional casualties—erroneously blocked legitimate email—are mounting. On top of all of this, federal legislation has begun to crack down on email marketing operations. Clearly, the medium is facing greater challenges than at any time in its history, which is why it is now more important than ever for responsible email marketers to adopt best practices.

As an Internet industry analyst, the most common question I am asked is about frequency: "How often can I send campaigns to my customers?" This is really an elegant way to disguise the real question: "How often can I hit my customers with email before they complain?" My answer, "Whenever the email is relevant" is often met with a quizzical stare. My point is that, although the number of messages will vary based on the goals of the business and of the email campaign, the overall arbiter of frequency should always be relevancy. Understanding how your brand and email offering is relevant to your customer is one of the first steps toward adopting a Customer Communication Management (CCM) strategy.

Many executives realize that email is important and cost effective, but they can't pinpoint its true value or understand where it fits into the company's overall marketing plan. Traditional marketing metrics lead marketers to measure the value of an email "campaign" as a singular event in time (similar to a catalog drop) rather than as a mode of communication that is managed over a period of time to influence customer behavior as well as drive satisfaction and brand equity.

We've failed to move forward in our perception and use of email, in part because we've been caught up in the feeding frenzy of the last five years. The frenzy began with our race to feed off of the Internet phenomenon. We aimed for explosive growth by gathering eyeballs, growing house lists, and blasting email to as many addresses as we could collect. When the economic downturn hit, and we had to learn how to live lean, email became a cost-effective way to communicate en masse to clients. Through the frenzy and the lean years, marketers have missed the real value of email as a vehicle to facilitate relationship marketing and manage customer communications. Perfecting email requires marketers to look beyond the fancy wizardry that the Internet affords us, and renew our passion for the classic business practices—identifying objectives, assessing corporate readiness, measuring success, and focusing on our customers.

Bill Nussey's book masterfully presents best practices and tactical advice to help marketers transform their email programs from a broadcast medium driven by frequency, to a valuable relationship-marketing tool driven by the principals of Customer Communication Management. Bill offers compelling and insightful approaches to limiting email marketing risks while exploiting its rich opportunities. I am sure that you will learn from this book, and I hope that you enjoy reading it as much as I did.

David Daniels, Research Director—JupiterResearch
June 2004

Part I

THE END OF THE BEGINNING

PART 1
THE END OF THE BEGINNING

This is not the end. It is not even the beginning of the end.
But it is, perhaps, the end of the beginning.
—Winston Churchill

The world of marketing is quietly undergoing an enormous shift.

Every day, more and more people are going online for commerce, community, and information. They are being driven to the Internet by the relentless forces of cost reduction, time savings, and convenience. The online migration is forever altering advertising, customer relationships, and the communications that support them.

The changes are already apparent. Mass marketing is slowly giving way to direct marketing. Online marketing has begun building momentum over traditional offline media such as TV, newspapers, and magazines.

Underlying and interwoven with these tectonic shifts is the Internet's original pioneering application, electronic mail. There is no single better example than email to highlight how the world of marketing and customer communications is being irrevocably changed. Email is more measurable, more flexible, and more affordable than any marketing tool that has come before it. Its unmistakable advantages are driving a quiet revolution in the way that customers and companies communicate.

Unfortunately, the very characteristics that give email its promise are undermining its effectiveness and threatening its success. Email transforms the economics of marketing. No longer are cost, execution time, and expertise barriers preventing marketers from reaching out to prospects and customers. Anyone with Internet access and a mail server can now be an email marketer. In unscrupulous hands, marketing's greatest tool has become one of its greatest threats: spam. Even well-intentioned marketers are seduced by the siren call of low-cost blasting, flooding their customers with incessant and irrelevant communications.

The role of email and its ultimate impact on the world of marketing has barely begun to unfold. Many marketers remain unaware of the changes reshaping their industry. They have not even begun to consider how email, and the online world in general, are affecting the way their customers and prospects want to interact with them.

Customer Communication Management (CCM) is a new solution to a new problem. CCM enables companies, especially large multisender organizations, to not only deal with, but also to embrace the email marketing revolution. CCM helps companies understand their customers and prospects in a much deeper and more insightful way. CCM allows companies to elevate email from a marketing afterthought to a highly strategic communications tool that cuts costs while establishing new levels of customer loyalty. And CCM gives companies a new framework and set of tools with which to manage their email communications at an enterprise level. Ultimately, CCM offers companies the strategic competitive advantage to move from the marketing sidelines to the forefront of their industries.

In trying to capture the new spirit of marketing communications, this book brings together insights from the brightest and most experienced marketing pioneers in the online world. It presents frameworks, concepts, and tools that will enable marketers in all business sizes—big and small—to apply CCM practices to their existing marketing strategies and use them to transform the way they communicate with prospects and customers.

INTRODUCTION

I always get asked what I do for a living. Now, to most people, that question is fairly benign. But I tend to do a lot of tap dancing whenever the subject of my occupation comes up. Whether I'm on an airplane, at a cocktail party, or even at a family reunion, I often find myself in the same uncomfortable question-and-answer scenario. It goes a little something like this:

"Hi there, I'm Ted Smith from XYZ Corporation."

"Bill Nussey," I mumble through a mouthful of mini quiche. "Nice to meet you."

After the obligatory discussion of how we came to be at this cocktail party, he throws the big question at me: "So, what do you do for a living?"

I take a quick swallow from my drink and, as casually as possible, reply, "Marketing."

I hope this response will satisfy him; but no, he's in for the long haul. "Oh really. What kind of marketing?" he presses.

"Interactive marketing," I answer after another brief hesitation.

He probes deeper. "What kind of interactive marketing?"

I can feel the sweat break out on my brow. "Email marketing," I respond, trying to sound as nonchalant as possible.

Then it comes—the response every legitimate email marketer dreads: "Oh, you do *spam!*"

I find it funny that so many people in my industry have had an experience like this. For those of us who orchestrate email marketing campaigns for a living, the difference between legitimate permission-based email and spam is the difference between making a withdrawal at an ATM and holding up the bank. But outside our profession, that seemingly monumental difference is usually lost. If you send large volumes of email, consumers see you as "one of those people who send all that crap into my inbox."

Spam has touched off an escalating war that pits legislators, consumers, and Internet Service Providers (ISPs) against an invisible and growing army of spammers. Unfortunately, legitimate, well-intentioned marketers are getting caught in the crossfire. The popular press makes no distinction between email marketers and spammers. ISP filters mistakenly toss out our permission messages and write them off as collateral damage. Politicians who disagree on everything find a common cause in regulating email.

But many legitimate marketers are not simply innocent casualties. As the battle rages, we keep our fingers crossed, hoping that the outside world won't figure out that some of the most well-respected brands in the world are actually feeding the problem, not helping it. Hard-driving executives marvel at email's success and return on investment (ROI). If three campaigns did well, they suggest, why not send ten; and if ten worked, why not send twenty-five; and so on. Relevancy plummets, response rates drop, frustration grows, and brands are undermined. As long as the revenue stream sustains, email programs continue to get pushed uncomfortably close to the spamming tactics we all despise so much.

I Love Email

Few marketing tools are more misunderstood, maligned, or abused than email. But despite the obvious missteps, email marketing not only survives; it thrives. The possibilities of this marketing medium are so profound that it promises to change virtually every aspect of company-customer interactions.

As you are beginning to suspect, I am more than an optimist—I love email. It's important to point this out, since my passion for the medium and the industry will inevitably color everything in this book. My love affair with email is not surprising. I have been in and around email for almost twenty years. As CEO of Da Vinci systems back in 1989, I was privileged to have worked on one of the first widely used email programs, Da Vinci eMAIL. Over the past few decades, watching email grow from a simple desktop application into an engine for a multibillion-dollar marketing industry has been both a privilege and a real learning experience. Da Vinci's product has long since faded into obscurity, but my belief in the medium remains as strong as ever.

When I joined Silverpop a few years ago, I told my wife what my new job entailed. I will never forget her response. "Oh geez, not email again!" But for me, it was like coming home.

The Birth of Customer Communication Management

In our day-to-day work at Silverpop, my colleagues and I regularly guide companies through the inevitable growing pains that accompany the development of any successful email initiative. A couple of years ago, I was invited to consult with a client that was really struggling with its email program. This company knew that the cost savings and measurability of email made it a powerful competitive weapon, yet the old blast-away prospecting approach was failing. They wanted to elevate their email program into a strategic initiative that would help them pull ahead of their competitors, yet their email program was mismanaged and disorganized. Multiple lists were scattered throughout various divisions, customer profiles lacked any real coordination, and there were no clear owners or policies to guide the program. Just as the promise of the medium was growing by the month, this company was seeing their response rates slipping.

Back in mid-2000, when I had first joined Silverpop, I was fortunate enough to meet with Stephen Diorio, the author of a pivotal book on electronic marketing called *Beyond-E*. Diorio made the somewhat radical proposition that response rates were not the biggest problem facing online marketers. Instead, he said, their real concern should be how to manage customer relationships over the new interactive medium. He suggested that marketers move away from using email as an advertising and prospecting tool, and to begin using it as a retention and relationship-building tool.

As Diorio and I collaborated over several months, the framework of his ideas really began to take shape in my mind. Corporations had already begun to make the shift toward his vision of relationship marketing, but they were still stuck in several areas: how to build their lists, communicate more effectively over the medium, and consolidate and coordinate their email efforts throughout their organizations.

As my colleagues and I at Silverpop began to help our client work through its email challenges, we implemented some of these new ideas and watched as a once-disparate and uncoordinated email effort was transformed into a highly effective communication vehicle. The company was able to turn potential risks into strategic advantages that have since helped them rise above their competition. Out of the new strategies and policies we developed to guide this new email program, the early ideas behind Customer Communication Management (CCM) were born.

How This Book Came to Be

While I was addressing my clients' questions and helping reshape their email strategies, I decided to look beyond my own experience. I actively sought out executives from a diverse range of companies, from Fortune 500s to thriving dot-coms. I asked them how email was evolving within their companies, and how its use was shifting from advertising to relationships. As I spoke with each of these executives, I realized that many of their problems *and solutions* were remarkably similar. There were clearly "best practices" that crossed industries and company sizes. Much of what these executives were learning wasn't new, yet forums for publishing and sharing their ideas were nonexistent.

After six months of asking and listening, I confirmed what I had suspected all along: there were approaches and strategies out there that already worked. The email programs that succeeded didn't necessarily spend the most money or blast out the most messages. Instead, they focused on building meaningful, long-term customer relationships.

It became clear to me that a valuable commodity was locked up in the heads of my colleagues, my clients, and other industry leaders. It became clear that I needed to put these new ideas into writing.

What Is This Book About?

It's easier to start with what this book is *not* about. This book is not about choosing the right colors or fonts for your email. It is not about crafting the most perfectly worded subject line. It is not even about developing the best promotional offers to increase your conversion rates. Although I will touch on some of these subjects, they are not the driving forces behind this book.

What else is this book *not* about? It's not about using email as a lead-generation tool. Many good sources of information exist on how to buy lists, target new recipients, and drive conversion rates from complete strangers. This book is not one of them. Although there are certainly circumstances in which email-based lead generation makes sense, I firmly believe that this aspect of email marketing will continue to decline in effectiveness until it is no better than any other medium, offline or online. Unless a recipient knows the sender, messages are very unlikely to be read.

So what *is* this book about?

As I spend more time traversing our industry and addressing the needs of my clients, it is becoming increasingly clear to me that email marketing is changing. It is evolving beyond a tactical line item for an interactive marketing project. It is becoming more than compiling the biggest list for message blasting.

In the new world of marketing, the rules are changing. What has worked for direct marketers over the last thirty years will not necessarily work now. Email marketing practices must change in the years ahead. If not, companies will risk wasting precious marketing dollars, damaging their brand value, and alienating their customers. And, in light of the new anti-spam legislation, the penalties for doing email poorly can now be measured in the millions of dollars and even jail time. Marketers must shift their thinking if they want to achieve the promise of email marketing while avoiding the pitfalls of the new marketing environment. Forget advertising. Think loyalty and communication.

Email is undergoing a quiet revolution. It is changing from a poorly utilized marketing tool into a strategic, enterprise-wide communication tool.

At Silverpop, we consider the driving force behind this revolution Customer Communication Management, or CCM. And *that* is what the book is about.

Chapter 1

THE QUIET REVOLUTION

Every generation needs a new revolution.
—Thomas Jefferson

Long Live Email Marketing

In the late 1800s, an amazing new technology was sweeping America and the world. From big cities to small towns, it was transforming the way people lived. At home, it allowed people to enjoy greater comfort than ever before. At work, it dramatically increased productivity and paved the way for the development of new goods and services.

Yet even as people everywhere were marveling at how this new technology was improving their lives, they were anxious about its drawbacks. When used incorrectly or irresponsibly, it could literally kill—and it did. As the death toll rose, newspaper headlines began to predict the demise of this otherwise amazing technology.

This story always comes to mind when I think of our industry. A little more than a century later, the newspapers are predicting the demise of our industry's technology, email. "Is the Future of Email Under Cyberattack?" warns *USA Today*,[1] "Email is crippled, concussed by an irrepressible spam stream," moans the *New York Times*,[2] and "Email: Killer App—Or Just a Killer?" asks *Business Week*.[3]

A few years ago, email was poised to revolutionize the marketing industry. Marketers were touting the medium as their next Holy Grail. It was faster, more measurable, and more personalized than traditional marketing campaigns—plus it was about 99 percent cheaper. Now, email has become overused, abused, and rendered all but useless. So what happened? The same assets that made the medium so revolutionary—its speed, cost-effectiveness, and unprecedented reach—also created its greatest stumbling block.

The public once welcomed the open flow of ideas and information that email delivered. Today, they are left reeling under an assault that clogs their inboxes with offers to "Get a Ph.D. online," "Earn million dollar commissions for moving money out of Nigeria," or "Add inches to your..." You get the picture. In 2003, unwanted messages (the ubiquitous *spam*) accounted for about 50 percent of all email.[4] The total number of spam messages sent out is expected to reach more than 645 billion per year by 2007.[5] A quarter of users polled by the Pew Research Center said spam was driving them so nuts that they were forced to cut down on their overall email use.[6] The Holy Grail had turned into a holy nuisance.

So why does everyone keep using email?

The answer is simple: It still works. Despite the assault of spam, most people still prefer email communication over the telephone and fax. In a recent survey by META Group, 80 percent of businesspeople said they would rather communicate by email than by traditional mediums such as phone or postal mail.[7]

History will most likely view electronic mail as one of the most profound inventions of the late-twentieth century. Ever since a young computer engineer named Ray Tomlinson sent the very first electronic message (to himself) in 1971, email has slowly and irrevocably been changing the way people communicate. What other technology can make these boasts?

- Email instantly crosses time zones, erasing geographical boundaries.
- It allows communication with one person—or a thousand—with equal ease.
- It enables people to easily store, retrieve, and organize their communications with unprecedented speed.
- It automatically creates an audit trail whenever it is used.
- It can deliver information in practically any format to almost any device: desktop computer, cell phone, wireless personal digital assistant, or printer.

- It can enhance plain text with pictures, video, sound, and animation.
- It can communicate with virtually anyone, anywhere on the planet, within seconds via a simple address.

The Promise of Email Marketing

A friend of mine, Susan White, runs a well-respected email marketing firm out of Southern California called WhiteSpeed. She tells a story that describes the unique value of email more effectively than anything else I can think of:

So there I was, sitting in the office of the head of marketing for one of the world's top fragrance companies. I noticed a copy of *People* magazine on his desk, opened to a full-page ad for one of his latest perfume products.

"Do you know how many people actually saw this particular ad?" I asked him.

"Well, circulation on that magazine is approximately 25 million and we assume a percentage saw that ad," he answered.

"No," I responded, "Exactly how many people read this article, and who were they? Where do they live? Are they customers already?"

He looked at me for a moment and then said, "I have no idea."

"Okay then," I continued, "How many people actually purchased something from this ad?" Again he could not give me an exact number.

"Do you think any of your readers will rip out this page, stick it in an envelope, address it, stamp it, and send it to a friend who they are sure will want to buy your product?"

"No."

"How much did you pay for this?" I asked him.

"About $50,000," he answered.

Now that I had his full attention, I asked, "What if I could tell you how many and exactly which people read your ad, what they did after they read it, and then I could ensure that thousands of them would send a copy of it to their closest friends?"

His answer was instant, "I would do it in a heartbeat."

I crossed my arms, stared him straight in the eye and said, "Then why won't your marketing department allocate $15,000 so that I can give you these real-time results?"[8]

Even as a customer-acquisition tool, email has profoundly and permanently changed how customers and businesses interact.

Let's step back for a minute and look at just how pervasive this new medium has become. International Data Group (IDG) estimates that *1 billion* email boxes were in use at the end of 2003. Email volume is expected to increase to 60 billion by 2006.[9]

Email use is growing in virtually every demographic. An estimated 92 percent of teenagers in the United States send email on a regular basis.[10] Nearly two-thirds of employed Americans have Internet access, and 98 percent of them use email at work. And 88 percent check their email account at least once a day.[11]

The statistics are impressive...but they don't even scratch the surface. Add the rapid growth of email use over wireless devices, the explosion of the technology in developing nations, and the increased access to broadband in the United States, and you can see that email has not even begun to reach its potential. The reason people use email, and the reason they will keep using email, is that it saves them time and it makes their lives easier.

Email is an effective tool for recipients, but it is an even more effective tool for organizations that need to communicate with large groups of stakeholders. Compare the cost and effort of putting together an email campaign to that of email's close relative, traditional direct marketing. Email costs about $5 to $7 per thousand. The cost of direct mail can reach *$500* to *$700* per thousand.[12] And whereas the cycle time of a direct mail campaign is usually measured in weeks or months, email campaigns can be executed within days, or even hours.

Beyond cost, email has several unique characteristics that set it apart from traditional marketing mediums:

- Email allows for greater personalization with little or no additional cost.

- It provides greater insight into the reader's actions through measurable events such as message opens, hyperlinks clicked, and messages forwarded.
- It allows marketers to quickly and easily test the success of promotions and creative treatments.
- It enables mass customization so that the content and timing of each message is unique to each recipient.

Sophisticated marketers exploit these advantages every day. As Matt Corey, vice president of marketing at furniture retailer The Bombay Company, says, "Email is the perfect tool to manage short-term communications and challenges. We never plan in advance for situations where we are undersold on a piece of furniture, so we have limited resources in place to deal with the problem. Email is an ideal solution. We can put together a targeted campaign to drive sales. It takes very little time and costs almost nothing. No tool can match email in this capacity."

The Perils of Email

When it comes to understanding explicitly and implicitly what customers want, and being able to individually (and cost-effectively) target customers with just the information or promotion they need, email has no peer. So why do so many email marketing campaigns still miss the mark? Because marketers fail to do just those things—they don't understand their customers, and they don't target them.

Many marketers have taken advantage of email's relatively low cost by building the largest lists possible, and then *blasting* out the same message to every address they have collected. They seem to forget that every recipient has unique wants and needs.

Imagine that a bachelor is looking for the woman of his dreams. He could start by walking up to every woman he meets and asking for her hand in marriage. After a few slaps in the face (or worse), he might step back and think about his predicament. He might consider what kind of woman would be compatible with him, and frequent the places where this type of woman would be likely to hang out. After striking up a conversation with several different women, he might ask one out on a date. Only after narrowing his search down to one woman and dating her for several months (or years), will our bachelor get a "yes" in response to his proposal.

Now, if the bachelor had persisted in his first approach, he might have eventually found one woman who was crazy enough to marry him. Say that he was successful, and he wound up engaged. What would happen if the other bachelors in town saw his success and tried to mimic his approach? Every self-respecting woman would run at the sight of an approaching male. An aggressive proposal strategy might work for one bachelor, but the same strategy would fail if hundreds tried it. And, even if one hasty proposal received a "yes", the resulting marriage would have little chance of lasting without a meaningful relationship behind it.

It seems obvious, but yet many marketers have been following the bachelor's first approach. Rather than engaging in a communication with their customers, finding out what they want, and then asking for their *permission* to send them information that is relevant to them, many marketers are sending out reams of unfocused, irrelevant messages and then crossing their fingers, hoping that their customers will respond.

The famous author Mark Twain once wrote a friend, "I would have written you a shorter letter but I didn't have time." If Twain had been an email marketer, he might have said, "I would have targeted you with more personalized messages, but I didn't have the budget." An industry CEO I know says that his biggest challenge is to sell his clients on the benefits of segmenting and targeting, when it is generally easier and less expensive for them to blast messages to their entire list.

Yes, email communication is inexpensive. Yes, blasted messages reach a lot of inboxes. But the practice of "Spray and Pray" just doesn't work as well as it used to. People simply get too many messages and they don't have time to read them all. Irrelevant messages are deleted, regardless of permission, time of day, or stylishness of design.

And while consumers are busily deleting this deluge of irrelevant, yet legitimate, messages, they are simultaneously being pummeled by the largest deluge of all—unabashedly illegitimate, inappropriate, and sometimes nasty email offers. As legitimate marketers have used email (albeit misguidedly) to expand their customer base and increase revenues, a number of far less scrupulous entrepreneurs have grabbed hold of the technology and gone hog wild.

A Few Bad Apples

The problem with any truly worthwhile revolution is that somewhere along the way, the bad guys will always try to get a piece of the action. They take an otherwise great cause (or idea or technology) and twist it to fit their own agenda. In the case of email, these scoundrels are creating the greatest scourge of the Internet era: spam.

In the neighborhood of email, spammers are bringing down property values and giving legitimate email marketers (see my cocktail party story at the beginning of the Introduction) a bad name.

The economics of sending large volumes of email is one of the chief reasons that spam exists. "If the U.S. Postal Service announced today that third-class mail was now less than a penny, within one week, our driveways would be covered with third-class mail," says John Ripa, head of e-products at Acxiom.[13] Spammers have capitalized on the speed, reach, and affordability of email to pummel our email boxes with billions of unwanted, unsolicited, and irrelevant messages.

But the efforts of spammers have not gone unnoticed. The outcry against these high volumes of irrelevant and often inappropriate messages has been loud and nearly universal. The cries have echoed through consumer households, the boardrooms of Fortune 500 companies, the data centers of large Internet Service Providers, and the halls of governments around the world.

One Internet vigilante was fed up enough to take matters into his own hands. After receiving countless ads promising to enlarge his organ (not the musical kind), a frustrated Silicon Valley computer programmer threatened employees of a Canadian Internet advertising agency with torture, mutilation, and castration. It was the first (and it probably won't be the last) documented case of "spam rage".

The war on spam may not always be this extreme, but it is well under way, and the battlefront is changing every day. The combined efforts of legislators, technologists, and consumers are proving a formidable opponent, forcing spammers out of the shadows and hopefully, out of business. While I was working on this book, the federal government passed the first sweeping anti-spam legislation (the *CAN-SPAM Act of 2003*), which, among other things, makes it criminal for spammers to hide their identities. We probably won't feel the full implications of the new law for another year or more, but hopefully CAN-SPAM will prove a serious combatant in the war on spam.

Unfortunately, even if the email overload eases, spam will never be fully excised from the Internet. Even though the law should slow down the flood of fraudulent email over the long term, it will continue to allow unsolicited email, provided that unsubscribes are honored. And even with spam significantly curtailed, blasting and other questionable tactics are likely to remain. The email glut may never go away—*but it doesn't really matter.*

"What?" you might be thinking, "If the glut gets any worse, people will stop using email altogether, right?"

Wrong. It doesn't matter how full people's inboxes become. They will adapt. People continue to drive cars despite the traffic, deadly accidents, and pollution. They continue to watch TV despite the commercials and questionable quality. The fact is, people have adapted to much worse than overflowing inboxes for the sake of something they want. Email may not be as straightforward as it once was, but it is far from being rendered ineffective.

Changing Attitudes

Thanks to email abusers, we have begun to regard our inboxes with a significant amount of trepidation. Remember when we could leave the house without worrying about locking the front door? There was a time when we could leave our inboxes similarly unguarded. Back then, we received only good messages. Those innocent times are no more. Now, just as we buy sophisticated alarm systems for our homes and refuse to open our door to strangers, we buy spam filters and hesitate before giving out our email address to those we don't know. The new economics of marketing and the global nature of the Internet will probably require us to continue looking over our proverbial shoulder when it comes to managing our inboxes.

The inbox environment has changed—that much is undeniable. But people are amazingly adaptable. Just as they have adapted to changes everywhere else in their world, they will adapt to changes in email practices. Think back about thirty years, when there were only three or four networks on television. Back then, parents could leave their children in front of the set without having to worry about what they'd see. About the most questionable show airing was *Gilligan's Island*. Today, leave kids alone in front of the set with a remote control in their hands, and they're likely to be exposed to explosions, bloody fights, and some rather provocative views of the human anatomy. So what did parents do? They adapted. They took away the remote. They purchased parental-lock technology. They began to watch with their children. People haven't turned off their TVs, just as they will not stop reading email. They will continue to develop simple techniques that will enable them to manage ever-increasing volumes of irrelevant email.

Ask yourself this question: If you get a message from your mom (or your spouse, best friend, boss, or anyone else you care about), can you find that message amid the clutter of your inbox? Most people immediately say "yes." Next question: How hard was it to find that message or to recognize that its sender was someone you wanted to hear from? Again, most people say, "pretty easy." Has the lightbulb gone off? The fact is, most people can easily separate the messages they want to read from the trash.

To put themselves in the former category, marketers need to do two things: First, they must adapt to the reality that email may be less effective for introductions and prospecting than it used to be. Second, they need to get themselves on the short list of senders their customers want to hear from.

A New Way of Thinking: Customer Communication Management

As I've mentioned, email is driving a quiet revolution, and it has permanently shifted the fundamental economics of marketing (not to mention communications in general). It has given marketers an unparalleled opportunity to understand and reach their stakeholders.

But its rampant abuse has also made consumers more cautious about sharing information and pickier about which companies they invite into their inboxes and wallets.

How do we as marketers make sure that our messages are read and acted upon by the stakeholders we want to communicate with? We do it by building a relationship with our customers. Think about it this way: Who would you be more likely to trust—a guy who pulls you aside in a parking lot and tries to sell you stereo equipment out of his car trunk, or a friend from work who invites you to her home to sample a new line of cooking products? The friend from work, of course. She has already earned your trust, and she will more likely earn your dollar.

Marketers must adapt to the new world of electronic communications by building trust with their prospects and customers. Befriend and learn about your customers rather than try to sell to them en masse. Make the effort to look at them as individuals rather than as a generic audience. Focus on what is relevant to them rather than on what you think you want to say. These are the simple principles behind *Customer Communication Management (CCM)*. To put it another way, CCM is about transforming email from a cheap communication tool that benefits marketers into a powerful relationship tool that benefits customers.

The Future of Email Marketing

Email marketers will undoubtedly face some rough roads ahead. Hopefully, by the time you read this book, some of the challenges facing marketers and email users will have been addressed by technology and legislation. But regardless of the path email takes, I firmly believe that it is going to significantly and permanently affect the way organizations communicate and build customer relationships.

Remember that technology I mentioned in the beginning of the chapter? Despite quite a bit of bad press in its early years, it prevailed. Electricity went on to transform every aspect of our civilization.

Looking back a hundred years, it's almost impossible to believe that anyone questioned the impact and the future of electricity. Any negative effects of the technology have been far outweighed by its positive life-altering contributions. Although I don't believe email will have anywhere near the world-changing impact of electricity, it is equally shortsighted to predict its demise at this stage in its life cycle. Provided that we learn how to handle it correctly, email will undoubtedly survive the challenges it faces. One day, we'll look back and laugh at the idea that we thought we could live without it.

Winston Churchill's quote is true of email today. "This is not the end. It is not even the beginning of the end. But it is, perhaps, the end of the beginning." The old era of email blasting and spam may never die, but it is slowly beginning to decay. The new era of email marketing will see a fundamental shift—from mass marketing to truly individualized conversations, one customer at a time.

I hope you find the rest of this book helpful and actionable. To adapt a bit from Mr. Churchill's brilliant words—On to the beginning of the middle…

Chapter 2

FORGET EVERYTHING YOU KNOW

It is not necessary to change. Survival is not mandatory.
—W. Edwards Deming

Email is a remarkable communications tool. It was powerful in its early days, when everyone was buzzing about what the new technology could accomplish, and it remains powerful today. The features that made email so effective years ago—its speed, low cost, and reach—are just as beneficial now. But a lot has changed in the email environment since then. *The world of email marketing has changed dramatically, and the old ways simply don't work as well as they used to.*

The original email marketing techniques—build a big list and blast to it all the time—struggle to work today because they can undermine an otherwise legitimate marketing effort. The approaches that *do* work aren't complex, but they do require email marketers to shift—and sometimes radically shift—their thinking. Some of the most flagrant examples of bad email marketing are no more than well-intentioned companies sticking blindly to the old ways.

A Story About My Credit Card Company

Like many businesspeople, I have one of those fancy corporate credit cards that I use for traveling and entertaining. The annual fee entitles me to a number of special services wherever I travel and for whatever items I purchase. And, to my credit card company's credit (pun intended), they provide great service. Most of the time.

About a year and a half ago, I received a letter inviting me to take part in my credit card company's email marketing program. The letter promised that I would receive offers, rewards information, statements, etc. Because *I love email* (have I mentioned that?), it was only natural for me to want to try it out.

I opted-in and began receiving a few emails here and there. Although the content was not eye-catching, I was enjoying the benefits of regular communication with a critical vendor. Then I started receiving Concert Promotions. It is important to capitalize "Concert Promotions" because my credit card company clearly believed that I absolutely needed to receive concert information. In reality, I'm not much of a concertgoer, and I am definitely not looking for my credit card company to handpick concerts for me. But, I figured, since the company had taken the time to send me weekly Concert Promotions, the messages must contain something worthwhile.

When I finally opened one of the messages, I discovered the single longest email I had ever received—almost eight pages. In it was a list of concert dates for about a dozen cities. I scrolled down to my city, only to find—*nothing*—a blank space with an invitation to click to learn more. About a week later, another message arrived. I scrolled down again and found—nothing. After opening several more of these messages, I decided to exercise my rights as a citizen of the Internet and unsubscribe from the Concert Promotions. My credit card company honored my request, and the emails stopped coming. Unfortunately, **all** of the emails stopped. Not just the concert emails, but **all** emails from my credit card company. The problem was, I had actually liked some of their emails. I just wanted to stop the Concert Promotions.

I called my credit card company to try to resolve the irrelevant email issue. The cheerful woman on the other end of the line apologetically explained that I had only two choices: I could receive all of the emails, or none of the emails. But she did have some "good" news. I could set up a spam filter in Outlook to block the concert emails. Let me say that again. My credit card company's call center was telling me that the only way I could stop receiving irrelevant emails was to manually configure my spam filter to block the messages *they were sending me.*

So I went back on the list and began a routine of manually deleting every Concert Promotion I received. Eventually, my credit card company must have heard from enough irritated customers that it decided to update its program. It sent me an email letting me know that I could now opt-in to Concert Promotions ONLY. If I didn't sign up immediately, the message warned, I would no longer be privy to the *valuable* Concert Promotion offers I had been receiving.

I deleted the message.

The Moral of the Story

My credit card company is not dumb. It clearly invests a great deal of resources to provide me with high-quality, highly responsive services. In many ways, its email program is a litany of best practices: consistent branding, 100 percent permission based, multiple ways to unsubscribe, and (in most cases) thoughtful promotions. However, while it was attending to these best practices, the company failed to address the most important issue of all: *relevancy.*

My credit card company probably has more computers than NASA. Why couldn't it figure out which concerts were coming to my city before sending me an email? From my perspective as a consumer, email has negatively affected my view of my credit card company's brand. The fact that it does such a great job of servicing me in traditional ways (great gifts, nice Web site, and responsive call center) is in sharp contrast to its willingness to waste my time on email.

Now you might say to yourself, "What's the big deal? It's just email. It's not like your credit card company is overcharging you or failing to answer its phones." To a certain degree, this is true—I am not likely to change my credit card company just because I'm disappointed with its email program. However, to put my experience into perspective, let's consider what this company is doing to its brand in unscientific, but quantitative, terms. Every month, I receive the following:

- Fifteen to twenty-five tiny brand impressions when I use the card
- Five to ten medium brand impressions when I receive postal promotions from my credit card company and its partners
- One to two high brand impressions when I receive gift catalogs
- One very high (but not necessarily positive) brand impression when my bill arrives

- Nine to twelve medium brand impressions per month from the emails I've described

Of the meaningful brand impressions I receive each month, email messages account for about half. Think about that. Almost half of the brand relationship I have with my credit card company comes from its email program. And about half of its emails are in the form of useless and irrelevant Concert Promotions. To put it another way, 25 percent of my brand exposure to my credit card company comes from one small group trying to sell me something I have repeatedly told them I have no interest in buying.

How much does that brand damage cost my credit card company? I am sure its advertising agency can tell it exactly how much it costs to increase customer loyalty, but I doubt the company has ever calculated the dollar value of annoying one valuable customer, let alone annoying hundreds, or even thousands, over an eighteen-month campaign of Concert Promotions. The effect of so many irrelevant messages most likely undermines the response rates of their other valuable and well-targeted messages. I can't say for sure, but I would venture a guess that the combined cost of lost customer loyalty opportunities and increased customer service complaints probably *exceeds what my credit card company spends on its entire email program.*

As a consumer, you can probably cite many other email programs from well-intentioned companies that are similarly broken or ineffective. My credit card company made the same mistake that the majority of large companies across the globe are making every day—it failed to realize the enterprise-wide potential (and risk) of email as a strategic, customer loyalty-building tool.

The moral of this story is simple. Even if you do everything right according to the old rules, you can still do meaningful damage to your brand and to your customer relationships.

How Does Your Email Program Stack Up?

Think about your company's email program (if you have one in place). Do you spend more time trying to grow your list than trying to target your customers? Are you interested in finding the maximum number of messages you can send without generating a spike in opt-outs? Are you more focused on subject lines than on brand impact?

If you answered yes to any of these questions, you're probably falling into the same trap as my credit card company. Every untargeted or irrelevant email your customers open from you puts a small dent in your brand. Every moment a customer wastes deciding whether to suffer through more unwanted messages or just opt-out erodes trust in your company. Every day in which your company continues to view email as an afterthought is another wasted opportunity to tap into one of the greatest sources of customer loyalty building that exists today.

That Was Then...This Is Now—The New Rules of Email Marketing

In this new era of CAN-SPAM legislation and ever-increasing customer expectations, many of the practices that worked for emailers in the past simply won't work anymore. The companies that can boast the most effective email programs today have been successful because they've completely overhauled their way of thinking. They have changed their strategy from blasting to an unsuspecting audience, to *communicating* with a willing and increasingly loyal customer base.

Figure 2.1 The new rules of email marketing

THE OLD WAY	THE NEW WAY
Interruption	Anticipation
List size	Active recipients
Subject line	"From" field
Prospecting for leads	Relationships with customers
Campaign success	Lifetime value of email customer (Email Brand Value)
Maximum frequency of campaigns	Recipient control
Communicate anything you want	Recipient control (Preferences)
Email is virtually free	Email is less expensive than other mediums
Email Marketing	Customer Communication Management

Let's explore a few of these strategy-shifts in more detail.

Old Way: Interrupt 'em Until They Respond
New Way: Turn Strangers into Friends and Friends into Customers

According to marketing guru Seth Godin, there are two types of marketers: interruption marketers and permission marketers. Interruption marketers break into your favorite television show to sell you shampoo, dog food, and jeans; they force you to flip through page after page of perfume and automobile ads before you can finish an article in your favorite magazine; and they disrupt your leisurely Sunday drive with billboards for local motels and diners. The idea behind *interruption marketing* is to get you to stop whatever you're doing and pay attention.

Interruption marketers have a good point: If they don't throw themselves in front of you, how else will you ever find out about them? Interruption marketing is undoubtedly an important marketing tool, but it can also be overused and abused to the point where it becomes ineffective. According to Godin, the average consumer is exposed to as many as three thousand interruption marketing messages *per day*.[1] By deluging unsuspecting inboxes with unwanted messages, interruption marketers have so abused email that they have rendered the entire medium far less effective.

Permission marketers, on the other hand, focus on building customer relationships. Effective permission marketers ask their customers about their wants and needs, request their permission to fulfill those wants and needs, gain their trust, and then elevate that trust into sales.

Imagine that you move into a new neighborhood. You haven't even had a chance to unpack when the neighbor from the house to your left bangs on your door. He has a timeshare in Miami that he knows you'll love, and he'd like to show you a few brochures. While he goes through his pitch, you look at your watch. When you're finally able to get rid of him and get back to unpacking, the phone rings. It's that pesky neighbor again. He wants to know if you've given the timeshare any thought. You hang up. This is getting annoying. As you take a break from unpacking to sit down at your kitchen table with a glass of iced tea, you happen to glance out your window. There, hanging down the side of your neighbor's house, is a huge banner advertising Florida timeshares. You're ready to call your realtor, right?

The next day your doorbell rings. "Oh no, not again," you think. But this time it is your neighbor from the house to the right. She says she understands that you're busy unpacking, but she just wanted to welcome you to the neighborhood. She hands you a basket filled with home-baked goodies. A week later, she calls to see how you're settling in, and to ask if you need anything. She invites you over to dinner and you reciprocate. Over time, this neighbor turns into a really good friend. During one of your conversations, you mention that you are looking to take a vacation over the holidays. She tells you that she and her husband have a condo in Hawaii they won't be using. Would you like to rent it? She has a sale.

Instead of interrupting you with a message you didn't request and don't want, permission marketers get to know you, earn your trust, and then send you personal messages that are relevant to you. As Godin puts it, *permission marketing* is about "turning strangers into friends and friends into customers."

Studies have proven Godin's idea right. An IMT Strategies survey of consumer email behavior showed that a trusted sender drove response rates higher more often than any other message characteristic, including relevancy and offer.[2]

Email, with its speed, low cost, and virtually unlimited reach, is the perfect vehicle to turn strangers into customers. But many email marketers are using the new medium to practice the old method of interruption marketing. Take my credit card company, for example. Technically, it asked for my permission. But once it had permission, it proceeded to badger me every week, hoping that I would eventually give in and travel hundreds or even thousands of miles to see a concert. Seth Godin and I would agree—that's not going to happen.

Old Way: Bigger Responses Need Bigger Lists
New Way: Size Isn't as Important as How You Use it

Shoot a thousand arrows at a target and you'll ultimately hit a few bull's-eyes. Send a few million messages and someone is bound to respond. In the early days of email marketing, messages were blasted as often as the marketer had something to say. Of course, marketers were under the mistaken impression that their customers wanted to hear everything they had to say.

But as inboxes overflowed with unrequested emails and customers' ire grew, marketers began to realize that sending more and more messages led to the phenomenon of the *incredible shrinking list*. The more emails a company sent, the more its customers opted-out or just stopped reading the messages altogether.

To combat the *incredible shrinking list*, marketers came up with a blanket rule to dictate email *frequency*. They called it the *Rule of 24*. According to this rule, twenty-four is about the right number of emails to send customers per year. Although there is no science behind this number, many companies have found, in the absence of any other approach, that twenty-four times a year is about as often as their customers want to hear from them.

Now, if your company lacks the technology, or the processes, to manage a variety of email transactions simultaneously, the Rule of 24 is a decent way to manage your frequency. But let's think about the philosophy behind this rule. It basically implies that twenty-four is the maximum number of messages your customers want to receive. Put another way, twenty-four is the maximum number of messages your customers *can stand*. Although the Rule of 24 technically moderates the number of interactions with your customer, it hasn't evolved far from the old method of sending your customers as many emails as they can stomach before they walk away from you.

Ultimately, owning a huge list does you no good if no one on your list wants to hear from you, and everyone on your list begins opting-out. Sending twenty-four emails a year is ineffective if the content is irrelevant and the timing inappropriate. On the other hand, twenty-four emails a year could be too few if your customers can't get enough of your promotions. The *New York Times* and the "Joke of the Day" both send well beyond the Rule of 24 and recipients don't complain a bit. If you focus excessively on list size and frequency, you ignore the three most critical tenets of any email marketing program: relevancy, recipient control, and relationships.

Old Way: Snag Them with a Snazzy Subject Line
New Way: Be the Friend in Their "From" Field

Nearly every email marketing book out there will tell you that your subject line is the cornerstone to a successful campaign. Adding a little "oomph" to your subject line, the thinking goes, is the best way to increase your response rates. I can't deny that subject lines impact response rates—the old way still works, in a sense—but if you focus solely on your subject line, you'll neglect an equally critical asset: your Email Brand Value.

Let's go back to a point I made in the last chapter. If you get an email from a friend (or your mother), can you find it among the clutter of your inbox? Of course you can. You look at the "from" field, see that you have a message from your friend, and open it because you're interested in what he or she has to say. Now, say your friend sends you an email from a different email address. The subject line is the same—but now that you don't recognize the name in the "from" field, will you be as likely to open the message? Probably not. The "from" field has lost most—or all—of its value.

Nearly two-thirds of email users say the name in the "from" field is what most compels them to open an email, according to a DoubleClick 2003 Consumer Email Study.[3] With the proliferation of spam, and the increase in overall email traffic, sender recognition has become increasingly more important.

When your customers and potential customers look at the "from" field of your emails, they are focusing on one thing—your brand. Only if they trust your company name and what it represents will they continue to read over to your subject line. If your name in the "from" field has come to represent irrelevant and useless emails, even the most enticing subject line is unlikely to convince people to open your messages.

When you think about it, moving just a few words from the subject to the "from" field changes your entire marketing strategy (and influences your chances of getting your message through spam filters— see Chapter 19). You're no longer solely focused on catching the customer's attention for *this* mailing; you are also ensuring that you leave a good impression for future mailings. In the end, you're focusing on the lifetime of your email relationship with your customer. *Customer lifetime value* is what turns one transaction into numerous sales over multiple years.

The subject line will always be critical, especially for promotional mailings. However, the "from" field goes beyond a single mailing—it is your brand. You need to focus on how you use it with as much scrutiny and zeal as you would give any branding effort, online or offline.

To succeed in the new world of email marketing, you need to move away from the old assumptions and adopt a new way of thinking. Rather than asking, "How big is my list?" you need to ask, "How engaged are my recipients?" Instead of asking, "What does my subject line say?" you need to ask, "How am I building my brand over this series of campaigns?" And instead of asking, "How frequently should I send my customers emails?" you need to ask, "How relevant is my email to each of my customers?"

The truth is, you don't really need to forget everything you know, as this chapter title suggests. Many of the lessons learned when email was in its infancy remain as valuable today. But a lot *has* changed. Email marketers are now operating in a radically different environment. Customers are far more sophisticated than they were a few years ago, and they have come to expect much more from the companies they interact with electronically. What's more, the penalties for practicing poor email tactics have become far steeper. Without changing your mindset or without understanding the new context, you significantly risk your customer relationships and your brand.

The first part of this book focuses primarily on the changes transforming this new world, and how they impact what we do as email marketers. As we move toward the next part of the book, we'll begin to focus on the specific rules and processes that take Customer Communication Management (CCM) from theoretical approach into practical, real-world use.

Chapter 3

THE THREE LEVELS OF EMAILERS

There are no limits. There are only plateaus, and you must not stay there, you must go beyond them.
—Bruce Lee

In the early days of long distance communication, having a conversation either meant traveling a great distance to talk to someone in person, or sending a letter and waiting weeks for a response. However, the last century has seen a communications revolution that has brought people together globally and instantaneously. Technology and the incredible pace of innovation behind it have fueled most of this revolution. First came the telegraph, followed by the telephone. Teletype machines paved the way for fax machines, which evolved into the Internet and email. Today, we have cellular phones, broadband digital video, and instant messaging. Technology continues its relentless push forward, and it is forever changing the world.

Just as technology and more sophisticated processes have enabled a revolution in traditional communications, advancements in email marketing solutions are transforming the way companies attract and retain customers. But with every new technology and every new way of thinking, adoption does not occur at the same pace and at the same speed for all participants. Just as many people waited to sign up for Internet service until they saw all of their neighbors happily surfing the Web, many email marketers have hesitated to move beyond the simplicity of blasting to more sophisticated, and more effective, techniques.

I am regularly asked to assess the maturity of email initiatives. Companies always want to know how well they stack up against their competitors, what kind of return they're getting on their investment, and what changes they can make to increase their level of maturity. After considering the question on so many occasions, I have begun to view email sophistication as a series of levels or steps.

Although there are an infinite number of ways to segment the various levels of email marketing sophistication, I have chosen the three that appear to be the most indicative of email program maturity.

The higher an emailer moves up the ladder, the more sophisticated that emailer's capabilities become. All marketers may not follow these steps in the same order or along such clear boundaries. But as they move up the list, they generally see an unmistakable improvement in overall customer satisfaction and, as a result, a real upsurge in lifetime customer value.

LEVEL ONE

Legitimate Level One emailers are just beginning to explore the medium and do not require complex technology. Level One is characterized by some combination of simple personalization and basic measurement.

In the early days of email marketing, message blasting was considered state of the art, and was nearly ubiquitous in its application. In many situations (for example, small company newsletters), it may still be the best approach. Blasting essentially involves three steps: building a general list, writing a message, and hitting send. Because it is the simplest method to execute, blasting remains the launching pad for most neophyte email marketers.

The most obvious example of the blast technique is spam. (I refer to spammers as level zero.) With little planning and relatively basic technology, spammers can blast an email promising lower mortgage rates or cheap Viagra simultaneously to millions of recipients. Spammers are the most egregious example of email misuse, but many legitimate marketers actually come closer to abusing the blast approach than they realize. If they grow their list too large and send their messages too frequently, they will find it difficult to remain relevant with every message and for every recipient.

Personalizing a message means adding unique information for each recipient. The most obvious and simplest form of personalization is an individual salutation (for example, "Dear Rick," rather than "Dear Customer,"). More advanced personalization may include the customer's account number, products purchased, or rewards points balance. Nearly 60 percent of email marketers use some form of personalization, according to a *Direct Marketing Association (DMA) study.*[1]

Technically, personalization is only a bit more complex than raw blasting, but the underlying information-gathering process is what makes the difference significant. To personalize an email, you must *know something about your recipient.* Customers are generally reluctant to share even their email address these days. When they *are* willing to provide you with personal information (their name, age, address, or shopping preferences, for example), they have indicated a high level of trust.

A study by email marketing provider YesMail found that simple personalization increased their clients' response rates from 4.7 percent to 14.8 percent.[2] And as significant as those numbers are, the real power of personalization comes from its higher upfront trust requirement. In a sense, personalizing an individual email message reflects back the trust your recipient initially provided. You've told them that you know who they are, and you've indicated that you're willing to go through the trouble to show them.

Measurement takes advantage of email's unique ability to track recipient actions. When a recipient clicks on your message to open it, the act indicates either a compelling subject line, or more likely, a respected brand name in the "from" field. When they take the next step by clicking (click-through) a link in the message to reach your Web site, they have indicated an interest in your product or service. And when the click-through results in the intended action (a sign-up or sale, for example), the conversion proves that your email campaign has resonated with at least some of your recipients.

Measurement can tell you volumes about your customers, but only if you use it. A study by email service provider e-Dialog indicated that fewer than half of all email marketers have the ability to measure their campaign effectiveness.[3] And many of those who *can* measure fail to incorporate what they've learned into campaign planning. Measurement is not just about reading reports—it's about acting on them.

LEVEL TWO

Level Two email marketers take one giant step toward relevancy and customer-driven communications. Their more sophisticated email initiatives include some combination of testing, targeting, and preference gathering. The resulting campaigns often require more work, but are far more relevant to most recipients. The work versus response trade-off is an essential component of Level Two.

If you advertise in traditional media (radio, TV, magazine), you already understand the basics of testing and its power to improve response rates. Perhaps you've analyzed Nielsen ratings, or brought a group of demographically diverse people into a room and watched from behind a two-way mirror as they discussed their preferences for soap, Internet service, or salad dressing. Traditional marketers test constantly—at great effort and at great expense.

Testing an email campaign is far less expensive than testing in traditional media, yet surprisingly few email marketers make it a regular part of their campaign execution. Testing is an integral part of designing an email campaign. You can (and should) routinely pull apart every element of your email—the look and feel, offer, subject line, etc.—to find out what works and what doesn't.

The easiest way to test is to randomly select several subsets of your target list and send each one a separate mailing, tweaking one or more elements at a time. You may try different subject lines, or experiment with content layout or colors. You may offer a percentage discount in one email, or extend your customers a free trial offer in another.

After each test, you use the elements that earn the highest response as a foundation to design subsequent mailings. Developing a test requires additional technical work, but once you have your test set up, you'll quickly realize the benefits of increased response rates and improved customer loyalty.

Testing will drive your relevancy higher for each campaign. But another aspect of Level Two email—*targeting*—enables your messages to become even more relevant. Targeting takes you far beyond list blasting by letting you select a subset of customers that are more closely aligned with the content you want communicate. Targeting finally moves you beyond the one-size-fits-all model.

The first step in targeting is to make educated guesses or smart choices about what specific recipient groups want to hear. For example, Tommy Hilfiger could send a winter wear promotion to people in New York City immediately after a big snowstorm. Similarly, American Airlines could target upgrades to customers who have flown more than fifty thousand miles within the year, or Drugstore.com could send reminders to people who have not logged in or made a purchase within the last year. You get the idea. We'll discuss targeting and testing in greater detail in Chapter 20.

A more precise variation of targeting factors in customer *preferences*. (See Chapter 11 for more on preferences.) If you visit the Lands' End Web site, you will be invited to opt-in to the company's newsletter. When you enter your email address, you'll be asked to choose your preferences: Would you like to receive emails weekly, monthly, or twice monthly? Do you want to receive product news for men, women, women's plus, kids, or the home?

Lands' End does not assume that every one of its customers wants to receive email on every topic. And rather than make a guess based on customer demographics, Lands' End explicitly asks each person for their preferences—what messages they want to receive (preferences) and how often they want to receive them (frequency). Lands' End builds its list based on these customer preferences, and then sends newsletters only to people who have asked to receive them, when they have asked to receive them.

Targeting, despite its obvious benefits, is an underutilized tool. The DMA study referenced earlier in the chapter revealed that just under half of email marketers surveyed do some kind of targeting.[4] Regardless of whether you are asking customers what type of information they want to receive, or making smart guesses based on demographics, targeting takes you one step closer to ensuring that your messages are relevant.

LEVEL THREE

This highest level of email sophistication goes beyond blasting and even beyond selecting subsets of a list. Level Three email programs take relevancy to the highest possible degree, using such techniques as dynamic content, life cycle automation, and deep analytics. These approaches combine the best of personalization and targeting, plus they add in the dimension of time to improve relevancy. Level Three treats each outgoing message as unique and each recipient as an individual.

Many marketers see *dynamic content* as a form of personalization, but it goes far deeper than just filling in the customer's first name or account number. Dynamic content rewrites entire sections of a message in a way that is unique to each recipient. If you owned a clothing company, for example, you could create two content blocks for your monthly mailing—a promotion for pink sweaters for the women, and a promotion for blue sweaters for the men. The benefit of dynamic content is that each customer receives a highly customized, and thus highly relevant, message. If each message contains four or five dynamic sections with fifteen or twenty content options per section, the number of permutations becomes so high that each recipient can end up receiving a completely unique message. Dynamic content offers a dual benefit: it dramatically increases relevancy while being automated to the point that it can still achieve some of the cost savings of mass mailings.

Life cycle automation (or campaign automation) takes personalization to the highest level. Whereas blasting sends to everyone on a list, and targeting sends to a specific subset of a list, life cycle automation sends one message to one person at a time. Sequencing messages allows for one of the most underutilized but powerful aspects of relevancy—timing. Examples include individual renewal notices sent a month or two before a magazine subscription is set to expire, or bill reminders sent when payment is due and followed up when the account is past due. Rather than sending messages in a large-volume blast, life cycle automation uniquely times each message (using business rules and analytic tools) to be relevant to each recipient. Life cycle marketing automates communications between a company and its customers for the lifetime of a campaign.

Chapters 6 and 20 discuss dynamic content and life cycle automation in more detail, but they are mentioned here because they are both great examples of Level Three emailing. These advanced techniques should be distinguished from *auto responders* and similar mechanisms which, although automated, are very limited and therefore probably do not qualify for Level Three. True Level Three techniques combine timing and content to target the user with a highly relevant, highly personalized message.

The last component of Level Three is *analytics*. Every few weeks, Amazon.com sends me an email recommending the latest book, DVD, and CD releases. I don't necessarily need to buy a new book, DVD, or CD every few weeks, but I always open the email. Why? Because nearly every email contains something of interest to me. Amazon.com knows what I like to read, what movies I like to watch, and what recording artists I like to listen to, because every time I make a purchase on its site, it makes a note of it. When a new book by Jim Collins comes out, they remind me. When a new Disney DVD is released, Amazon lets me know ahead of time so I can pre-order a copy. Amazon.com not only meets my needs as a consumer—it anticipates them.

The sort of advanced targeting that Amazon.com practices not only requires sophisticated technology, but it also requires a unique kind of marketing expertise. By analyzing past data (in Amazon's case from past purchases and searches), database marketing experts can target customers by their interests or predicted behavior.

Examples of predictive analytics can range from simple approaches, such as matching author names from past purchases, to more complex systems, such as automated collaborative filters (ACFs). ACFs look at groups of users and find similarities between them based on common interests. Using this technology, a company can predict that you will like a certain product because *people just like you* have already said that they like the product.

Advanced predictive modeling goes even beyond matching and ACF by incorporating statistics. In one predictive approach, you can determine a customer's likelihood to purchase based on past purchases made by individuals in the same demographic. In another, you can analyze historical response patterns and send out a specific promotion to those who would be most inclined to make a purchase.

A 2004 survey by *USA Today*, CMO Council, and *B2B Magazine* indicated that top marketing decision makers viewed customer profiling and analytics as the number one way to improve email marketing effectiveness.[5] When used in conjunction with dynamic content and automated sequencing, robust analytics can do more to increase relevancy than almost any other direct marketing approach, online or offline.

Technology

As you read through the three levels, you may have noticed a not-too-subtle thread through all of them—technology. The more sophisticated the email program, the more complex the underlying technology needs to be. Blasting, because of its simplicity, requires a relatively low level of technical sophistication. At the other end of the spectrum are highly personalized, precisely timed email programs, which require a platform that can not only keep track of customer data, but that can also analyze and react to data in real time.

As you climb the ladder in email sophistication, your reliance on technology increases dramatically. I have met with many companies whose IT departments initially insisted upon developing their email system in-house. In almost every instance, the system was eventually moved out of house to a specialized email vendor. The reason so many IT departments underestimate their in-house capabilities is that they view email marketing purely in terms of Level One. And even then, they often fail to consider the sophistication of basic measurement and reporting requirements. Specialized *email service providers (ESPs)* have the advantage of being able to spread their development costs over dozens, or even hundreds, of customers. Very few IT departments can similarly match the level of investment, or meet the level of functionality, that a single marketing department may demand.

Whether you outsource entirely, use an online self-service solution, or develop all of your technology internally, you need at least a basic understanding of the technology you use today, *as well as the solutions you think you will use in the future.* Ignoring the technology side of email marketing can cause your costs to surge, and/or inhibit your ability to reach the level of sophistication your marketing objectives require.

The Three Levels and CCM

The techniques used within each of the Three Levels can exist independently of CCM. You can begin to apply concepts such as Email Brand Value (EBV) and Campaign Value Exchange (CVE), regardless of your technical or process sophistication. But as your list grows in size and in diversity, you can't expect to evolve far beyond the level of blaster without relying on higher-level techniques. The more sophisticated your email program becomes, the more completely the Three Levels become wrapped up in your CCM strategy.

■ ■ ■ ■

The Three Levels are a simple measuring stick that can help you understand the state of your current initiatives and provide a roadmap for future initiatives. Surprisingly, few companies are forging beyond the most basic techniques. Although there are no hard statistics, I estimate that fewer than a quarter of large companies have even attempted Level Three techniques. Most are working hard just to build in the regular workflows for testing and targeting.

Companies that can master Level Two and move into Level Three dramatically increase their relevancy, thereby increasing customer trust and lifetime value.

Part II

THE FOUNDATIONS OF ENTERPRISE EMAIL

PART 2
THE FOUNDATIONS OF ENTERPRISE EMAIL

As any reputable builder will attest, every good house starts with a solid foundation. Likewise, every world-class enterprise-level email program begins with strong fundamentals—a set of foundational ideas and processes on which marketers can build their strategies and techniques.

Part 2 will cover five concepts that support any enterprise-wide email marketing and communications strategy. Chapter 4 discusses the book's core concept, Customer Communication Management (CCM). Chapter 5 introduces one of the more important concepts behind CCM, Email Brand Value (EBV). If, as I've mentioned many times throughout the book, relevancy is the heart of CCM, then Email Brand Value is the cumulative measure of that relevancy. Chapters 6 and 7 cover the basics of email marketing and its underlying technology. Even if you are already familiar with email marketing concepts, you should find these chapters useful because they cut through the clutter of misused terms and provide a single lexicon for the rest of the book. Finally, Chapter 8 explores the evolving legislation that is playing an increasingly critical role in the marketing world.

The following section will introduce you to the fundamentals of CCM and help you grasp the language and concepts used throughout the remainder of the book.

Chapter 4

CUSTOMER COMMUNICATION MANAGEMENT

*He who has not first laid his foundations may be able with
great ability to lay them afterwards, but they will be laid
with trouble to the architect and danger to the building.*
—Niccolò Machiavelli, *The Prince*, 1532

Email marketers in the twenty-first century are facing a paradox. On one hand, both business partners and customers are increasingly demanding that their vendors communicate with them electronically. Fifty-one percent of business users cite email as the most effective communication method.[1] Almost two-thirds of people who use email at work say they prefer it for making arrangements and setting appointments over talking on the telephone or communicating in person.[2] On the other hand, email users are straining against a flood of messages. They are responding by reading a decreasing percentage of their messages, and are often deleting any messages from unknown senders.

Companies are faced with a dual challenge: To satisfy customer needs, they must migrate their communications to email, yet they are having to work harder and harder to get their messages delivered and read.

Customer Communication Management (CCM) is an idea and a strategy that addresses this paradox. CCM changes an organization's view of email away from a tactical, departmental-level marketing line item and turns it into a highly effective tool for building and sustaining customer relationships across the enterprise. In shaping this critical transformation, CCM restores email and other digital communications to a higher-impact, higher-response medium.

In my role as CEO, I am asked the same question over and over: Won't the huge volumes of spam kill the medium? Won't spam make email useless as a communications tool? To answer these questions, I return once again to my point from Chapter 1: In the seemingly bottomless clutter of your inbox, can you find a message from your mother? Your boss? Your friend? Of course you can. You can find any message you truly want to receive.

So why do people often fail to make the connection? I believe the problem is that most consumers associate commercial email with solicitations. They see email primarily as a mass-marketing medium, because they are constantly receiving messages they don't want and don't need from companies they know nothing about. Because prospecting accounts for the vast majority of messages in our inboxes, it is not surprising that most people fail to look past it. If we go back to the origins of email, however, we see that it was not designed for commercial communications. It was meant to be—and was originally used as—a basic interpersonal communication tool, like the telephone. It was about relationships.

CCM is about moving your organization's email strategy back to where the medium started. It is about taking email away from its current status as a mass media promotional tool, and remaking it into a one-to-one relationship tool. Understanding this fundamental difference is the key to unlocking the promise of CCM.

The Cocktail Party and Your Customer's Inbox

Imagine walking into a crowded cocktail party filled with dozens, or even hundreds, of people you've never met. Each time a stranger approaches you, you respond politely, but you don't want to divulge any personal information or invest too much time listening to their stories. Your walls go up when you are around people you don't know. But when you spot a group of your friends through this sea of strangers, your comfort level rises. You head in their direction. Once you've reached your friends, you spend some time catching up. You tell them about recent happenings in your life, and you react to their latest news with great interest.

This party is a parable for your customer's inbox. Like the party, your customer's inbox is filled with strangers and friends. Although strangers may approach your customers through mass-marketing emails, they're unlikely to get much of a response because your customer's walls are up. CCM helps you transform your email from a stranger to a friend that your customers will not just respond to—but will also readily seek out.

Let's go back to the party and this time, we'll turn the tables. Assume that you are the stranger, and one of the other guests is a person you would like to meet. How might you make an introduction and try to turn that stranger into a friend? You could go to the middle of the room, stand on top of a table, and shout the person's name until he turns around and notices you. Or, you could simply follow your prospect around the room, talking incessantly about whatever is on your mind. Needless to say, all of these ideas are ludicrous. The host would call the police and have you thrown out.

Why mention such inappropriate ways of meeting people? Because in the world of email marketing, these tactics are seen as "best practices" by a disappointingly large number of organizations.

The key to meeting people at a party and the key to using email as a marketing tool are simple: It is your responsibility to be interesting and relevant to your target. Find a common friend to introduce you. Join the same club or organization. Learn about a subject that interests him. Get to know your target as a friend, so the next time you find yourself at the same party, you can walk right up to him and say "hello".

The last part of the party parable involves an old friend from college. You haven't seen him in years, yet he shows up at the party uninvited. You greet him, trying to be polite. He corners you. He tells you that he has been married a few times and has spent several months in jail, but now he has really turned his life around. He is an independent salesman for a vinyl siding company. By telling you his life story, it appears your old friend has an ulterior motive. He wants to come by your house next week and show you the marvels of his product line.

So you stand there—cornered, thirsty, and watching your good friends talking happily fifteen feet away. You've given your old college chum permission to talk to you, but did you really want to hear his sales pitch? As you're designing your email strategy, ask yourself this question: "Even though my customers have given me permission to send them email, can I really say whatever I want, whenever I want, and still expect them to want to hear from me?" Probably not.

CCM is not just about getting your messages read; it is also about making sure they are read in the future. CCM builds relationships and makes them last. If you measure the success of your email program by the highest frequency of messages you can send before customers unsubscribe, go back and think about that vinyl siding salesman and how you felt about him and his brand. You might have listened the first time to be polite, but you will probably avoid him like the plague the next time you are at a party together.

Your Top Twenty

If you were single, you could conceivably date hundreds of people at the same time. You could also surround yourself with thousands of friends. Yet why do most of us gravitate toward monogamous relationships and maintain small circles of friends? Because the smaller the number of relationships we maintain, the more time and attention we can give to each relationship.

The same is true of customer-vendor relationships. When companies reach out blindly to the maximum number of names they can compile on a list, they are unable to cultivate any meaningful customer relationships. Research shows that customers are willing to "befriend" only a select number of vendors. The growth rate of Internet users has continued to slow over the last few years, and current users are becoming more discerning about which emails they open and read. A recent study conducted by my colleagues at Quris revealed that most email users maintain an email relationship with no more than ten to twenty organizations at a time.[3] Beyond that, correspondence winds up in the virtual trash bin. Once you're in that group of ten to twenty, or what Quris calls the "inner circle," waste even a moment of your customers' time and they'll drop you from their inner circle. The bar is getting higher.

You gain entry into your customers' inner circle by building relationships. Customers say brand loyalty is one of the top factors that motivates them to opt-in to a company's email program. What makes customers loyal, and keeps them loyal? Knowing that the company in question is responsive to—and can meet—their needs. The first step in meeting customer needs is asking for their permission. But once you have that permission, don't make the mistake of regarding it as a permanent yes. Assume that your customer is granting only *provisional permission*. In other words, each time you ask for permission, you're granted it only for the very next message you send. You must re-earn your customers' permission for every subsequent message to ensure that they remain interested in—and tuned into—what you have to say.

Why Doesn't Everyone Use CCM (or Something Like It) Already?

If CCM is such a potentially lucrative and easy-to-implement strategy, why aren't more companies jumping on the bandwagon? The answer may be as simple as they haven't yet identified the enterprise impact of their email programs. Like most new mediums, email marketing is not always on the radar of corporate policymakers and executives. Email marketing campaigns are often built and implemented within the ranks of an organization. Centralization is rare, and coordination is even rarer. Several departments within the same company may be working on campaigns simultaneously, targeting the same core group of customers, yet one will have no idea what the other is doing. For most companies, email marketing started at the departmental level. For many of them, it has yet to elevate beyond that point.

For example, say you own a department store. Your women's sportswear department decides that it wants to build a Web site to help promote a new designer line. It pulls the entire list of store customers and sends them weekly emails, alerting them that the line is set to launch. At the same time, your housewares department decides to send customers an email inviting them to participate in a sweepstakes, and your public relations department sends out a release spotlighting your store's charitable contributions that year. The poor customer has received three (or more) emails within one week, all from different departments within the same company, none of which he or she really wanted.

If this department store had had a viable CCM strategy in place, it would have established preferences by which customers could specify which kinds of messages they wanted to receive, and how often they wanted to receive them. Through the store's customer relationships, it would have learned which customers wanted to hear about the new designer line, and which customers wanted to sign up for the sweepstakes. If this department store had used CCM, it would not only have increased its response rates and generated more sales, but it would have also gained something even more important and long term: Email Brand Value (EBV).

Email Brand Value

Several times now I've raised the question of whether you can find your mother's email message within your cluttered inbox. You are able to find your mom's message because her name has value to you. (After giving birth to you and raising you, she *should* have value.)

You can make your company name have so much value to your customers that they're willing to open your messages after looking at the "from" field. It's a concept I call Email Brand Value, and it forms the cornerstone of CCM.

It is easy to juice up your responses by sending huge volumes of email or by using attention-grabbing subjects ("READ THIS MESSAGE NOW"), but these tactics can backfire and diminish future responses if the message itself lacks real value to your recipients. The idea is to focus less on near-term response rates, and instead focus more on the lifetime value of a customer. Would you rather have one quick and easy sale here and there, or a pattern of regular transactions with a customer over the course of several years?

Building EBV is essential to establishing long-term customer relationships, and it absolutely hinges upon the relevancy of your messages. Send out a boring, irrelevant newsletter and your customers will decide not to read it. Send it to the wrong people, and they'll no longer want to have anything to do with you. Angry customers are not customers for long.

Seth Godin refers to relationship building as "dating your customer." In the old days (and still today), companies would start right in with a marriage proposal. They would spend a lot of money on a fancy television ad and hope that it would entice new customers to buy their product. But this tactic assumes that consumers have loads of time on their hands (which they don't), and that they have few alternatives to your brand (which they do).

When you date your customers, you woo them slowly. The process takes longer, but it yields powerful long-term results. Offer an incentive, use that incentive to build the customer's understanding of your product, reinforce the incentive to gain even more permission, and over time, you can use the permission you've earned to change your customer's purchasing behavior.[4]

Solidifying customer relationships and building EBV requires moving your company's email program from an isolated marketing endeavor to a consistent, enterprise-wide strategy. Your brand is what keeps your customers reading past the "from" field. Your brand is what lays the foundation for every interaction you have with your customers. And every department within your organization needs to be focused single-mindedly on maintaining the value of that brand.

A Tale of Two Email Marketers

It was the best of email marketing strategies, it was the worst of email marketing strategies. It was a campaign that tried to exceed its customers' expectations, and a campaign that tried its customers' patience.

Once, there was a credit card company that invited their customers to take part in its email marketing program. Its customers, eager to receive valuable offers and rewards information, gladly opted-in. The company grew a big list. The company executives were pleased.

But then the company did a bad thing. It abused its precious list. Instead of asking its customers what they wanted to receive and honoring that request, the company sent them useless, irrelevant messages. When recipients tried to remove themselves from some of the mailings, the company removed them from all mailings. Customers were not pleased.

In the same virtual universe, there existed another company—a large media outlet. This company too amassed a large email list. But this company did so by allowing its customers to choose from a variety of channels that suited their interests. When customers grew weary of one channel, they could easily switch to another or cease all correspondence. Customers were pleased. The company name became even more valuable.

You may recognize the first story as that of my credit card company from Chapter 2. The other marketer—the one that had its email strategy right—was the *New York Times*. Part of the irony is that my credit card company is making money off of me, and they've got their email all wrong. The *New York Times*, on the other hand, is making nothing off of me, yet they've got their strategy right. Whereas my credit card company takes my loyalty for granted, the *New York Times* earns it every day. They've realized the value of their list, and they have no intention of abusing it.

As you'll see in Chapter 11, the *New York Times* has built one of the most successful email programs in the world. They have more subscriber growth, higher open rates, and greater EBV than most other companies. Every email offering begins with customer preference selection. Message frequency is carefully managed and monitored. And, as you'd expect from a respected brand like the *New York Times*, all content, both editorial and promotional, is scrupulously managed.

What have we learned from this story? We've learned that relevancy and relationship building are the keys to customer satisfaction. When consumers were recently asked what factor most often drove them to make a purchase from a permission-based email, nearly 38 percent said it was content relevance.[5]

Every contact you have with your customers is another opportunity to learn more about their wants and needs. Remember that email is as much a brand-building tool as it is an advertising tool. A poorly executed email strategy can kill your brand just as surely as a poorly conceived product.

Why Do You Need CCM?

CCM will help you lose weight, whiten your smile, and improve your sex life! Just kidding. I won't make the kinds of false claims spammers have become famous for, but I can promise you that a well-thought-out and well-executed CCM strategy will deliver a number of significant benefits:

- When used correctly, CCM takes advantage of the best that email offers—its speed, reach, and affordability.
- A well run CCM program provides senior management a higher level of visibility and control over email communications. This increased insight drives awareness, which in turn often drives increased budget allocation.
- Increased control over email at the enterprise level enables companies to better manage risks and to comply with CAN-SPAM and other legislation.
- By shifting the value of email toward recipients, and more importantly, letting recipients have some control over the communications they receive, CCM drives relevancy and customer lifetime value.
- CCM builds upon preexisting database marketing and *customer relationship management (CRM)* efforts, further increasing their value.
- CCM expands email beyond a product-pushing vehicle and into a powerful brand-building tool.

But one of the most important justifications for using CCM is not how it benefits your company, but rather how it impacts your customer. There is a battle being waged on your customer's property—her inbox. Every day, countless trespassers walk freely through her front yard and drop off their garbage (in the form of irrelevant messages). No matter how many spam messages are weeded out by legislation and the latest high-tech filters, your customer's front yard will always be littered with garbage. And as her yard becomes more and more cluttered, it becomes harder and harder for you to stroll up to her door and drop off your message unchallenged. As an email marketer, you have to make your way through the mess to deliver your important package intact, on time, and professionally. You also have to ensure that your customer opens the door.

Unless you and your company adapt to the new world of commercial email, you risk having your messages sit in your customer's front yard along with all of the garbage: never read, never responded to, and hardly worth the effort you made to send them.

Of course, the biggest reason to apply CCM is the new legal environment. Since January 1, 2004, the cost of launching a misguided commercial email campaign is no longer measured in brand damage or reduced sales alone; it is now measured in the millions of dollars, and (for the most egregious offenders) jail time. To stay within the bounds of the new law, some companies will simply choose to choke off their email programs by centralizing every initiative or, worse yet, by eliminating their email program entirely. Unfortunately for them, some of their competitors will quickly fill the void and take advantage of the open email channel to pull ahead in their market.

CCM is one of the first comprehensive strategies for aligning email marketing across an enterprise, and it is one of the most efficient ways to ensure that your entire company's email program is complying with the evolving legislation.

CCM and the Rest of the Book

CCM is about three core concepts. I call them the three Rs: recipient control, relevancy, and, above all, relationships. How well your email program implements the three Rs will determine how your messages will be received.

Although there are countless ways to implement a CCM strategy, in this book I have divided the fundamentals into three sections. First, I'll cover the foundational elements of an effective CCM strategy: email types, permission levels, channels, and opt-outs. To achieve the three Rs, you must handle all of these elements well. Second, I'll discuss *governance*, or managing an email program across an enterprise. Governance consists of several elements: creating policies, building a governance model, sharing lists, and integrating with other business systems and processes. Finally, in the last section, I will bring CCM into the real world, illustrating the day-to-day execution and technology issues that will help drive a world-class email initiative.

■　■　■　■

Customer Communication Management is not only a new term, it is also a new concept to fit a new era of customer communications. For decades, managing customer communications was intrinsic. The cost and expertise required to launch a traditional mass marketing campaign prohibited all but a select few within an organization from initiating customer contact. That changed with the introduction of the Internet and email. Suddenly, anyone with an email program could talk to customers; the costs were nominal and the technology was easy to use. The ensuing communications glut, both from well-intentioned companies and far-from-well-intentioned spammers, changed the entire nature of email as a commercial communications vehicle.

The "Management" in CCM replaces the former budgetary and expertise limitations with benchmarks such as Email Brand Value and Campaign Value Exchange (CVE), to help ease marketers through the transition from grassroots self-management into enterprise-governed communications. CCM enables organizations to maintain much of the incredible cost-effectiveness and measurability of email, while instilling the discipline and expertise that is now needed to surmount the inbox glut.

Chapter 5

EMAIL BRAND VALUE

*We will increasingly need to know how much satisfaction
our products, services, and prices provide. Is that
satisfaction growing, lessening, or staying the same? Is it
more, less, or the same as our competition's? But we will not
be able to know or find out unless we create some kind of
dialogue and information exchange with customers.
Knowing their needs is the first step toward satisfying them.*
—Les Wunderman, founder of the Wunderman agency,
considered to be the father of direct marketing

Brand value. It is arguably one of your company's greatest assets.
Your brand is what drives customers to choose your product over your
competitor's. It's what keeps them coming back to you, even if you
make a mistake. It is the essence of their trust in the things you say and
do. Remember the New Coke fiasco back in 1985? Coca-Cola was able
to come back from the edge of the soft drink abyss and regain its place
as market leader, thanks to a century of advertising, shelf dominance,
and established customer loyalty. Interbrand estimates that more than
two-thirds of Coke's current market value can be attributed to its brand
alone.[1]

Most companies have realized the benefit of building a strong
brand. They go through great expense and effort to hire a top-shelf
agency, design a logo that catches the eye, and write a slogan that says
volumes about their corporate identity. But while they're massaging
their offline brand, a lot of companies are ignoring a critical
opportunity to build real, long-term brand value—online. Although
many companies see email as a valid medium to express their brand,

disappointingly few understand the unique role that email can play in developing that brand.

As I pointed out with my credit card company story in Chapter 2, your email program can be a significant source of your company's brand impressions, good or bad. In a recent Quris study, 56 percent of respondents said the quality of a company's email program influenced their opinions of that company.[2] When the opinion was favorable, and customers stayed on as subscribers, they were more likely to actually read and respond to their emails than non-subscribers. When the impression was negative, customers shied away not only from the email program, but also from the company as a whole. Nearly half of the people who responded to another Quris study said they stopped doing business entirely with companies that had poor email marketing practices.[3]

The cost of making a mistake with your email program is higher than the cost of making a mistake in other marketing ventures, because email is by nature interruptive. If your Web site is visually unappealing and tough to navigate, only those who visit will know about it. Even the customers who *do* visit may not notice, because chances are they were only there to look up something specific (a product in your catalog, or your mailing address, for example). But if you send an irrelevant and unrequested email to thousands of customers, you'd better believe they'll know about it, and they'll be a lot less likely to let you interrupt them again in the future.

Companies that focus on short-term customer acquisition at the expense of relevance sacrifice most, if not all, of their positive brand impact. Companies that take the time to develop long-term relationships, on the other hand, gain equity in the form of increased customer lifetime value. Having a well-designed email program is like putting money in the bank and watching it earn interest.

How Do You Measure the Value of a Brand?

Building a brand takes time and effort, so companies feel that they must constantly justify their brand's worth. Executives know intrinsically that their brand is critical to their company's financial well-being, yet few can put a real value on it. Brand value is probably the most elusive asset to measure because it is defined by intangibles. How do you measure the value of name recognition, company reputation, and customer attitudes?

In the past, efforts to put a figure on brand value focused on such attitudinal measures as "awareness," "recall," and "feelings"; in other words, these measures were used to gauge consumer reactions when they see a company's name or logo, and the likelihood that those brand symbols will entice a purchase. But any attempts at brand valuation across the wide spectrum of an organization's marketing efforts have been indirect, imprecise, and very difficult to measure in hard, financial terms.

Email Brand Value (EBV), while still about attitudes, is somewhat easier to measure, because it is real time, single channel, and because it provides a bounty of data chronicling each recipient's responses. Companies can not only analyze that data; they can also use it to further target and personalize, building greater value with each message they send.

But trying to measure EBV using traditional short-term metrics is like trying to capture a flower's bloom in a single photograph. A snapshot reveals just one instant in the life of a flower. To capture the entire bloom requires a whole series of photographs over an extended period of time. In the world of email, measuring the success of a program requires you to look beyond the metrics of the most recent campaign and view responses and trends over a long period of time.

EBV is not about individual campaigns; it's about the lifetime of your email program. If one campaign fails, your numbers may shrink momentarily. But if you send the wrong message to the wrong customer enough times, you forfeit the EBV of that customer forever.

A Formula for Measuring Email Brand Value

EBV is difficult to distill into black-and-white financial terms because, like offline brand value, it is based on attitudes—specifically, your customers' attitude when they see your company name in their "from" field. You can see how your brand influences customer actions by watching how they respond to your email: they may read it, click through to your site, or throw it in the trash bin; but you'll have a tough time pinning down its actual economic value.

That said, you *can* isolate the individual elements of EBV to help you get a better handle on your campaign and determine how well it's working, without actually using hard numbers. I've come up with a decidedly nonscientific formula that can help you "calculate" your EBV in relative terms. The goal is not to produce a single number but, rather, to show how a select set of tangible components can work together to drive the intangible idea of EBV.

EBV = existing brand (+/-) relevancy + content value - frequency

Let's break this formula down into its core components:

Existing brand: Unless your company is new, your name already holds some value to your customers. The name recognition you've already earned from your Web site, advertising campaigns, products, retail stores, and other exposure will give you a big head start on your EBV because your customers will already recognize your name in the "from" field.

That your email brand and your offline brand are so tightly connected can be a blessing—or a curse. Any harm that results from an interruptive, irrelevant email campaign is certain to bleed over into your overall brand. You will not only ensure that your customers won't want to hear from you via email, but you'll also leave a lasting negative imprint on their perception of your entire brand.

Relevancy: The core tenet of CCM is also the central component of the EBV equation. Relevancy ties into every aspect of the formula, and it is woven into every facet of your brand. By itself, irrelevance can damage your brand. When exacerbated by frequency, it can cause irreparable harm.

Relevancy is considered positive when the content of the message is highly applicable to the recipient. It is neutral when the content is aimed at a very wide group, which just happens to include the recipient. Relevancy becomes negative and begins to undermine your brand when the message content has absolutely no applicability to the recipient.

Content value: Even though the value of a message differs for each recipient, the overall value of your campaign is determined by how much your recipients, as a group, can benefit from your content. If the content of your campaign is poorly targeted, the value to the entire audience is lower because only a few recipients benefit.

Content value is not just about money. For example, an offer of 50 percent off a large office supply purchase is more valuable to customers than a free ream of paper. An e-bill can be quite valuable to customers who prefer the ease and time savings of online bill payment.

Frequency: The goal in setting frequency is to squeeze the maximum benefit out of the minimum number of messages by making each message relevant. The lower the frequency, the more relevant each message must be. Clearly, frequency is not always negative, as my equation suggests. Some of your recipients may, in fact, like hearing from you regularly. But I've put a minus sign in front of frequency because, in general, recipients prefer to receive fewer, rather than more, messages.

As I mentioned above, the benefit of this formula is that it distills EBV into four simple drivers: existing brand value, relevancy, content value, and frequency. Even without plugging in specific numbers, the formula shows that relevancy can hurt or help EBV, and increased frequency almost always detracts from EBV.

The list of factors that affect EBV goes beyond the four listed here. But hopefully, this formula will provide you with a simple and useful way to start evaluating this critical aspect of CCM.

Plugging in Numbers

I've told you that applying real numbers to brand value is difficult. It is not impossible, however. Back in 2002, American Airlines began an initiative to place an economic value on its email program. Elaine O'Gorman, who ran a large part of the program at the time, wanted to understand how her day-to-day email campaigns affected the airline overall. In many respects, she was seeking to put a hard dollar figure on the company's EBV.

American's "measure everything" culture gave Elaine and her team a solid head start. After years of performing analysis, American's marketing team had become expert at predicting and measuring their customers' relative value. But in order to translate raw research into an email specific value, Elaine's team had to perform a series of analyses comparing their email customers to a control group of customers that did not receive email. She knew she had to approach her research carefully, keeping in mind that loyal customers would have a natural affinity to American's communications and could possibly skew the results. But by defining a control group and an email group with similar characteristics, the team was able to minimize any bias.

After compiling the results from various communications and promotions to both groups over a series of months, the team applied American's relative value calculations to each group. By subtracting the calculated value of the control group from the value of the email group and extrapolating that difference over the lifetime of the customers, the American team arrived at a figure approximating the value of their email list. As it turned out, their list had about the same value as one of American's airplanes.

Of course, the point of the exercise was not to put a precise accounting value on the email list, but rather to put the value of the email list into perspective for Elaine's colleagues and peers. Before the study, Elaine regularly had to explain why a "free" resource like their email list should be treated with care. With the "value of an airplane" behind her efforts (when you work at an airline, an airplane carries great weight—both literally and figuratively), she found it much easier to gain support for the list allocation policies needed to run American's email program.[4]

Two Perceptions of Email Brand Value

Imagine that two companies are simultaneously preparing to launch their email programs. The first company is a well-known athletic shoe manufacturer. Executives of this company have decided that they need an email program because every one of its competitors already has one in place. The company sets aside a tiny cubicle within its marketing department, and "volunteers" one of its marketing professionals to spearhead the new venture. The newly appointed email manager scours the company's existing mailing list and past promotions to search for potential recipients. He then throws together a few promotional and sales messages, and blasts them to everyone on his new list every couple of weeks.

At the same time, the second company, a startup publisher, launches its own email program. Because this company doesn't have established contact lists, it sets up an opt-in program on its Web site. Visitors can sign up to receive a weekly or monthly newsletter alerting them to new book titles and sales on topics that interest them. After every mailing, the company carefully measures its results to find out which elements of its campaign are working. It uses the sum of its research and customer responses to further target and customize its email program.

The first company is probably under the impression that it doesn't need to expend much time and effort on email. The world is already familiar with its brand, and the public is already buying its athletic shoes to the tune of millions of dollars in yearly revenues. The second company, which is only getting started, realizes how powerful a tool its email program can be in building its brand. It is reaching out to new and existing customers, and forming long-term relationships in the process.

Why should the athletic shoe company care about its email program? Its brand already has built-in value from years of advertising and marketing campaigns. What this established company doesn't realize is that it has far more at stake than the unknown publisher. Customers hold email from well-known companies to a higher standard than they would email from an unknown company, according to an Executive Summary Consulting and Quris study.[5] When an established company uses its email blindly and for the sole purpose of pushing its products, it irritates its established customers, compromises their loyalty, and, in the process, puts its brand value on the line.

The second company, though still unknown, has realized the potential of email as an extension of its brand. It has asked its customers what messages they want to receive, listened to their responses, and responded with targeted, relevant emails. The company has collected the data from each campaign, analyzed it, and used it to fine-tune its program. This upstart company is taking advantage of the key CCM tenet, relevancy, and in the process is building lifetime EBV.

Making Sure Your Message Is Worth Reading

Acquiring a new customer is five to ten times more expensive than selling to an existing customer,[6] says Frederick F. Reichheld in his book, *The Loyalty Effect*. If you overuse your email list to boost your short-term numbers, you're passing up a critical opportunity to cement relationships with the valuable customers you already have.

Building customer loyalty requires a shift from acquisition to retention and from short-term campaign successes to long-term customer relationships. As I've said before—make a contact, and you have a one-time sale. Establish a relationship, and you have a loyal customer who keeps coming back for more.

■　■　■　■

In this chapter, I've used two of the three Rs in CCM—relationship and relevancy. EBV relies heavily on both. A relationship without relevancy dies a slow death. Relevancy without a relationship is nothing more than an advertisement. In a sense, a great EBV is the result of consistent relevancy (and value) over the life of a customer relationship.

Email Brand Value is a powerful concept that can help you understand how your customers perceive your company in the online world, and how that online perception affects your overall brand.

Chapter 6

A PRIMER ON EMAIL MARKETING

It is possible to fly without motors, but not without knowledge and skill.
—Wilbur Wright

Before we move forward, I'd like to take a step back and review some basic concepts I will be mentioning quite frequently throughout the book. We've already gone over the high-level theories that shape Customer Communication Management (CCM). But to fully develop your email program, you will eventually have to move from strategy mode into practical implementation. Putting CCM to work requires that all managers involved understand the core mechanics behind email, email marketing, and email marketing management systems.

Even if you decide to outsource with a *full-service provider,* you'll still want some degree of fluency in these basic concepts. Knowing the underlying mechanics will enable you to know what you can—and cannot—accomplish with your email program. Knowing the basics will also help you set realistic goals and develop strategies before your service provider even comes into the picture.

THE INGREDIENTS: EMAIL MARKETING FUNDAMENTALS

As email has become more firmly entrenched in the corporate consciousness, the basic terms have taken on a life of their own. Whether you are already fully conversant in the language of email marketing or just starting out, this chapter will help you navigate conversations with your vendors and colleagues. It will also set a standard lexicon for the rest of the book.

Lists

Any legitimate email campaign hinges upon the recipient's consent, or *permission*. Recipients give you permission to contact them because they have an interest in hearing from you. With permission, your message is more likely to be opened, read, and considered. Without permission, it will probably get deleted.

Permission is such a central concept that marketers have created a variety of synonymous and complementary terms to define it. You may hear the words *opt-in* or *subscribe* to describe the act by which customers grant their permission. Thanks to CAN-SPAM, the term *affirmative consent* has also entered the marketing lexicon. Affirmative consent is used to describe an even higher level of permission, in which recipients give their express permission in response to a clearly stated request.

Chapter 18 covers list building in great detail, but I want to introduce you to some of the basic concepts here. Your list can grow in one of three ways:

Opt-in: Whether customers surf your Web site, visit your physical store, or contact your call center to give their permission, their action is called an *opt-in*. Chapter 10 explores the various levels of permission in greater detail, and provides a roadmap for applying them. As a brief overview, this book divides permission into four levels: opt-out, opt-in (or single opt-in), confirmed opt-in, and double opt-in. Each represents a higher level of permission than its predecessor.

The list you generate internally from opted-in customer email addresses is known as your *house list*. The return on investment (ROI) on an internal list is usually higher than it is on a third-party list because you save on the cost of renting the list.

Third-party lists: You borrow or rent a prebuilt list from a third party, such as another division of your organization, a business partner, or a list aggregator. Many marketers use third-party lists purely to drive opt-ins to their house list. Others use them for advertising and promotional purposes.

Appends and Co-registrations: An email append process takes your existing offline (postal addresses) customer mailing list into the digital age. Third-party list append services maintain massive databases of consumer records. Each record contains both physical and email addresses. You can pay these firms to *append* the records in your postal address list with email addresses from their databases. *Co-registration* lets you "rent space" on a well-trafficked site. You put a small promotion for your email list next to the site's own registration page. When a site visitor checks the box next to your offer, the site sends you the opted-in individual's contact information.

Growing your lists takes work. Unfortunately, shrinking them requires no effort at all. You can lose addresses during the natural transition process as your recipients change ISPs or companies. When you try to send an email to an invalid address, you will get a return bounce from the old server. After a certain number of bounces, you will have to remove each old address from your list. Or, you can lose addresses if recipients no longer want to hear from you because your message is no longer relevant to them. They may choose to *opt-out* (also called *unsubscribe* or *remove*) of your mailings.

Testing: Lists can prove a valuable tool for testing your message to ensure that it remains relevant to your customers. You test by *segmenting*, or dividing your list into random groups and trying out various elements of your message (creative, subject line, etc.) to determine which variations garner the most responses. Or, you can divide your list by specifics such as demographics, purchasing behavior, or interests, to target your message to only the people who want to receive it. If you test and target appropriately, you should see results in the form of improved click-throughs and conversions (both of which we'll discuss later in this chapter).

A common mechanism for creating random segments is called *nthing*. Yes, you read it right. Nthing is a technique which pulls every *nth* record from your list to create a near-random set of subgroups. For example, if you have one thousand names, and you *nth* on every ten, each of those one thousand names is assigned a value of 0, 1, 2, 3, 4, 5, 6, 7, 8, or 9. If you wanted to create two random "test" segments, you would send one offer to segment 0 and another to segment 1. You would then send the best-performing offer to segments 2 through 9.

Another segmenting technique, called *A/B splits*, divides a list randomly into two equal parts. One part of the list is the control group;

the other is the test group. Using the control group as a baseline, you send your test group messages in which you change one element at a time (subject line, offer, graphics, etc.). Then you measure the response of one group against the other. By changing one piece of your message at a time, you can really gauge what works and what doesn't.

Both nthing and A/B splits are mechanisms for creating *test cells*—a term used to describe the combined list segment and the message variation being tested. A marketer might say, for example, "We will create seven test cells for this campaign before we send out the final message."

Segmenting is not only used to test message elements, such as creative or subject line; it can also be used to *target* your message to a particular audience. Borrowing a term from the direct marketing world, creating a segment is also referred to as performing a *select*. You can send to multiple targets to test one group's response relative to another (for example, men vs. women). But more commonly, you target simply to increase relevancy, by sending messages only to people on your list who you know will value your communication.

The Basic Email Campaign

Most of your campaigns will go through a fairly consistent and straightforward cycle: campaign objectives, execution, and analysis. Each campaign's objectives should fall within an enterprise-wide strategy and adhere to an enterprise policy (see Chapter 14) to ensure that your email program is integrated with your broader marketing efforts and that all of your campaigns are aligned across your organization.

When planning your campaign, you might find it helpful to think of the process in terms of the following three steps:

1. Set up a campaign strategy. Determine who your audience will be, how you will contact them, and what you will offer or communicate.

2. Outline your campaign objectives. What action do you want your recipients to perform? Should they click through to your Web site, sign up for a newsletter, or make a purchase?

3. Write a measurement plan. Determine which metrics you will use (click-throughs, conversions, etc.) to gauge the effectiveness of your campaign, and set clear goals for the numbers you want to hit.

Now that you've outlined your objectives, it's time to execute the campaign. Generally, you start by building out the actual content. Your message may be formatted in text only, HTML, or, if you have more sophisticated capabilities, AOL and even rich media. At this stage, advanced emailers (especially those with particularly important campaigns) will test their message by trying out various combinations of offers, subject lines, creative designs, etc. against a tiny subset of their list. Finally, you select your target audience from your overall list—and send.

The actual path that your message will take to and from each recipient is outlined in the following section. Assuming your execution is complete, the final step in your campaign life cycle is analysis: reviewing the results of your campaign and using those results to refine your plans for future campaigns. I could devote several chapters to email marketing analysis and action plan development, but these subjects are far beyond the scope of this book. Read through Chapter 20 for a few general ideas on the analysis process.

The Life Cycle of the Individual Message

In this section, we'll follow the course of a single message as it makes its way to its intended recipient. Assuming that you have good technology and/or a solid Email Service Provider (ESP), a lot of the steps in this process are invisible. But if you were to examine it in detail, you'd see that the execution process is truly amazing. A single campaign kicks off thousands, even millions, of independent messages that each begins its own unique life cycle. The course of that life cycle varies for each message based on the actions of your recipient. This section will illustrate the details of execution and explain email metrics by taking you through the major events that occur in the lifetime of a message.

Figure 6.1 The email message life cycle

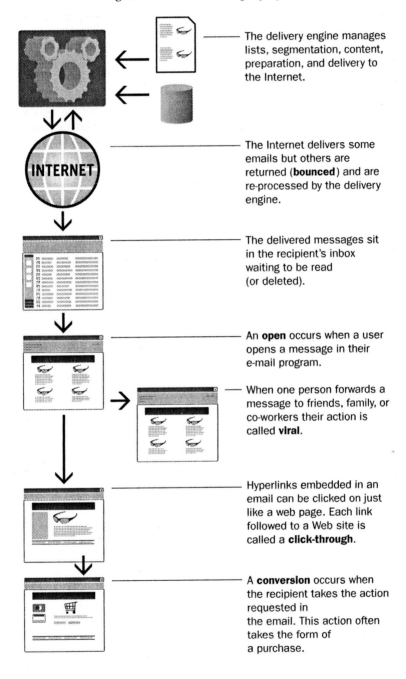

The delivery engine manages lists, segmentation, content, preparation, and delivery to the Internet.

The Internet delivers some emails but others are returned (**bounced**) and are re-processed by the delivery engine.

The delivered messages sit in the recipient's inbox waiting to be read (or deleted).

An **open** occurs when a user opens a message in their e-mail program.

When one person forwards a message to friends, family, or co-workers their action is called **viral**.

Hyperlinks embedded in an email can be clicked on just like a web page. Each link followed to a Web site is called a **click-through**.

A **conversion** occurs when the recipient takes the action requested in the email. This action often takes the form of a purchase.

Let's look at each of these terms in more detail:

Bounce: If you send a message and either the receiving server does not exist or it sends back an error, the return is called a *bounce*. For example, a message may bounce when the text sets off an alarm in the spam filter, or when the recipient's address is no longer valid.

Bounces are divided into two categories: *hard bounces* and *soft bounces*. A fair amount of debate surrounds the use of these terms, but a hard bounce is generally taken to mean that the email is permanently undeliverable because the address is invalid or has expired. A soft bounce occurs when the email is returned, usually with an error message telling the sender to try to send it again later. With a soft bounce, the recipient's email server recognizes the sender's address, but a temporary problem—e.g., the recipient's mailbox is full or the incoming server is swamped—prevents the email from getting through. Most ESPs will attempt a certain number of resends on a bounced email before removing the name from the sender's list.

Open: An *open*, also called an *impression,* occurs when your recipient clicks on your message and her email program opens a window to display it. Add up the number of opens, divide by the total number of messages sent, and you have your open rate. If you send twenty thousand messages and you get five thousand opens, you have an open rate of 25 percent. Opens are perhaps the simplest way to measure your EBV. The more recipients that see your name in the "from" field and open the message, the higher your EBV.

Sometimes open rates are not one hundred percent accurate. Preview windows and remotely viewed emails can skew the numbers. It's impossible for any email program to tell, for example, whether a user actually opened an email or whether their preview window opened it for them automatically. To measure open rates more precisely, many marketers look at *unique opens.* Whereas total opens count each time a recipient opens a message, unique opens count only the first open. For instance, say you send out two messages. One recipient opens the message four times; the other opens it only once. From those two messages you would have five total opens, but only two unique opens. When you read your final numbers, you need to know whether you are looking at *opens* or *unique opens* to avoid misinterpretation. Despite the potential confusion, open rates are effective for detecting large statistical swings. Any meaningful dips in your open rate should raise a big red flag that something is wrong with either your message or delivery.

I need to point out here that opens will work *only* in HTML messages. Opens are measured using an image embedded in the HTML message. When the recipient opens the message, the image sends a request to the sender's Email Marketing System (EMS). Text emails do not contain HTML or images, and are therefore unable to measure direct open rates. Opens in text (and AOL message bodies) can be inferred only when a user clicks on a link within the text, which does not necessarily occur with each open. Chapter 7 discusses in greater detail the technology behind measuring opens.

Viral: In the 1970s, a shampoo commercial became an instant hit thanks to the now famous words, "I told two friends, and they told two friends, and so on, and so on..." As the commercial artfully showed, people value recommendations from friends or family members and respond to them with far greater frequency than they respond to corporate promotions. In a study by IMT Strategies, consumers said they would rather receive email from a friend than from a company or any other sender. The biggest reasons people forwarded messages were relevance and, interestingly, humor (41 percent and 25 percent, respectively). Forty-four percent of people reported that they had forwarded messages; 65 percent said they had received viral messages. The last two statistics support the idea that a small group of your customers instigates a disproportionately large share of your brand development via email.[1]

Email, with its speed and ease, is the perfect vehicle for passing along recommendations. The "sneezers" as Seth Godin describes them, are the individuals who like your message enough to *forward* it to people they know. Marketers love sneezers; they get the word out about products or services without any added cost—or effort. Because of the negative association with the computer term "virus," many marketers refer to viral email as *forward to a friend, referrals* or *pass along*.

Recipients can forward your message in one of two ways:

1. They can click the forward button in their email program.

2. With more advanced email marketing systems, recipients can either click on a special link that takes them to a Web page, or enter their friend's email address in an embedded form within the message itself.

Viral messaging raises several interesting issues, which we will touch upon in later chapters. Briefly, the line between viral messaging and spam is often thin, especially when promotions ask customers to pass the word along to, say, five friends in order to earn a reward. Yes, the message is coming from a friend, but it's still unsolicited and non-permission based, and that negative reputation can be associated with the company's brand. In light of CAN-SPAM legislation, the question remains as to whether certain types of viral messages will be regarded as *commercial electronic mail messages (CEMMs*—the legal word for commercial email). As of this writing, the Federal Trade Commission (FTC) and the courts were still undecided on the issue.

Click-through: The term *response* has many meanings, but we'll treat it as synonymous with click-throughs in this book. When a customer clicks on a link in your email and travels to your Web site, the action is called a *click-through. Click-through rate* (CTR) measures the percentage of people who clicked on the link (number of click-throughs divided by number of recipients). Click-throughs are a good measure of your message relevancy, but *conversions* are by far the more coveted measure. Conversions occur when the recipient takes the desired action: asks for more information, subscribes to a new list, registers for a seminar, or buys your product.

A few other metrics warrant a mention here, as they will help you track your campaign success:

Replies: Some messages explicitly request "no replies" and ask that customers respond by clicking on the various links within the message. But if you do set up your email system to receive responses (or if you want to capture replies from people who ignore your "no replies" request and respond anyway), you can keep track of each customer question, follow up, or unsubscribe request.

Web page clicks: This metric goes one step further than the click-through, enabling you to track your customers' movements once they reach your Web site from the email link. If you have Web analytics tools in place, you can follow the path your recipient takes around your site. With basic email tools, your tracking ability is more limited, but you can still measure your recipient's movements across a finite number of pages. Many ESPs do not offer Web-tracking tools, but if yours does, you'll have an easier time setting up Web page clicks than trying to orchestrate a full-blown Web analytic solution.

Getting Help with Your Execution

When it comes time to implement your email program, you can decide to go it alone, or hire an outside company to do all or most of the work for you. To choose the right option for your program, you need to know what you're trying to accomplish, what percentage of the project you can reasonably complete in-house, and how much you're willing to spend.

Although we discuss execution models in great depth in Chapter 17, I want to provide an overview earlier in the book. Here are a few of the execution models from which you can choose:

Full service: If you outsource to one of the many ESPs that offer total email marketing solutions, you can pretty much sit back and watch your email program take shape. Full-service agencies take care of everything from campaign planning to results analysis.

Self-service: Several ESPs offer self-service packages as a less costly alternative to their full-service options. If you choose the self-service option, you will handle most of your own campaign execution from a Web-based interface, but your ESP will be available to provide technical support along the way. The self-service model is often referred to as an *ASP*, which is IT-speak for *Application Service Provider*. ASP basically means that your email vendor hosts and runs its software for you, saving your IT department the trouble of having to install and maintain it themselves.

Service Bureau: The most popular model among sophisticated emailers, Service Bureau provides a hybrid solution. It not only offers a complete self-service platform like the self-service model, but it also provides account management, various professional services (e.g., best practices), and on-demand fulfillment. The Service Bureau model is appealing because it offers the cost savings of self-service with the availability of ESP assistance when campaigns become too complex or the internal workload increases.

Install: If your technology team members are willing to tackle the entire email program in-house, they can purchase email marketing software and install it in your data center.

Adding Pizzazz to Your Message: Rich Media

If you have an advanced email system, you can jazz up your messages with embedded *rich media.* Although the term rich media has many definitions, it is almost always used to describe video, animation, and audio. Video and audio are usually delivered via a plug-in such as Microsoft Media Player or Java. Animation, the most commonly used variety of rich media, is almost universally created with Macromedia's Flash technology. Flash is available on more than 90 percent of personal computers. Compared to video and audio, Flash is inexpensive to produce and takes up less bandwidth. A number of studies indicate that response rates to rich media messages are significantly higher than responses to traditional, HTML-only messages.

Unfortunately, rich media has its challenges. With the war on spam and email viruses raging, Microsoft and other email client manufacturers are continually upping their security settings, to the point where many users can no longer see video, audio, and Flash animations. The good news is that smart emailers (using good email technology) can add a "click to view" option at the top of their message, which immediately opens a browser window, enabling them to see the message as the sender intended it to be viewed. HTML pages can also be coded so that they will display a static image if the email client is not capable of displaying rich media.

HTML, though considered the standard for email graphics these days, faces its own *deliverability* issues. Even if an HTML message makes it into someone's inbox, there is no guarantee that it will display properly, if at all. Unlike simple text messages, HTML email must overcome the challenge of *renderability.*

Renderability is a two-part challenge: First, the HTML must be designed so that it will display correctly. Second, HTML emails often run into disabled graphics, a technique many email programs employ to stop spammers from using Web beacons (message open tags). The first challenge requires human expertise or a smart rendering engine; the second can be resolved by asking the recipient to add the sender's company name to his address book (more on this subject in Chapter 19). Advertising marketers are not always concerned about renderability, because the extra effort required to make each message readable is often more costly than the decreased response rates. But for brand-sensitive relationship marketers, renderability is paramount, and it is generally worth the extra effort.

Deliverability Issues

The rise of spam and other unwanted messages has put consumers—and their Internet Service Providers (ISPs)—on high alert. ISPs have thrown up mile-high barriers (in the forms of blocks and filters) to protect their valued customers from this ongoing attack. Unfortunately, filters are often turned up so high that they mistake legitimate, permission-based email for spam and block it, too. This phenomenon is known as the *false positive*. Recent studies indicate that almost 20 percent of legitimate emails are mistakenly blocked.[2]

It's not surprising that ISPs have trouble identifying spam. Until very recently, no one in the marketing industry seemed to be able to agree on a definition—or even a name—for the stuff. Even as late as 2002, the terms Unsolicited Commercial Email (UCE) and Unsolicited Bulk Email (UBE) were still being used interchangeably with spam. Various groups have tried to push these more scientific terms, but the 2003 CAN-SPAM Act appears to have finally cemented spam as the official term.

Most of my clients (and most readers of this book, no doubt) consider spam to be any messages sent without permission, whereas the majority of consumers have a much broader, and less tolerant, definition. They consider any message irrelevant enough to waste their time to be spam.

The consumer definition of spam is more important than most email marketers realize. ISPs are not telephone companies—they are NOT required by law to facilitate communications between their constituents. Their only constituents are their customers, who pay them for broadband and dial-up connections. If a customer says a message is spam, then as far as the ISP is concerned, the message *is* spam, regardless of whether it was an opt-in. The imprecise way in which ISPs handle spam complaints, compounded by the high volume of well-intentioned but irrelevant messages from permission mailers, only serve to drive up the overall numbers of false positives.

Advanced Email Marketing

In Chapter 20, we'll cover some of the cutting-edge techniques marketers are using as part of their CCM strategies such as dynamic content, segmentation, and life cycle automation. For now, we'll just touch on these terms:

Dynamic content: Also referred to as *dynamic message assembly* or *content blocks*, dynamic content uses a message template to deliver unique content to each recipient based on his or her profile. Dynamic content goes beyond simple personalization by varying entire blocks of content (you can interchange a photo, a few links, or sections of text) from message to message. Each content block is selected from a library created for the campaign. The selection is usually based on simple business rules, such as: "display content block A for men" and "display content block B for women." Companies using dynamic content have reported results that are four to eight times better than the results of static campaigns, according to a 2003 JupiterResearch report.[3]

Behavior targeting: This advanced technique analyzes the course of your customers' actions on previous campaigns to help you target them with future marketing efforts. For example, if you know that a certain group of customers clicked through on a jewelry promotion, you could *re-market* them with a new, exclusive diamond sale. Or, you could send follow-up messages to customers who did not respond to a particular campaign (sometimes called a *drip campaign*).

Life cycle automation: Also referred to as *sequenced messaging, curriculum-based campaigns,* and *campaign automation,* life cycle automation is perhaps the most exciting of all the emerging email marketing techniques. Using a series of external triggers and internal rules, the system automatically finds and sends the appropriate response to a given situation. The simplest form of life cycle marketing is called *triggered* or *event-triggered messages* (also called auto responders). Triggered messages are sent one at a time in response to a single action. For example, when a customer opts-in to your newsletter, your system would generate and send a welcome message. In a more advanced form of life cycle marketing, a bank could send a series of messages to a new online banking customer. The first message might be a generic welcome from the bank, but the content of subsequent messages would vary depending on the level of activity in the online account. High activity could generate a thank you; low activity could prompt a promotion encouraging greater use. Life cycle marketing automates the entire process and times each message precisely to the needs of the customer.

Now that we've covered marketing terminology, let's turn to the next chapter to review some of the fundamental technical concepts underlying most email marketing solutions.

Chapter 7

A PRIMER ON EMAIL TECHNOLOGY

Any sufficiently advanced technology is
indistinguishable from magic.
—Arthur C. Clarke, science fiction writer

If the message is the heart of every email campaign, technology is the blood that keeps it beating. A fabulous marketing plan can't deliver text, graphics, and animation to thousands of inboxes. A great strategy can't track how many customers are clicking through and making purchases on your site. Technology is central to interactive marketing, and particularly so with email marketing. Few business computing systems will generate as much data as quickly, or require as much analysis, as email marketing.

The goal of this chapter is to expose you to the basic concepts involved in your day-to-day processes and systems. Obviously you don't need to be fluent in email technology, but without at least a basic understanding, you risk making mistakes that damage your brand and jeopardize your customer relationships.

Constructing an Email Message

The history of email dates back almost as far as the Internet itself. Although email has evolved over the years to offer a broader range of features, the basic technology remains as simple as it was thirty years ago. Tens of billions of messages traverse the Internet each day. Every one of those messages starts with the same framework: A simple text file, just as you would create with a word processor.

The simplest kind of email, a basic text message, consists of a single text file divided into two sections: a *header* and a *message body* (see

Figure 7.1). A header is like an addressed envelope—it contains the information that the outgoing and receiving email servers use to process and deliver the message. The header typically includes information such as the sender's address, the recipient's address, and the time and date the message was sent. The message body is the part your recipient sees when he opens the message.

Figure 7.1 An example of an HTML header and message body

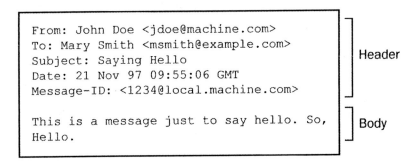

With *HTML (Hypertext Markup Language)* email, the structure of the message gets a bit more complicated. As you know, HTML is a set of codes that tells Web browsers how to display the pages you and I see when we surf the Web. Most email programs use only a subset of the HTML codes used by modern browsers, but the basic idea is the same.

In 1999, one of the Internet's governing bodies, the Internet Engineering Task Force (IETF), formally gave birth to HTML email by defining the way codes could be embedded and delivered via email. To send multiple forms of media within the same message relies on another IETF standard, called *Multipurpose Internet Mail Extensions (MIME)*. MIME divides the simple text message body into multiple sections, each capable of containing a different element of the message. One section might contain an attachment, another might contain a simple text body, and yet another might contain the HTML codes for an HTML message.

Although MIME goes a long way to standardizing how email messages work, it does not ensure 100 percent interoperability. Not all browsers and email programs play by the same rules. For example, when America Online (AOL) launched its 5.0 product in 1999, the company decided to introduce its own version of *rich text* email with its own unique MIME type. Even though newer AOL versions will work with standard HTML specifications, the millions of AOL subscribers who still use the older version create a never-ending challenge for email marketers.

And AOL is not the only exception marketers must consider when sending MIME and HTML messages. Various email clients, from online systems such as Yahoo! Mail, to enterprise products such as Lotus Notes, react differently when faced with the same MIME and HTML message formatting. In the wild world of email, simply following the standards is not enough to ensure that your messages are delivered and readable. As your technology team constructs your campaigns, they—and your tools—must be able to accommodate the huge variety of nuances and incompatibilities that still exist across the Internet.

Sending an Email Message

Similar to a postal message, an email must be processed on the outgoing end, transferred en route, and then processed again at the receiving end. The journey of a single (not bulk) email message almost always starts and ends with an *email client*. Some of the more popular clients are Microsoft Outlook, Netscape Messenger, Eudora, WordPerfect Office, and Lotus Notes; their online cousins are Yahoo! Mail, Hotmail, and AOL Mail (as in, "You've got mail!").

When the email leaves the sender's client, specialized servers called *Message Transfer Agents* (MTAs) convey it to the recipient's server. Some products, including Microsoft Exchange and Lotus Notes, come with built-in MTAs. In other cases, MTAs are stand-alone servers that do nothing but move messages along their route from sender to recipient.

Email messages travel between MTA servers via an Internet standard called *Simple Message Transfer Protocol (SMTP)*. SMTP ensures that the text files containing the actual email message make it to their intended destination intact. When a message finally arrives at the recipient's server, the email client retrieves it using standard protocols such as *Post Office Protocol (POP3)* or *Internet Message Access*

Protocol (IMAP), as well as proprietary protocols from vendors such as Microsoft or Lotus.

As you can see, email delivery and design are governed by a number of stringent Internet standards. Yet huge variations have crept in over time in the way servers and email clients interpret these standards. It is to your advantage to choose well-established, proven technologies and to work with vendors who not only adhere to standards, but who also have the experience to deal with the variety of nonstandard approaches that exist in the world of email.

HTML: A Unique Set of Delivery Challenges

You *could* simplify your email delivery by sending text-only messages. You could also trade in your brand new, leather-interior Mercedes Benz for a ten-year-old Yugo. The latter is easier on the wallet, and it will still get you from place to place, but which car would you rather drive? Text messages are great for personal email, but they are not as effective at creating a strong brand impact and improving the readability of your content. Text also won't do much for your response rates. In fact, a 2002 DoubleClick report[1] found that HTML messages generated about 40 percent more responses than text-only messages. (HTML is better than text in general, but, as I mentioned earlier, it does carry certain renderability challenges. I would advise that you test both formats to see which performs best for your particular campaign.)

HTML enlivens your messages not only with a variety of fonts and colors, but also with images. Following Internet standards, you can deliver your HTML images in one of two ways: embedded in the message, or hosted externally on a standard Web server. Embedded graphics are by far the more problematic of the two methods. First, embedding requires that every graphic be delivered with every message. Because graphics take up more space than text, their delivery not only increases download time for many users, but it also raises the sender's bandwidth requirements. Second, many email clients, particularly online Web clients, cannot process embedded graphics very well. Customers who use one of these clients can wind up with gaping holes and little red X's where graphics should have been—a gaffe that does not reflect well upon your company.

To avoid the potential complications of embedded images, nearly all email marketers use *image hosting*. A third party, usually the Email Service Provider, hosts the images and delivers them only when a recipient opens the message (see figure 7.2). This method does have a slight drawback: email clients that are running offline are unable to download hosted images. Fortunately, the number of Internet users accessing email offline is rapidly shrinking. Given the tradeoffs between the two approaches, losing a few graphic views to the small number of recipients who view their email offline is by far preferable to potentially alienating the larger number of recipients whose online email clients cannot display embedded images.

Figure 7.2 illustrates the route by which HTML messages and their associated images are delivered over the Internet to the recipient's email client

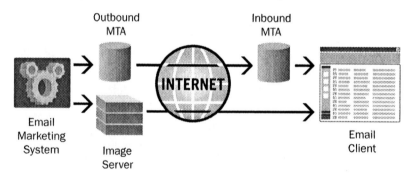

Specialized Email Marketing Technology

In the old days, email marketing pioneers would often use the same tools to send marketing messages as they used to send *interpersonal emails*. Outlook, Netscape, and other, similar clients unwittingly became the technology platforms for sending large volumes of messages. But as recipient lists began to climb into the thousands, these desktop tools became inadequate. Marketers responded by modifying popular MTAs such as SendMail to handle larger email volumes. But even these souped-up applications could not satisfy their demands for more sophisticated accessories such as Web beacons, MIME messages, image hosting, and real-time reporting.

Between 1998 and 2000, a new breed of software tool evolved, focused exclusively on the needs of high-volume email marketers. These tools, which I will refer to as *Email Marketing Systems (EMSs)*, can handle high-volume email delivery as well as the far more complex content management and reporting aspects of email marketing.

The need for full-blown, specialized EMS solutions is now universally recognized. But companies are still unsure of the best way to build their EMS system. Should they take on the task internally, or outsource it to a specialized software or service firm? Several years ago, when specialized software was in its infancy, many IT departments believed (with good reason) that they could create "best in class" solutions using only internal staff. But with recent technology advancements, most IT departments would now be hard-pressed to match the features and sophistication of even the simplest commercially developed solution.

Regardless of whether you decide to tackle your email marketing system in-house or outsource it, you'll want to understand the components of your system. The goal for this section is *not* to drive a deep understanding of the technology behind EMSs, but rather to help you appreciate the complexity of the systems you will come to rely upon.

First, I'd like to address a common misperception surrounding EMS solutions. A number of marketers, and an even greater number of IT professionals, jump to the conclusion that EMSs are little more than beefed-up delivery engines (outbound MTAs). Although this may have been the case several years ago, it is no longer true today. Email marketing systems are actually quite sophisticated multicomponent, multifunctional units.

To help simplify these complex systems, I have created a general overview of a real-world EMS. This overview could be used to describe any popular system, including the one we offer at Silverpop. Keep in mind that my representation is simplified and may not take into account every possible nuance you might encounter with your own EMS.

The typical email marketing system (see Figure 7.3) consists of four basic sections: the data systems, the user-facing components, the Internet-facing components, and the internal management systems.

Figure 7.3 A typical EMS internal architecture

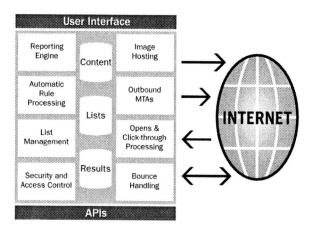

Data storage: Like all marketing efforts, EMSs revolve around data. Email data come in three forms: content (images, rich media, and text), mailing lists, and results. Content is usually stored as files on one or more servers in the EMS. Because lists and, particularly, results, can often be enormous—sometimes reaching into the billions of records— most EMSs utilize commercial databases, such as Oracle or Microsoft SQL Server. The sheer size of a large email marketing database is one of the many reasons marketers choose to outsource these solutions. Managing such an unwieldy database requires a great deal more expertise than do more traditional Web-based business applications.

User interface: Any interfaces that marketers or their full-service vendors use to set up, execute, and report on campaigns are considered user-facing interfaces.

Figure 7.4 shows an example of a typical reporting screen for an EMS

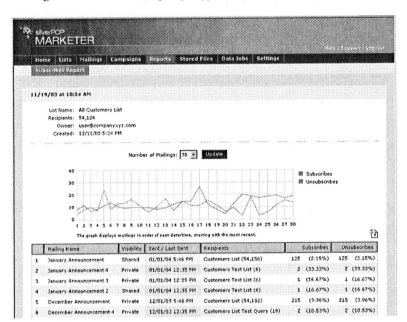

APIs: Not all interfaces are designed for human interaction. An increasingly critical aspect of mature EMS solutions is their ability to interface with marketers' preexisting systems and databases.

Software programmers use a term called *Application Programming Interface (API)* to describe the mechanisms by which data and commands move in and out of different computer systems. For example, APIs in an EMS solution can automatically link customer data between the marketer's IT systems and its email marketing vendor's EMS. APIs can be as simple as automatically importing updated lists from a CRM system, or they can be as complex as XML-based, two-way, real-time data feeds for event-triggered and automated message sequences. If the latter part of the previous sentence doesn't make sense to you, don't be concerned. All you really need to know is that the growth in EMS technology has allowed marketers to get whatever data they want, whenever they want it, from their EMS.

Internet-facing components: Also referred to as *recipient-facing* components, Internet-facing components are usually invisible and (hopefully) automatic for the marketer. These components enable a huge number of recipients to interact with your messages (via opens, click-throughs, conversions, forwards, etc.). They deliver message images and record recipient actions.

The following are examples of Internet-facing components:

- The outbound MTA servers transmit your messages across the Internet to your recipients' servers.

- Image-hosting servers deliver graphics to your message when the recipient opens it.

- Bounce servers handle undeliverable messages that are returned from ISPs and corporate email servers.

- Internet-facing servers deliver Web beacons, track click-throughs, follow opt-ins and opt-outs, and perform every other real-time recipient-facing action.

Most marketers think of the size or *scalability* of their EMS in terms of the number of messages it can send over a given period of time. But in reality, scalability is far more crucial to the other Internet-facing components of an EMS. Think about this scenario: You send a message to millions of recipients and, within the space of an hour, 50 percent of your recipients open your message. Of those opens, 50 percent click through. Your EMS could become so bogged down in tracking opens that click-throughs could take minutes to redirect. The bandwidth of the EMS could fill up so fast that images don't get delivered and recipients see errors or blanks in your email message.

If your outbound MTA takes a few extra minutes to send out several million messages, the delay probably won't hurt your campaign. Your recipients probably won't even notice. But if the other components slow down, your recipients may get broken messages or inactive links. Clearly, the consequences of broken links and images are far worse than the results of delayed delivery.

Most of the EMS providers I know are asked by at least three or four clients per month to *slow down* their rate of message delivery. Many of these clients have learned the hard way that too many simultaneous responses can overwhelm and even crash an e-commerce system, as well as the web sites they've linked to in their email. Talk about negative brand impact.

Internal management systems: The final set of email system components tie all of the other components together:

- The *reporting engine* takes the countless clicks, opens, and forwards, then slices and dices them and serves marketers the critical behavioral and response data they need to measure campaign success. For many marketers, the reporting engine is the most important component of an EMS.
- The automatic rules processor handles event-triggered messages, sequenced campaigns, scheduled mailings, and every other part of the email marketing campaign that occurs outside of the marketer's direct control.
- List management provides the processing power to set up lists, perform segmentation, modify records, and maintain overall data hygiene.
- Administration, security, and control systems complete the email solution.

The Big Mistake

A few years back, one of the top ISPs delivered an HTML message to its entire customer base. Upon opening the message, millions and millions of customers saw a red X where every graphic should have been. The mistake was huge and the ISP was, needless to say, embarrassed.

I wasn't a subscriber, but several of my colleagues used this ISP's service at home. A few of us got together and took apart the message to see what had gone wrong. We immediately saw the problem. Rather than pointing to an Internet location, each image (URL) referred to a file on the hard drive of a woman named Jane (name has been changed to protect the almost-fired). Apparently, Jane had constructed the message using files from her hard drive (a common practice), but she had forgotten to reset the links to her company's image server when she was finished. (Her company's EMS requires that this be done manually.) The irony was that Jane had tested the message by sending it to herself, and it had worked perfectly. (Her email client had no problem finding the images because they were on her PC.) Fortunately for Jane, she kept her job, but she came within a millimeter of slinging burgers at the local fast-food joint.

Email facilitates really big mistakes more so than most of its Internet peers. If a company puts up a broken Web page or fails to process an e-commerce transaction in a timely manner, the mistake can be caught and fixed fairly quickly. Only those users who come to the site during the error are affected by it. But once an email message has been sent, it cannot be recalled, and *it cannot be changed or updated.* If you misspell a word or link to a nonexistent image, you can do nothing (in most cases) to fix it. I sometimes think that it is this aspect of email—its ability to make massive, unrecoverable mistakes—that has pushed so many organizations to use outsourced services and expertise.

Companies that specialize in email fulfillment need to have processes and technologies in place to minimize human error. And if a massive mistake does occur, the ESP, and not our friend Jane, gets the boot.

Jane's story also speaks to a key point about EMS technologies. It is never enough to simply ask if a feature or capability exists. You must also ask how easy that feature is to use or, more importantly, how easy it would be for one of your employees to make a devastating mistake with it. The best EMSs support a wide range of key features, and do it in a way that catches human error. A solid EMS solution can provide all of the features I've outlined, prevent embarrassing technical mistakes, and enforce compliance with CAN-SPAM and other legislation.

Tracking Message Opens

Do you know whether your customers are actually reading your emails? Most sophisticated email marketing systems will automatically place a small *Web beacon* (also called a *Web bug*) in your HTML messages that invisibly tracks when your recipients open a message. The technology is the same one used by Web analytics tools to track visitors' movements through a site. Although Web beacons have raised privacy issues, they are immensely valuable to both marketers and recipients. Web beacons enable one of the big benefits of email marketing over traditional direct mail: They measure when someone has been *exposed* to a communication, not just when they *act* upon it.

Technically, a Web beacon is nothing more than a small, invisible image placed at the top or bottom of your HTML message. Each beacon image is uniquely coded for the individual email message and the recipient. Every time a user opens a message, the beacon alerts your server, saying, "Hi, I'm on the email you just sent out, and this particular recipient has just opened it." Beacons tell you who reads your email, on what date and time they open it, and how often they re-read it.

Many spammers have latched on to Web beacon technology, but with an aim far less noble than measuring recipient interest levels. Spammers can charge their customers a premium for email addresses of "confirmed openers," so they understandably want to know which of their recipients are most likely to open their messages. In the continuing battle to thwart spammers, some new email programs have gone so far as to turn off *all* email graphics unless the message is from a name in the recipient's address book. (See Chapter 19 for more information on renderability.) This draconian reaction hurts legitimate marketers, who generally use beacons for more benign purposes. But the fact that such extreme measures exist only confirms the need to build customer relationships. When customers know who you are and anticipate your messages, they are more likely to add you to their address book, and your messages are more likely to display properly.

Tracking Click-Throughs

Hypertext, the technology that allows users to travel via a link from one Web page to another, was one of the breakthroughs that enabled the World Wide Web. Email marketers use the same basic technology in their email links, but with a slightly different approach. Rather than sending users directly to a page on the sender's site, the email link takes them on an almost instantaneous detour. A basic Web technology called a *redirect* routes the user through the sender's EMS. The EMS records the click, notes the recipient and message, then redirects the recipient's Web browser to the final Web site destination. Sophisticated EMSs make the setup, execution, and tracking of the redirect invisible to both marketer and recipients. The recipient has no idea she has been detoured, and the marketer sees nothing but a highly accurate final report detailing which recipients clicked on which links.

Tracking Conversions

Conversions can be tracked in many ways. The simplest method uses Web beacons in a manner similar to open tracking. But instead of placing the beacon on the email, marketers place it on their Web site at the exact location where the customer would complete the conversion (purchase something, sign-up for an event, etc.). The Web beacon can be used in conjunction with *cookies* to further track the user, or it can be used to pass along simple information, such as the type and price of the product purchased.

■　■　■　■

I hope you come away from this chapter with a greater understanding of the software and hardware systems that are at the heart of your day-to-day activities. As email marketing becomes more complex and more relationship driven, the need for sophisticated technology will only continue to rise. One of my clients, Beth Fisher of the American Management Association, put it best when she said, "Technology is at the heart of email marketing. If you don't understand the technology, you will never be able to master the medium."[2]

Chapter 8

THE LEGAL ENVIRONMENT—CAN-SPAM

Laws control the lesser man. Right conduct controls
the greater one.
—Chinese proverb

Email was once a wild, untamed land where outlaw spammers roamed unchallenged. By the late 1990s, a few states had become fed up and began passing their own rules in an attempt to stop the spammers. But many of the state laws were convoluted and hard to enforce. While many of the bad guys slipped through town without notice, the good guys became entangled in a legal mess. Every time they tried to follow one law, they broke another. And the lawlessness continued.

In 2003, a new sheriff finally rolled into town. It was called CAN-SPAM. Some citizens of the Internet had high hopes that the sheriff would clean up the land. Others were afraid that it would never be tough enough to stand up against the spammers. But when CAN-SPAM went into effect on January 1, 2004, no one could argue that it would forever change the land of email.

Although few people agree on how CAN-SPAM will affect the problem of spam, no one can deny that it will profoundly influence email marketing. The act has driven a clear stake into the ground that legitimate email marketers have no choice but to recognize. While I was writing this book, nearly every company in the United States was scrutinizing the newly enacted legislation, trying to fully comprehend its intent and implications.

As we get ready to maneuver through the precarious legal implications of CAN-SPAM in this chapter, I must remind you that I am *not* a lawyer. In fact, I am far more likely to play a lawyer in the next

John Grisham film than I am to become one. My goal is to simply give you a high-level perspective on the history, architecture, and impact of the laws that now govern our profession. Therefore, I urge you to seek guidance from your own counsel as you attempt to make sense of the issues I will touch upon here.

A Look Back at U.S. Marketing Legislation

Reactions to CAN-SPAM have ranged from the optimistic, to the skeptical, to the unabashedly pessimistic. When the law passed, legislators lauded it as a victory for consumers. But industry experts predicted that the measure would do little to stem the growing tide of unsolicited email. Stanford Law School professor Lawrence Lessig went so far as to call the law an "abomination," not only ineffective but harmful because it overrode previously enacted state legislation.[1]

Many people argue that anything less than a complete ban on spam falls far short of protecting American consumers. Others say that government intervention in any technology serves only to worsen the problem.

The only point everyone seems to agree on is that CAN-SPAM will not make spam go away. In fact, the bill has been jokingly referred to as the "YOU-CAN-SPAM Act" because, rather than banning the practice, it actually legalizes unsolicited commercial email (provided that marketers follow its rules). What CAN-SPAM *does* do is finally provide guidance at the federal level, offering a realistic framework for legitimate marketers to follow. It also defines what practices are illegal federally and how they will be punished.

CAN-SPAM has not eliminated the legal labyrinth at the state level. The new law only preempts state statutes that regulate the use of email to send commercial messages; it does not necessarily override state statutes that prohibit the sending of fraudulent messages. In other words, as long as a message is not fraudulent in nature, CAN-SPAM governs. But as soon as a sender uses email for fraudulent purposes, state laws come into play as well. Also, broader state laws (e.g., those that cover trespass or fraud outside of email) can remain in force under CAN-SPAM.

A History of Media Legislation

Email is far from the first public medium to face regulation. As each new technology (radio, television, and the telephone) has gained popularity the government has stepped in and passed laws to protect consumers from those who would misuse or abuse the medium. Here are just a few examples of past media regulation:

- The Public Health Cigarette Smoking Act of 1969 banned cigarette advertising on radio and television.
- The 1991 federal Telephone Consumer Protection Act (TCPA) prohibited the use of fax communication for junk mail and allowed recipients to sue any business that sends junk faxes.
- The Children's Television Act of 1990 required broadcasters to air at least three hours per week of educational programming.
- The Children's Internet Protection Act of 2000 required schools and libraries to block or filter pornographic materials on computers with Internet access.

The Birth of CAN-SPAM

The Internet and email are in their infancy compared to television, radio, and other more established media. As had been the case with radio and television, the government at first adopted a hands-off approach to email. The Direct Marketing Association (DMA), arguably the most influential trade association overseeing email marketing, was firmly behind the government's laissez-faire stance.

But eventually spam made the issue of regulation unavoidable. By 2002, spammers were launching approximately 15 billion messages at consumers each day. AOL and MSN, two of the biggest Internet Service Providers (ISPs), reported that they were blocking 2.4 billion spam messages (or about 67 emails per customer inbox) daily.[2] While it irritated ISPs, spam drove consumers crazy. A 2003 study found that 75 percent of email users were bothered that they couldn't stop the flow of spam, and 25 percent were using email less as a result of it.[3] That same year, the DMA finally reversed its position and began working with state legislators and the federal government to craft anti-spam laws.

As legislation was evolving at the national level, nearly forty states passed their own anti-spam laws. Legitimate marketers trying to keep pace with the dizzying array of local laws found it nearly impossible to send a campaign without violating at least a few of them. The toughest and probably the most contentious of these laws was California SB 186, signed by Governor Gray Davis in September 2003. The law prohibited companies from sending commercial emails to people who hadn't specifically provided consent or who didn't have a preexisting business relationship with the sender. The law allowed individual consumers to sue spammers for up to $1,000 per email and $1 million per incident. For legitimate marketers trying to play by the rules, California SB 186 was volatile, imprecisely aimed, and generally unmanageable.

The California law was set to go into effect on January 1, 2004. As the date loomed, the DMA and most marketers warned that SB 186 would bring legitimate commercial email marketing to a virtual standstill. They pressured the U.S. Congress to pass more manageable legislation that would preempt at least some of SB 186 and other statutes like it. In December 2003, with a near unanimous vote, Congress passed the Controlling the Assault of Non-Solicited Pornography and Marketing Act of 2003, or CAN-SPAM.

Much to the chagrin of privacy and anti-spam advocates, CAN-SPAM is very much in line with the United States' overall approach to privacy issues. Despite its name, it definitely does NOT outlaw unsolicited commercial email, but only seeks to regulate it. CAN-SPAM does little to restrict the ways in which email addresses are gathered and managed, other than outlawing certain questionable practices, such as *harvesting*. And, it creates few constraints that limit how a company can communicate commercially with a prospect via email.

To get a perspective on privacy and spam legislation, I sat down with John Delaney, a partner with the international law firm Morrison & Foerster, LLP, and a leading expert on CAN-SPAM and general privacy legislation. According to John, the government views an email address as a form of personally identifiable information. As such, its collection, management, and usage fall under the privacy umbrella.

Most federal privacy legislation in the United States is administered and interpreted by the Federal Trade Commission (FTC), which follows a disclosure and notice approach. The FTC's position is to promote full and fair disclosures to permit consumers to make informed decisions. If a company clearly spells out how it will use personal data (including email addresses), then it is generally up to the customers to determine whether they want to do business under those terms. The United States also takes a strong First Amendment approach to marketing communications. Freedom of speech is often the starting point from which issues of privacy are addressed.

The Vision behind the Original Legislation

After CAN-SPAM became law, I lost track of how many conference calls and webinars I attended on the subject. Every pundit and so-called expert I listened to seemed to have a different interpretation of how the new law had come into being. Rather than accept a secondhand explanation of the vision behind CAN-SPAM, I decided to go to the source. I was fortunate enough to spend some one-on-one time with CAN-SPAM co-author Conrad Burns, the three-term Senator from Montana.

Senator Burns told me he had never envisioned that CAN-SPAM would rid the world of spam. Instead, he had designed it to make email a viable and safe place to do business. "The idea behind CAN-SPAM was to get rid of the scoundrels on the Internet so that legitimate advertisers and businesspeople could use the medium safely," he explains.[4] Although CAN-SPAM didn't live up to every expectation of consumers and anti-spam groups, Burns believes it was an important first step.

To understand the rationale behind CAN-SPAM requires some insight into Senator Burns's view of the Internet. He sees it as a means for moving rural Americans into "downtown America." In other words, the Internet makes distance and location irrelevant. Anyone, no matter where he lives, is an equal citizen online. The problem with cyberspace is that it changes the way most Americans are used to interacting with companies. Without face-to-face contact, consumers have fewer tools with which to judge businesses. Burns was concerned that consumers burned once too often by online swindlers would shun the medium entirely, undermining its ability to act as a place of commerce and community.

Spam has had a particularly detrimental impact upon Burns's constituency because many Montana residents rely on long distance dial-up connections to access the Internet. Every unwanted email message has a real cost to the people in his state.

But despite his concerns about spam, Burns was—and still is—a firm believer in advertising. He feels that advertising has a place in email, just as it has a place in radio and television. "Listen, I watch TV," he says. "I wish I didn't have to see those ads, but advertising is just a fact of the medium."[5] To Burns, the Internet and email are the same in this regard as all the mediums that have come before them.

Regardless of Burns's original vision, as soon as the bill was signed into law, interpretation and enforcement fell into another set of hands—the FTC. Hopefully by the time you read this, the FTC will have clarified much of CAN-SPAM and marketers will have a much better roadmap by which to navigate. But regardless of the outcome, I think we owe our thanks to Senator Burns, as well as to Senator Ron Wyden, co-author of the bill. They had the vision to create a single, federal standard that addresses consumer needs while allowing email to continue to evolve as a marketing medium.

The New Language of CAN-SPAM

One of the side benefits of CAN-SPAM is that it defines a few key terms that were previously confused or unclear among email marketers. Of course, CAN-SPAM's language is limited to the law's primary purpose—regulating commercial electronic mail. As such, the terms are not sufficient for the kind of brand-sensitive, enterprise initiatives that legitimate marketers require. I'll touch on the definitions outlined in CAN-SPAM, and I'll put them into the more brand-focused context of CCM. But for a more comprehensive set of terms that cover the entire spectrum of CCM, refer to Chapters 9 and 10.

CAN-SPAM defines two types of email messages:

Commercial electronic email messages (CEMMs):
Section 3(2)(A)

IN GENERAL—The term 'commercial electronic mail message' means any electronic mail message the primary purpose of which is the commercial advertisement or promotion of a commercial product or service (including content on an Internet website operated for a Commercial purpose).

Transactional or relationship messages (TRMs):
Section 3(17)(A)

IN GENERAL—The term 'transactional or relationship message' means an electronic mail message the primary purpose of which is—

(i) to facilitate, complete, or confirm a commercial transaction that the recipient has previously agreed to enter into with the sender;

(ii) to provide warranty information, product recall information, or safety or security information with respect to a commercial product or service used or purchased by the recipient;

(iii) to provide—

(I) notification concerning a change in the terms or features of;

(II) notification of a change in the recipient's standing or status with respect to; or

(III) at regular periodic intervals, account balance information or other type of account statement with respect to,

a subscription, membership, account, loan, or comparable ongoing commercial relationship involving the ongoing purchase or use by the recipient of products or services offered by the sender;

(iv) to provide information directly related to an employment relationship or related benefit plan in which the recipient is currently involved, participating, or enrolled; or

(v) to deliver goods or services, including product updates or upgrades, that the recipient is entitled to receive under the terms of a transaction that the recipient has previously agreed to enter into with the sender.[6]

(If you want to impress your friends, you can use "insider's" slang and refer to the two types of message as, respectively, "sems" and "trims.")

The law is primarily focused on regulating CEMMs, the most egregious example of which is spam. But the term CEMM is also used to define legitimate email. A CEMM is basically any message that is commercial in nature, whether it is unsolicited or permissioned. Transactional and relationship messages, which are generally part of a preexisting business relationship, are treated more leniently and require less stringent labeling. Both CEMMs and TRMs are discussed in greater detail in Chapter 9.

CAN-SPAM boils the idea of permission down to a concept called "affirmative consent," which, when used with respect to a CEMM, is defined as:

```
Section 3(1)
(A) the recipient expressly consented to receive the
message, either in response to a clear and conspicuous
request for such consent or at the recipient's own
initiative; and

(B) if the message is from a party other than the party to
which the recipient communicated such consent, the
recipient was given clear and conspicuous notice at the
time the consent was communicated that the recipient's
electronic mail address could be transferred to such other
party for the purpose of initiating commercial electronic
mail messages.7
```

Affirmative consent means that the recipient has granted his or her express permission to receive the message. Although the statues are not specific, best practices are emerging as companies attempt to comply with CAN-SPAM. For example, if you use a check box for a recipient to provide consent, a prechecked box may not qualify as affirmative consent. And even if the box starts out unchecked, it still may not be sufficient affirmative consent if the text next to the box does not clearly and conspicuously disclose which option the recipient is choosing.

CAN-SPAM has also added several new concepts that define the various participants and actions involved in the creation and delivery of an email message:

Initiate refers to the "execution" of the email, or the person(s) who wants the message sent.

> Section 3(9)
> The term 'initiate', when used with respect to a
> commercial electronic mail message, means to originate or
> transmit such message or to procure the origination or
> transmission of such message, but shall not include
> actions that constitute routine conveyance of such
> message. For purposes of this paragraph, more than one
> person may be considered to have initiated a message.[8]

According to this definition, if a magazine publisher hires Silverpop to run an email magazine promotion, both the publisher and Silverpop may be considered initiators. An initiator should not be confused with a sender, which CAN-SPAM defines as:

> Section 3(16)(A)
> ...the term 'sender', when used with respect to a commercial
> electronic mail message, means a person who initiates such
> a message and whose product, service, or Internet web site
> is advertised or promoted by the message.[9]

The *sender* refers to the person whose product or service is advertised or promoted by the message. For example, if a soft drink company rents an email list and sends those addresses a promotional message for its product, it is considered the sender, even if a list owner handles the message delivery. However, if an airline and a hotel team up to create a *promotional email* that contains advertisements for both partners, many people would interpret CAN-SPAM to mean that both the airline and hotel are considered senders. But if the hotel simply places an ad banner in the airline's email newsletter, many lawyers would argue that only the airline is the sender because the hotel was not involved in *initiating* the message.

The law specifically singles out the messengers—the organizations or technologies that deliver the message to its final recipient—with the term *routine conveyance*:

> Section 3(15)
> The term 'routine conveyance' means the transmission,
> routing, relaying, handling, or storing, through an
> automatic technical process, of an electronic mail message

```
for which another person has identified the recipients or
provided the recipient addresses.10
```

On the surface, the definition appears to exempt email inbox providers, ISPs, and other companies that process the CEMM on its route from the initiator. Less clear is the responsibility of Email Service Providers (ESPs). Logically, full-service providers would have some culpability, considering that they play a role in the message creation. But what about self-service ESPs? Should they be liable for every piece of content that advertisers send across their network? The law might say yes, but trying to monitor and infiltrate thousands, if not millions, of messages a day would be a logistical and fiscal impossibility. The FTC has not yet begun to address this question, although I believe it's inevitable. My advice to my ESP colleagues: Screen your customers. Work only with clients who are fully CAN-SPAM compliant. Otherwise, the law-defining court case may be about you.

Penalties and Enforcement

Legitimate marketers following generally accepted best practices are likely to avoid much of the sting associated with CAN-SPAM penalties. If you focus on permission and play by the rules, you're not likely to run afoul of the law. That said, the consequences are pretty severe if you do make a misstep.

The act does not allow for a "private right of action"; that is, individual recipients cannot sue spammers directly (as the California measure would have allowed). It does, however, allow suits by the FTC, state attorneys general, and ISPs. The severity of the penalty varies based on which entity initiates the suit. Depending on the violation, ISPs may be able to sue for up to $100 per illegal email message, to a maximum of $1 million, and state attorneys general can sue for $250 per illegal message, up to a maximum of $2 million. But the fines can go even higher if the spammer is found to have violated the prohibition on transmitting false or misleading information, in which case aggravated penalties may be imposed. The most egregious offenders can find themselves behind bars for up to five years.

The nation's four biggest ISPs were quick to test the new law. Just under ninety days after CAN-SPAM went into force, Yahoo!, Earthlink, Microsoft, and AOL launched a coordinated legal attack, firing off six lawsuits against hundreds of "kingpin" spammers. For the sake of all legitimate marketers, we should hope that future legal action will similarly focus on the spammers who send billions of illegal and sometimes illicit messages, rather than the legitimate business owners who accidentally omit their physical mailing address in their latest newsletter. (See page 65 for CAN-SPAM requirements.)

If you're still having trouble navigating the CAN-SPAM labyrinth after reading this section, or you're simply looking for a legislative update, you can find one of the best sources of information on U.S. and international spam laws at http://www.spamlaws.com.

International Spam Laws

The Internet has truly globalized our world. Email can cross borders just as easily as it crosses your office. But regulating and enforcing across such a vast playing field is difficult, if not impossible.

Numerous countries have enacted their own laws that specifically govern electronic mail. But a country-by-country approach may be insufficient to catch spammers who disappear across virtual borders without a trace. As John Ripa, head of e-products at Acxiom, puts it, "If 4 billion messages are sent out tonight from Nigeria, I seriously doubt we'll send troops over there to do anything about it."[11]

"Spam is a global problem," explains Delaney. "It doesn't lend itself well to local solutions."[12] World governments may need to work together, he says, to come up with a unified, global legislative solution.

Most of the world takes a different approach to anti-spam laws than the United States, which wraps its anti-spam legislation within the greater context of free speech and privacy. Whereas U.S. privacy laws tend to protect citizens against abuses by the *government*, European Union privacy laws are more likely to protect citizens from abuses by *businesses*. Also, whereas the United States favors business self-regulation, the European Union leans toward governmental regulation.

Two EU directives focus on privacy and spam. In 1995, the European Union passed Directive 95/46/EC (often referred to as the

Data Protection Directive), which addresses the way personal data is processed and transferred. This directive protects consumers by stipulating the way in which companies can collect, process, and transfer personal data. As of this writing, the majority of EU member countries had put the Data Protection Directive into law.

Then in 2002, the European Union enacted the Directive on Privacy and Electronic Communications, which speaks more directly to email and spam. The directive prohibits companies from sending *any* direct marketing electronic messages without <u>first</u> obtaining recipients' express opt-in permission. The American law, by contrast, allows companies to send to consumers, without permission, at least until they say "stop."

American companies need to take the European laws into consideration. Multinational companies, in particular, are not beyond the reach of EU law. If you can remain compliant with the directives (obtaining upfront permission, for example), you will avoid a lot of legal headaches down the road. Because most of the world takes its privacy and spam cues from the European Union, compliance will likely put you in good stead with a large portion of the rest of the planet.

Navigating CAN-SPAM Legislation

CAN-SPAM does not prohibit the sending of commercial email. Rather, it prohibits fraudulent and misleading practices and requires that marketers include more identifying information in their messages. The law should have relatively little impact on legitimate, responsible emailers, provided that permission is granted and all opt-outs are honored. Aside from some tactical items, such as clear labeling of advertisements, inclusion of physical addresses, and legal scrutiny of email programs, most marketers will need to make only minor adjustments to their programs.

Although a full review of CAN-SPAM is well beyond the scope of this book, I can offer a few suggestions to help your organization adapt to the new legislation. My colleagues and I recommend that our clients focus on four specific areas when reviewing their email initiatives for CAN-SPAM compliance:

1. Add a physical address to all of your mailings. Although the law is not specific, many experts are recommending against the use of P.O. boxes.

2. If your message does not meet the definition of "affirmative consent" (the recipient expressly consented to receive the message), add a notice clearly identifying your message as an advertisement or solicitation. The FTC will eventually specify how commercial messages must be labeled, but in the meantime, make sure that your intent is clear.

3. Review each of your mailings to ensure that your opt-out mechanism is "clear and conspicuous."

4. Review your opt-out process to ensure that all opt-outs are handled within the ten-business-day period required by the law. Also make sure that you provide a global opt-out that covers your entire organization. A line of business exception (i.e., a separate brand owned by the same corporation) may apply in some cases; consult the legislation or talk to your attorney for more specifics.

CCM and the Law

The irony of this legislation, both in the United States and abroad, is that legality is only the first step to becoming a good marketer. Truly effective email marketing requires a great deal more effort than mere CAN-SPAM compliance. Remember, the legislation is designed to protect consumer resources: their time, their privacy, and the sanctity of their inboxes. Although CCM also aims for these goals, it takes a giant step further by helping build positive, long-lasting customer relationships between customers and companies.

I remember one instance in which Silverpop had to sever ties with a client that was slipping into spammer-like habits. In our final conversation, the company's marketing director practically screamed at us, "Everything we do is completely legal!" She had completely missed the point. Following the law will probably keep you out of jail, and it may even help you keep your job, but it certainly won't win you customers. The government does not mandate high standards—its role is to make sure standards don't sink too low. Even if you follow every aspect of the U.S. legislation, ISPs and their customers always have the final say as to whether your email is spam.

CCM, on the other hand, is all about high standards. It's about understanding your customers' wants and expectations, and designing your email program to ensure that everything you communicate is relevant to them.

Nonetheless, CAN-SPAM has served CCM well. First, it has reduced the conflicting obligations imposed by individual states. Rather than having to deal with each state's legal stipulations on a case-by-case basis, companies can now implement simpler policies that comply with the overall federal legislation. Second, because CAN-SPAM requires extensive coordination across enterprises (and because the cost of screwing up an email campaign is now so high), senior management is forced to take notice and to devote much-needed care and resources to their email program. Such high-level involvement also ensures that opt-outs are handled universally and that the company presents a unified face to its consumers (both of which are good practices). Most important, because CAN-SPAM mandates a more appropriate use of the email channel, it might finally bring well-intentioned email marketers the credibility they deserve.

Down the Road

Those who question whether CAN-SPAM will have any real impact must understand that the legislation is still in its infancy. Congress has written a fine roadmap, but the road ahead is long and twisted, and many of the directions are still unclear. The law has left many issues open for the FTC to clarify in the years to come. By the time you read this, many of these issues will hopefully have been resolved. But as I sit here writing, the process has just begun.

To fully understand the next steps in the evolution of CAN-SPAM, I spent some time with Michael Goodman, a staff attorney at the FTC who was involved in the interpretation and "rule making" effort.

As Goodman explained to me, the FTC is required to interpret and define six specific rule-making areas of the CAN-SPAM legislation:

1. Adult Content Label—Effective May 19, 2004, the FTC ruled that all CEMMs containing sexually oriented material carry the warning label, "SEXUALLY EXPLICIT:" in the subject line. The rule also specifies which kinds of content can be initially viewable in the message without prior recipient consent.

2. Definition of "Primary Purpose"—The authors of CAN-SPAM realized that the definition of CEMMs needed some serious review. Although many emails will be overtly commercial in nature, Congress recognized that there will likely be some hazy messages that warrant more specific classification. Congress asked the FTC to enact regulations that provide criteria for defining "Primary Purpose" as it applies to electronic mail messages.

The next set of rules are optional and have no specific deadlines:

3. Further Define Transactional or Relationship Messages ("TRMs")—Congress gave the FTC the authority to review and modify which types of messages constitute TRMs. The FTC may decide to either broaden or narrow its definition of TRMs.

4. Opt-out Period—CAN-SPAM gives marketers up to ten business days to honor opt-out requests. Although the FTC does not have to change the rule, it has the option of modifying the time period.

5. Aggravated Violations—The act defines certain practices, such as address harvesting, as aggravated violations. The FTC may decide to define additional aggravated violations. Anyone who breaches one of the Act's provisions and commits an aggravated violation may face increased penalties.

6. General Rule Making—The FTC has an open invitation to create additional rules that help implement the act.

In addition to these six areas of rule making, the FTC is required to deliver four reports to Congress:

1. Do-Not-Email Registry ("DNE")—One of the most controversial aspects of the new law was a proposed "Do-Not-Email" list. The legislation allows consumers to opt themselves out of unwanted messages, but only after receiving the first email. Similar to the FTC's "Do-Not-Call" list aimed at telemarketers, the "Do-Not-Email" registry would bar marketers from sending unsolicited email to anyone on the list. In June 2004, the FTC recommended against a DNE list until the industry developed more mature sender-authentication technologies. See Chapter 19 for more detail on these technologies.

2. Reward or Bounty System—Another report, due in September 2004, will offer recommendations on establishing a public reward or bounty system. People who supply information about CAN-SPAM violations could receive 20 percent of civil penalties collected from the spammers they nab.

3. A Commercial Email Label—Before CAN-SPAM, many states required that commercial emails include the code "ADV" (for "advertising") in their subject line, to give consumers and ISPs an easier way of filtering out unwanted messages. Congress asked the FTC to analyze this and other labeling possibilities and submit a report by June 2005.

4. CAN-SPAM Effectiveness—Two years after CAN-SPAM's enactment, the FTC will report back to Congress on the law's effectiveness.

When Will CAN-SPAM Finally Become Clear?

Marketers, lawyers, and consumers want to know: When will we really understand how to interpret the law? I fear the answer will not come anytime soon.

The good news is, if you apply a CCM strategy to your email, you'll already be one step ahead of the legislation. Generally speaking, CCM practices are higher and harder to manage than either the U.S. or EU legislation. The higher you aim, the more you'll protect your marketing effort from any potential legal repercussions.

In the meantime, we'll have to keep an eye on the FTC's rule-making efforts. We'll also have to watch as individual states battle it out with the federal government over jurisdiction. Ultimately, the courts will probably give marketers the answers we seek. Hard-fought cases will likely be the final judge of how CAN-SPAM is to be interpreted.

And CAN-SPAM is just the first chapter of email legislation. There will undoubtedly be more to come.

The Future of Legislation

As I write this book, the newspapers are filled with stories predicting the failure of CAN-SPAM. Spam counts are still as high as ever; therefore, CAN-SPAM has failed, they contend. I agree that CAN-SPAM has missed the mark in some respects. American consumers have been trained to avoid the opt-out. But by doing so, they risk handing their email address on a silver platter to spammers. And without the opt-out, CAN-SPAM gives spammers the go-ahead to persist in their practices.

But before you condemn the measure for its downfalls, you have to remember that CAN-SPAM was never written to outlaw spam, at least not in the way most consumers define it (unsolicited commercial email). Expecting CAN-SPAM to stop spam is like expecting speed limits to eliminate automobile accidents. CAN-SPAM only regulates and controls commercial email—it does not purport to end it.

That said, CAN-SPAM may still get tougher on spammers. Unless spam begins to slow, consumers will grow ever more impatient. Foreign governments have already begun to push the United States to comply with their more restrictive email legislation. Perhaps the combined weight of consumers and international legislators will finally put spammers on notice, and force Congress's hand to the point where it will update the existing CAN-SPAM legislation or enact new, stricter legislation.

■　■　■　■

CAN-SPAM is not going to erase the problem of spam anytime soon. Combating this scourge will require both marketers and consumers to adjust their perceptions and practices over the long term. Consumers will have to start trusting the opt-out process to make the current provisions of CAN-SPAM work. Marketers will have to focus even harder on building customer relationships.

But over the long term, CAN-SPAM has given us many reasons to be optimistic. The measure is a true call to arms. It finally gives enforcement agencies and consumers the weapons they need to go after spammers.

As John Delaney pointed out, spam is a global problem, requiring a global solution. As I write this, I read daily pronouncements of new technologies created to combat spam. Technology is the ultimate global solution—it has no borders and it works the same wherever it is applied. Without a doubt, it will be the one-two punch of technology and legislation that will finally begin to erode the Internet's greatest scourge. Marketers must fully understand and embrace both aspects of the counterattack if their customer relationships are to thrive in the email channel.

Part III

MANAGING PERMISSION

PART 3
MANAGING PERMISSION

The simple act of asking for permission before sending a message sets off a powerful positive momentum that reverberates throughout an entire email program. Permission is what separates legitimate marketers from spammers. Permission is what earns customers' trust. Permission is what drives relevancy—the foundation of CCM.

Permission is the tool that turns prospects into customers, and customers into lifelong customers.

Requesting permission would appear as easy as asking a simple question: "Do you want to hear from us, yes or no?" In reality, gaining permission is a complex process requiring both insight and subtlety. Managing permission across the scope of an organization is an even more complex process requiring fairly sophisticated technology, active coordination among all departments, and a cohesive, company-wide policy.

The next section will take you through the fine points of permission. I'll show you how this critical concept fits into your overall CCM strategy, and advise you how to manage your permissions under the new CAN-SPAM legislation.

First, I'll distinguish between the various "types" of email, for example, prospecting versus promotional. Next, I will dissect the various levels of permission. Then, I'll introduce a concept called *preferences,* which helps put recipients in control of what they receive from you.

Once we've established permission, we'll turn our attention to what is probably the most complex and tightly regulated element of permission marketing: managing opt-outs. I'll show you some of the challenges companies face when trying to manage organizational opt-out programs, and I'll give you some ideas on how to manage your own opt-out solutions.

Finally, I will try to clarify the most confusing and risky aspect of permission—the use of third-party data and lists to build your CCM programs.

Chapter 9

TYPES OF EMAIL

Divide each difficulty into as many parts as is feasible and necessary to resolve it.
—René Descartes, famous seventeenth-century mathematician

If you're like me, you've probably found yourself driving with cell phone in hand at least once, and probably far more often. Without lifting our foot from the gas, we can conduct meetings, check on our families, or let our appointments know we're running late. I'm sure all of us realize on some level that juggling cell phone and steering wheel probably isn't the safest practice, but it's nonetheless one we've come to take for granted.

But some of us are now having to change our ways. With strict cell phone regulations already in place in a handful of states, and more states expected to follow, we've been forced to think about where—and how—we use our phones. Pick up the phone while you're driving in one of the cell phone—restricted states these days and you're looking at a steep fine.

Why do I mention cell phone laws in a chapter about email types? Because most email marketers are similarly having to start thinking about and changing everyday practices that, under CAN-SPAM, can now get them into legal hot water.

Think about your own email program for a moment. You may send one message welcoming a new customer and another promoting a sale, but have you ever thought to categorize each message by type? Do you ask yourself: Am I prospecting for new customers or promoting a product or service with a *commercial* message? Am I following up on a purchase with a *transactional* message, or is my message simply an extension of an ongoing *relationship*? By regulating certain *types* of messages, CAN-SPAM is now requiring that all email marketers make these distinctions.

In their effort to devise a simple regulation standard, the authors of CAN-SPAM have clearly delineated two types of email: Commercial Electronic Mail Messages (CEMMs), and Transactional or Relationship messages (TRMs). (See Chapter 8 for the legal implications of these message types.) The former are sent for the purpose of selling or advertising products. The latter are viewed as extensions of an existing company-customer relationship. Sometimes the line between the two email types is fuzzy.

Understanding the dividing line is important because each type of message must be handled differently. A simple greeting could fall under the CEMM category if it has a promotional overtone, for example, whereas a shipping reminder would normally be considered a relationship message because a transaction has already occurred. CAN-SPAM stipulates that all CEMMs be clearly labeled as advertisements and include a conspicuous opt-out somewhere within the message. Transactional and relationship messages are handled far more liberally and don't require the same labeling.

Differentiating message types is now de rigueur for marketers, but it is also a key part of CCM strategy. As email marketing programs diversify beyond "buy this now" advertising messages, organizations will find that types can help them strike the right balance between meeting their marketing needs and satisfying their customers. Message types can make frequency policies more meaningful. Types can help clarify recipient expectations and define the right type of communication for each kind of interaction. And types can allow organizations to define the appropriate workflows and approvals for each kind of message.

Types are also useful for determining the right level of permission for each message. Even though most legitimate emailers technically practice permission marketing, they have in place, at best, enveloping policies that cut a wide swath over their entire organization's email efforts. Permissions under these blanket policies can too easily be confused. For example, if you ask most companies whether they require permission for every customer email, they will usually answer yes. Then ask them if they should require permission to send a receipt for an e-commerce purchase, and they won't have a clue. (Don't laugh—I know a company that spent a month deadlocked on that very question.)

Without types, permission policies can be too imprecise because they fail to reflect customer expectations. With types, the focus shifts from the marketer to the customer. Types don't dwell on the marketer's desired outcome from the interaction, but instead revolve around the recipient's expectations and perceived value of the communication.

THE CAMPAIGN VALUE EXCHANGE

Virtually every email interaction revolves around an exchange of value. Customers grant their permission in exchange for what they perceive as valuable information or services from a company. The company gains value by converting those customer permissions into sales or loyalty. We can measure the value exchange of a campaign, to some degree, by what extent the sender or recipient benefits. I call this concept *Campaign Value Exchange (CVE)*.

It may not be practical, or even possible, to measure the value of every email you send your customers. But having the CVE on hand helps you easily gauge the overall impact of your messages on your customers.

Figure 9.1 Campaign Value Exchange

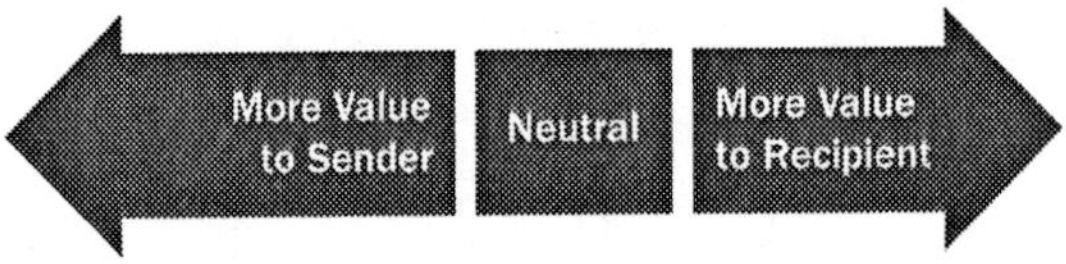

Most messages will fall somewhere within the spectrum of value shown in Figure 9.1. The diagram naturally skews to the left, because most email is sent to benefit the sender only (spam being the worst example of heavily sender-valued email). Such inequality persists because spammers can reach a nearly infinite number of recipients at virtually no cost. The recipient gains nothing from these unwanted interactions and, in fact, loses an extremely valuable commodity: time.

I'll give you an example using simple math. On a slow day, a spammer can send 50 million messages. Let's say 25 percent make it through the spam filters, and those 12.5 million messages find their way to their intended recipients. Let's assume that these recipients are extremely fast—they can read, evaluate, and delete one message per second. Valuing each recipient's time at a mere $10 an hour, the spammer has erased almost $35,000 worth of productivity. And that figure takes into account lost productivity from only *one spammer* on *one day*. Multiply that by the 3 trillion to 4 trillion total spam messages sent out by spammers each year and you start to get a sense of how skewed the CVE can become.

With permission-based messages, the value exchange tends to be more balanced. For example, say an airline sends out a notice promoting its new automated check-in feature to 2 million customers. Over the next three months, one hundred thousand of those customers take advantage of the new service. The airline saves $2.50 per transaction, and each customer saves fifteen minutes of precious time. This single campaign has been part of an astonishing $500,000 value creation. What's more, both sender and recipient have benefited.

Campaign Value Exchange under CAN-SPAM

As I mentioned earlier in the chapter, CAN-SPAM defines two types of emails: CEMMs and TRMs. As you can see from Figure 9.2, CEMMs sit squarely on the sender's side, and transactional or relationship messages are either neutral or in favor of the recipient. CAN-SPAM focuses almost entirely on legislating the CEMM, or "value to sender" side of the equation.

Figure 9.2 Campaign Value Exchange under CCM

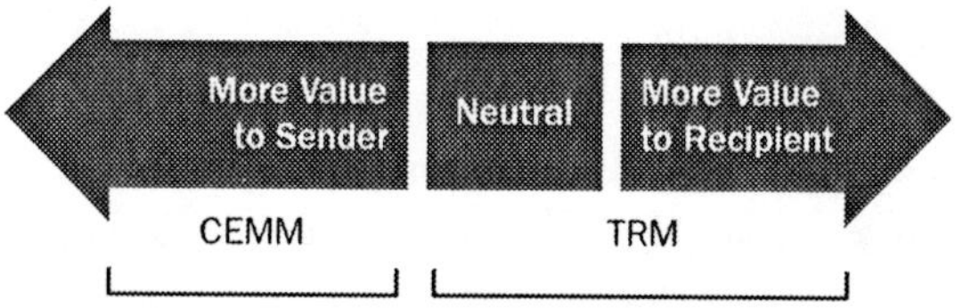

With CCM, the goal is to shift the balance in the opposite direction—to the recipient-value side. The idea is that by transferring the greatest value to the recipient, the marketer dramatically increases loyalty, repeat purchases, and lifetime value. I should mention that many commercial messages provide great value to recipients (for example, the airline's automated check-in feature mentioned on page 72) but, generally speaking, CEMMs lean in favor of the sender.

TYPES OF EMAIL

As CCM propagates throughout organizations and email expands beyond a mass advertising tool, the two types defined by CAN-SPAM become inadequate to describe all possible customer interactions. There are many ways to "bucket" the different types of emails. Your company may already have established its own types, or your types may evolve as your email program matures.

The six types I have listed here, though by no means the only possible descriptors, should provide good examples to fit the majority of your communications: interpersonal, informational, administrative, transactional, promotional, and prospecting. And, for the purposes of this book, these six types will be the basic "types" used in CCM.

Figure 9.3 Campaign Value Exchange with the CCM Types

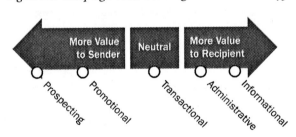

Figure 9.3 shows where each of the CCM types fits into the CVE chart. Of course, types can fall into more than one position within the range, depending upon the campaign execution. For example, a prospecting message offering $50 off a purchase, although unquestionably beneficial to the sender, would also have extremely high

value to a large number of recipients. The purpose in plotting the types this way is to show where they land *most of the time*.

Interpersonal

The classic definition of interpersonal communication is an interaction between two or more people. When applied to email, interpersonal communication is used to describe the act of one person manually composing and sending a message to another. Examples of interpersonal emails might be two friends chatting about their children, an engineer asking a colleague for feedback on a problem, or a hiring manager following up with an applicant.

You'll notice that I have not included interpersonal emails in Figure 9.3. I've omitted it because I view the interpersonal message as a special case that can fall anywhere on the CVE depending upon the intent of the message.

The basic mode of communication is the same in email as it is in other forms of interpersonal communication. Email does lack some of the immediacy of face-to-face or phone conversation, because messages normally take a few seconds to send and may take the recipient up to several days to read. Interpersonal emails should nonetheless be as individual and as relevant as a personal conversation.

Which brings us to the subject of permission. If you were to engage in a one-on-one conversation with a customer, would you need to first ask for his or her permission? The answer depends upon the nature of your message, and how narrowly you define the term "interpersonal." One of my clients was in a situation that threatened to pull interpersonal email into its more restrictive enterprise-wide email marketing policy. Each time the company's customer service agents went on vacation, they would send out a message to each of their customers (about seventy-five to one hundred people), providing contact numbers to be used during their absence. The company wanted to know, was this practice considered informational or interpersonal? Should the customer service agents have requested permission before sending the message? And did the recipients need to be scrubbed against the company's global opt-out mechanism prior to the mailing? In this case, we elected to have the message fall under the interpersonal category. But it would have taken just one customer service agent to embed a promotional message within their vacation notice to really muddy the waters.

Interpersonal email also gets confusing when it comes to interpreting CAN-SPAM. After discussing the legislation with co-author Senator Conrad Burns, I've come to the conclusion that CAN-SPAM was never intended to cover interpersonal emails. Unfortunately, my conversations with several FTC staff members have led me to believe that certain interpersonal emails will nonetheless be viewed as CEMMs and be subject to the same rules. The actual impact of CAN-SPAM on interpersonal commercial emails will take some time to unfold. The FTC and the courts will be busy fielding a range of viewpoints for quite a while. Until the issue is resolved, marketers are safest to manage their interpersonal sales and service emails under the guidance of CAN-SPAM. Most of my clients are already looking hard at including active opt-out mechanisms in the interpersonal emails that come from their sales and service departments, despite the technical and procedural challenges.

Another potential confounder of interpersonal email is viral messaging. Technically, viral falls under the interpersonal header because it is sent from one individual (the original recipient) to another (or several others). But the marketer's role in the equation makes the lines unclear. Marketers want to promote viral messaging because it gets the word out about their products or services. They construct their messages specifically to encourage pass-alongs. They even go so far as to get involved in the actual delivery of viral messages.

The marketer's role has people in the industry squabbling over how viral emails should be treated. Some say viral messages should be considered interpersonal because they are no different from personal recommendations sent from one friend to another. The recipient, they argue, cannot tell whether the message was forwarded via a pass-along feature in the Email Marketing System (EMS) or through the forward feature of the original recipient's email client. Others exclude from the interpersonal category any viral messages that reward the original recipient with an incentive (a cash prize, for instance) for forwarding the message. Regardless of how you view the viral message, the safest approach is to scrub every viral message delivered through your EMS against your organizational opt-out list before sending.

Hopefully by the time you read this, the FTC will have resolved the questions surrounding interpersonal email. Until then, leading-edge companies are playing it safe by defining permission policies for the use of their sales force and customer service representatives, and building global, organization-wide opt-outs that cover marketing, viral, and other interpersonal emails.

Informational

Informational emails transfer knowledge from company to customer. Customers are usually receptive to information from the companies with which they do business. They want the latest stock information, the quickest and easiest recipes, and the best parenting ideas from the pros. Companies fulfill those wants by sending newsletters, alerts, status updates, and product updates. Each informational email is (or should be) highly relevant and valuable to the consumer. The return value to the company comes in the forms of repeated brand exposure and, more important, increased customer loyalty.

As valuable as they often are to consumers, informational emails walk a fine line with CAN-SPAM. If they are sent in the context of an existing relationship, they might fall under the header of transactional messages and be spared CEMM restrictions. Examples include warranty information, product recalls or upgrades, and safety and security updates. But if even the merest hint of an advertisement or product solicitation slips in, the entire foundation of the message can change, which is why companies are safest getting help from their legal counsel or simply treating all informational messages as CEMMs.

Administrative

In the traditional offline world, administrative communications have a bad reputation, and for good reason. They are manual, tedious, and slow. If a company wants to update its customer service policy, for example, the policy has to be drafted, physically carried through all of

123

the approval points in the organization, copied thousands of times, and then mailed to each customer. Employees can spend days getting out a single message. Forests full of trees perish, only to line wastebaskets across America. It is only logical for companies to want to look for faster, cheaper, and less paper-intensive alternatives.

Email is a natural. Many companies have already eliminated the old paper trail. They now rely on email for communicating account status updates, billing information, policy updates, and other requisite administrative information with their customers and vendors. In many cases, *administrative emails* are a great solution for companies, and they provide a more personal and faster solution for customers.

Several years ago, American Airlines made a bold move by scrapping paper entirely from its frequent flier club communications. Now if a customer wants to participate in the airline's frequent flier program, she has to provide an email address and be willing to receive updates by email. By removing a paper-based component from the communication flow, American simplified its execution, dramatically lowered its costs, and was able to deliver key information to its customers faster than ever before.

Because administrative emails are, by their very nature, part of an ongoing business relationship, they have not surprisingly been spared the strictures of CAN-SPAM. The legislation appears to very clearly delineate administrative as a branch of transactional and relationship messaging, thereby bypassing most of the CEMM requirements. Specifically, CAN-SPAM allows administrative emails that notify customers of a change in their account status (for example, account balance or subscription statements), or that constitute employee communications (for example, benefits notices).

Transactional

Transactional email can be a powerful customer service tool and a persuasive brand ambassador. The strength of transactional communication lies in its origin point. Unlike virtually every other message type, transactional emails are initiated by the recipient, not the sender. Because they are requested and anticipated, they tend to cut more quickly through the clutter of a crowded inbox. Transactional emails are positioned as the first communication in the overall email relationship because the value is so high to both parties.

The transactional email chain begins with a customer action (a purchase, an opt-in, or a class sign-up), which triggers a reaction (or two) from the company. If you order a book from Amazon.com, for example, they will send you an electronic receipt confirming the sale, followed by a shipping notification. Amazon needs no permission (aside from the purchase itself) to contact you. But once your transaction is complete, the correspondence likely ends unless they can sway you to opt-in to a broader email program. Reservation confirmations, cancellations and returns, billing and payment notifications are all forms of transactional messaging.

CAN-SPAM is fairly lenient with transactional emails. Messages that "facilitate, complete, or confirm" a preexisting relationship (as transactional emails do) are clearly defined as noncommercial and are therefore not subject to CEMM restrictions.

Promotional

Promotional and prospecting emails have the same aim—to elicit a purchase. The difference is in the expectation. Promotional emails use existing customer relationships and active permissions to make their call to action. Because they have indicated their receptiveness, customers should anticipate—if not outright desire—these messages.

The reward for customers is in the message incentive, which could come in the form of a discount coupon or a weekend sale announcement. The reward to the marketer is in the purchase.

Some messages are inherently more promotional than others. To determine the slant of your own messages, ask yourself, "How much of my recipients' time, privacy, or money am I requesting?" The larger the gap between what you're offering and what you're requesting, the more promotional your message.

Regardless of the benefit to the customer, and regardless of how noble your aim might be, promotional email will almost always fall squarely within the realm of CEMM under CAN-SPAM.

Prospecting

Prospecting emails, like their promotional counterparts, are sent with the goal of enticing a purchase. The difference is that the potential purchaser is more of a stranger than a friend. The recipient has not initiated a relationship, offline or online, and is therefore not anticipating the message.

The most obvious examples of prospecting are sending an advertisement to a rented third-party list, or sending a promotion to a list borrowed from a business partner. More subtle, but potentially more damaging, is the unanticipated prospecting message. Borrowing a newsletter list from another division and blasting a promotion to it strains the original permission and will probably strain your customer's loyalty. In my experience, abusing a trust your company has worked hard to earn impacts your brand far more than never having established that trust to begin with. Prospecting is filled with risks, but it can still be effective if handled with the utmost delicacy. Chapter 18 offers some suggestions for using email to find new customers and grow your lists.

CAN-SPAM has had interesting ramifications for prospecting emails, especially for companies that prospect using third-party lists. In the old days, third-party list owners were responsible for handling unsubscribes and deleting names from their own master list. A marketer friend of mine complained that, post-CAN-SPAM, her third-party list provider was requiring her to process and manage unsubscribes on her own house lists. Under CAN-SPAM, my friend is now the sender, with all of the associated responsibilities (see Chapter 8). Despite her complaints, list management is now part of her job.

Although I can understand my friend's lament, I can also see the issue from the customer's perspective. Customers believe they are removing their name from a company's mailing list, not from a third-party list. They could care less about who is doing the sending—their only concern is that the emails stop.

Gray Areas

Not every type of email will fall neatly into one of these six categories. A newsletter may contain a sweepstakes invitation; an electronic receipt may include a coupon for a future purchase.

Surveys inhabit their own universe. In the past, my clients have treated surveys as they would promotional or even prospecting emails, but I've recommended that they create a specific channel and policy (see Chapter 14) to manage customer interactions and frequency for surveys.

Blurring the distinction between types when you compose your emails can sometimes actually be good for brand building. You're exposing your customers to a message they might not have otherwise seen. The question is, how many advertisements can you include in your administrative or transactional email before it becomes promotional? To recipients, the answer is a matter of perception. How do they view your email, and what do they wind up doing with it? Under CAN-SPAM, the answer becomes a matter of compliance. To comply with the new regulations, understanding the impact and perception of your message is an absolute necessity.

■ ■ ■ ■

Every email interaction involves an exchange of value between company and customer. Types are a useful way to classify the gap between value requested and value offered. The bigger the gap, the lower the value of the email to the recipient. Too many messages of negative value to the recipient will invite opt-outs, spam blocks, and deletes, all of which drive your overall Email Brand Value (EBV) lower.

Types not only allow you to manage the value of your messages to your customers, they also enable you to fine-tune your delivery to increase that value. When you segment your emails by types, you can set up specific policies, workflows, access controls, and metrics for each type. Each control you add can improve your relevancy and increase the value to your customers.

Chapter 10

LEVELS OF PERMISSION

The Permission Marketer knows that the first date is an opportunity to sell the other person on a second date.
—Seth Godin from *Permission Marketing*

A Permission Parable

Once upon a time, in a faraway forest, there lived a tortoise and a hare. The hare was a speedy fellow, and he spent his days selling bushels of carrots to the other woodland creatures. He would zip around from tree to tree and from hole to hole soliciting his bushels to anyone who would listen. On the other side of the forest lived the tortoise. He was a slow, patient creature who made his living by selling a wide assortment of vegetables to his friends throughout the forest.

As their businesses grew, it was inevitable that the tortoise and hare would start to compete for customers. Tired of being jaunted by the hare for his slow and deliberate selling technique, the tortoise challenged the hare to a contest.

"We will each have exactly one day to sell as many vegetables as we can. Whoever sells the most will be the greatest sales animal in the forest," he said.

"Are you kidding?" laughed the hare. "I can run circles around you. I'll have talked to a dozen animals before you can reach your first one."

And so, the tortoise and the hare set off on their race.

As the sun set on the horizon and the contest came to its end, the two animals gathered to compare notes. The hare boasted that he had talked to almost seventy-five animals and had sold six bushels of carrots. The tortoise sat back, smiled, and informed the hare that he had visited only eight animals. But, he said, they were all regular customers and had each bought several bushels of vegetables, just as they always did.

Aghast, the hare exclaimed, "I don't understand. How did you do that?"

"I learn what my customers want, earn their trust over time, and make sure I sell them only the vegetables they want to buy," the tortoise replied. "Oh, and like I told that Aesop guy, 'Slow and steady wins the race.'"

Epilogue

After the great race, the hare was so disillusioned that he quit the vegetable business, moved to the Cayman Islands, and opened an email business selling mortgages and body enlargement supplements. With one fewer competitor on the market, the tortoise was able to raise $50 million in venture capital and buy out the defunct assets of Webvan. He is now selling vegetables in over two dozen forests.

This send-up of the tortoise and the hare parable illustrates perhaps the most important concept to legitimate email marketers: permission. Permission is more than a principle—it is an essential for every email marketing campaign. Studies have shown that 80 percent of consumers delete unsolicited email without reading it.[1] Unless your recipients have granted you permission to send them email, they will view your messages as spam and send them careening into the virtual trash bin as quickly as they can press the delete key.

By granting you permission, your customers are taking a calculated risk. They are entrusting you with their time, and they are awarding you an expensive chunk of real estate in their inbox, with the expectation that you will provide them with something worthwhile in return.

What do your customers want before they grant you their invaluable permission? Several features:

- A clear notice stating exactly what you are going to do with their permission

- An assurance that their name will not be shared with other companies (but if it is going to be shared, exactly how and with whom it will be shared)
- Content that is relevant to them
- A quick and easy way to opt-out when they no longer want to receive your messages

Permission does not mean that you have carte blanche to send any kind of message as often as you like. The best kind of permission is easy for your recipients to refine (with preferences) and even easier for them to revoke. The safest way to think of permission is to *assume that you have to re-earn it with every message you send.*

Tricking customers into granting their permission, or abusing that permission once it has been granted, is worse than never having asked for it in the first place. Either tactic creates a negative image that becomes cemented to every aspect of your brand for that customer.

Abused and Confused

Marketers squander their customers' permission over and over again. Questionable marketers are notorious for stretching the definition of "opt-in" or "permission." For example, if you sign up for a sweepstakes and forget to uncheck the box that specifies, "I would like to receive promotions and offers from your partners," you may have unwittingly—and unwillingly—opted in to dozens or hundreds of new messages. Marketers who use this type of device will claim that they obtained your permission (after all, the box was checked), but it is a façade. If you didn't actively and knowingly grant your permission, they don't have it. CAN-SPAM does put some limitations on such sneaky tactics, but it has not eliminated them entirely.

Even with the best of intentions, legitimate marketers can easily confuse permission. They know they must get permission, but they are not sure what constitutes it. Unfortunately, there are no strict definitions for permission and no clear procedures for obtaining it. Some of the common questions I hear highlight just how unclear permission can be:

- If I gather a customer's email address for an electronic receipt, do I have enough permission to send a follow-up email inviting that customer to opt-in to my newsletter?

- If I collect a business card at a tradeshow, has the owner granted me permission to send her a single follow-up email? Do I have permission to add her to my newsletter list?

- Does permission fade with time? Do I still have permission if my opt-in list has been unused for two years?

- If another division in my company has an opt-in list, has permission for that list been granted to add those customers to my division's list?

Although the answers to many of these questions will vary by context, this chapter will lay out some of the defining characteristics of permission and demonstrate the accepted processes for gathering it for your email marketing and communications initiatives.

THE FOUR LEVELS OF PERMISSION

Permission is not simply a black or white issue. The type of permission you need will vary based on three things: the relevancy of the message to your recipient, the value to the recipient along the Campaign Value Exchange (CVE), and the extent of the call to action. Asking customers to receive a quarterly newsletter requires far less permission then asking them to receive daily promotions for various body part enlargements.

The trick to permission is finding the right balance. If you ask for too little, your customers may feel as though you are violating their inbox. If you ask for too much, your customers will give up or lose interest before they've completed the process—granting permission shouldn't require that much effort.

Permission is undeniably important to your recipients, yet it means nothing to their ISPs. There is a common misperception that ISPs view permission as the golden ticket that affords exclusive entry into their customers' inboxes. Not so. The notion of permission and opt-in has been so overused and abused that it has become meaningless outside of the recipient's perception. An ISP's only concern is whether its customers want to receive your email. Permission or not, messages that are unwanted will quickly get blocked.

Industry insiders have devised a number of ways in which to segment permission into levels. I've chosen the four that seem to best fit the needs of most marketers. They are, in order of least to most conservative:

- Opt-out
- Opt-in
- Confirmed Opt-in
- Double Opt-in

In describing these various levels, I will use several terms from CAN-SPAM. By referencing legal terms, one might assume that I am offering legal advice. I can assure you, however, that there is no legal advice in this book (otherwise, I'd have to charge you $300 an hour to read it). Only your counsel can tell you for sure whether you're complying with CAN-SPAM.

Opt-Out

Opt-out assumes that the recipient's permission is granted unless explicitly instructed otherwise.

In 2003, online megaportal Yahoo! sent its users a message indicating that it had reset their preferences to receive solicitations from the company's advertisers, regardless of their original permission. The company gave its users sixty days in which to change their preferences back to "No."

The backlash was immediate—and loud. Privacy advocates labeled Yahoo! a spammer, and customers were outraged. Why all the fuss? Yahoo! hadn't explicitly asked for permission, but it had given its users a clear opportunity to opt-out, right?

Allowing your customers to back out of your messages is *not* the same as explicitly asking for their permission. The ambiguity of the opt-out leaves recipients feeling as though they have no control over the messages they are receiving. Renting a third-party list is a good example. You can argue that customers granted their permission, but they never explicitly granted it to you. The same is true if you borrow a list from another division within your company. Although the customers on the list are accustomed to hearing from your company, they may not be anticipating messages from your division.

The term "opt-out" is itself confusing, because it also applies to the action of unsubscribing. Most marketers use it in both contexts. Be clear on your meaning whenever you use the term.

Although opt-out messages are legal under CAN-SPAM (to the disappointment of many industry watchdogs), the law shakes their foundations a bit. Under the new legislation, you are free to send commercial emails until someone tells you to stop. But given that the intent of opt-out permission is to communicate with someone who is not anticipating the message, opt-outs aren't going to fall under the more lenient category of "affirmative consent." In other words, if customers do not give their express consent to receive your messages, you must stick by CAN-SPAM's content requirements for CEMMs (clearly labeling your messages as advertisements and including a conspicuous opt-out).

To be clear—just because opt-out is legal does not make it a good practice. Marketers are always better starting off a customer relationship with a clear request for permission.

Sometimes permission is requested, but not so clearly. If you enter an online sweepstakes, you may notice (most marketers hope you won't notice) a phrase that reads something like, "Yes, I would like to receive special offers from XYZ's partners." Next to the phrase is a tiny box, which has conveniently been checked for you. If you fail to notice the tiny box, or forget to uncheck it, congratulations—you've just invited a bunch of marketers into your inbox. An obscured pre-checked box is only marginally better than list harvesting. It is deceptive and antithetical to creating real customer relationships.

Take the case of one large manufacturing company. Back in 2002, the company's email administrator noticed that employees were receiving large volumes of unsolicited commercial email, most for the first time. The administrator feared that the company's internal email list had been stolen. However, upon further examination, another culprit surfaced.

The company had recently begun to include video messages from its CEO in their internal emails. To support these emails, the IT department was for the first time allowing employees to download media players. Freed from their narrowband world, employees began to roam the vast plains of broadband media sites across the Internet. But some of the media player providers, one in particular, required users to enter their email address before they could install the player. This media player company was gathering customer email addresses under the guise of support and updates. Few of the users noticed the small scroll bar on the registration page. If they had scrolled down, they would have seen a pre-checked box granting the company the right to share their email address with its various "partners." Employees of the manufacturing company (and probably countless other recipients) not only viewed the media player's advertisers as spammers, but they also developed a scathing view of the media player company's brand.

The marketer who has acquired an email address (or thousands) via such a deceptive measure can claim, at best, a hollow victory. Yes, they've added more addresses to their list, but very few of those addresses asked to hear from them. Yes, they technically have permission, but they have gathered it without the user's active consent. Under CAN-SPAM, this type of opt-in still falls outside the range of affirmative action. In the realm of permission marketing, it is misleading and misbegotten.

Opt-in

A true opt-in requires the recipient's explicit and active permission. Explicit permission means that the recipient has entered her email address for the sole and clearly stated purpose of subscribing to a list, and she has performed some additional action (for example, checking a box), to confirm that she understands how her email address will be used.

Opt-in is the gold standard for permission marketing. It has also become the clear expectation among consumers and businesspeople. Only if you have opt-in level permission can you unreservedly call yourself a "permission marketer."

The one gray area surrounding opt-in permission is the affirming action. Many marketers would argue that a text-entry box that is clearly used to gather an email address is sufficient without a corresponding check box. By hitting the submit button, they say, the recipient has affirmed their permission. Whether you agree with this thinking or not, you must ensure that your recipients are absolutely clear that they are providing their permission and that they understand explicitly for what purpose they are granting that permission.

Despite the obvious difference in semantics, the concept of "affirmative consent" in CAN-SPAM is often considered to be similar to the definition of opt-in provided earlier in this chapter (explicit and active permission). The writers of the law were wise to avoid the term "opt-in," considering how widely it has been abused and misunderstood. Obtaining affirmative consent not only enables a marketer to bypass some of the CAN-SPAM requirements for nonconsent email, but it is also considered a best practice among legitimate marketers. By employing it properly and universally, organizations will get higher delivery rates (people click the "spam" button less often when they recall giving their permission), better brand perception (consumers do not think kindly of spam), and improved response rates.

Confirmed Opt-in

A confirmed opt-in takes place when the recipient opts-in and receives a follow-up message confirming that permission has been obtained.

You know you never signed up for the Britney Spears email fanzine, yet somehow it's landing in your inbox every week. Getting weekly updates on the pop princess's latest antics may be irritating, but it's not necessarily spam. You may be the victim of a well-intentioned friend (who could have sworn you said you loved Britney Spears) or a misspelled address, either of which caused you to receive messages you never requested and never wanted.

As powerful as the opt-in can be, it is not always enough to ensure that the recipient has granted permission. Conservative marketers often take opt-in one step further with a confirmation message, which verifies that you did, indeed, opt-in. ("This message is confirming that you want to join the Britney Spears mailing list. Click here if this is a mistake.") The confirmation message will also let you know whether someone else opted you in—either accidentally or maliciously.

The confirmed opt-in is the easiest and most effective way for a marketer to catch accidental opt-ins, as well as identify mistakes such as address misspellings. On the surface, accidental opt-ins may not seem to be a big concern for marketers. However, if unwitting recipients begin getting emails they never requested, and your name is in the "from" field, they will immediately brand you as a spammer.

Figure 10.1 The confirmed opt-in is the permission level
most desired by American consumers
Source: NFO[2]

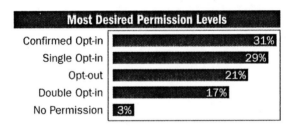

For maximum effectiveness, confirmed opt-ins should be sent within moments of an email sign-up to ensure that users remember that they opted-in to the message in the first place. Opt-in confirmations should also contain an easy opt-out to allow users to quickly back out of messages they hadn't intended to sign up for.

Double Opt-in

A double opt-in requires two explicit actions on the part of the recipient granting permission: First, the recipient must formally opt-in. Second, the recipient must actively respond to a confirmation. Only after the final response is received will the double opt-in be complete.

Anne Holland, publisher and managing editor of the MarketingSherpa Web site, tells a great story about the double opt-in:

"A few years ago, I was interviewing the marketing director of a large international company. When the topic of permission came up, he told me that his company used double opt-in. Knowing how low the company's response rates were, I asked him to clarify what he meant by double opt-in. He said, 'We get the email addresses from our customer database, and then we confirm that they're valid by checking that their email domains exist'.[3] This company was, needless to say, confused about the level of permission it had obtained."

The double opt-in is one of the most rigorous levels of permission that marketers use. It is also one of the least often used. A study by my company, Silverpop, revealed that only 5 percent of Fortune 500 companies were using double opt-ins. In fact, far more marketers (36.9 percent) use the opt-out permission level than the more conservative double opt-in (23.9 percent), according to MarketingSherpa.

Figure 10.2 Survey of permission levels used by marketers
Source: MarketingSherpa[4]

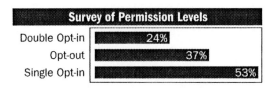

Perhaps so few companies use the double opt-in because of its downsides. Although this high level of permission undoubtedly reduces accidental and forged opt-ins, the added second step increases the effort for recipients, and, as a result, lowers the overall opt-in rate. When users are required to take a second action, many simply neglect to do so. In some cases, they forget to check their email. In other cases, they have second thoughts about opting-in. ClickZ estimates that companies who use double opt-ins can see as much as a 50 percent drop in recipients during the permission process.[5]

The cause of the double opt-in drop-off is not always just apathy or neglect. Spam filters can also be the culprits. If a filter snags your confirmation email, your recipients will never have the chance to grant their full permission. Ironically, the very process of gaining maximum permission can result in meaningful brand damage. If a spam filter blocks your double opt-in request and recipients never complete their permission, the messages they thought they were signing up for will never be delivered. According to a survey by Harris Interactive and Digital Impact, 29 percent of consumers said that not receiving messages they specifically requested is even more annoying than receiving spam.[6]

The double opt-in is best reserved for situations in which your recipient needs to be fully aware of your objectives or content. For example, if you are running a sweepstakes with the primary purpose of gathering a list of email addresses to resell, you might choose the double opt-in just to make absolutely sure your recipients know that their email addresses will be widely distributed. Alternatively, if your content is very sensitive (think medical advice for sexual dysfunctions), the double opt-in can prevent some heavy backlash if some joker opts-in his friend as a gag.

Confirming a double opt-in can be accomplished in one of three ways:

1. Reply: The recipient presses the "reply" button on his email client, which sends an immediate response to the sending servers for processing.
2. Embedded link: A link in the message drives the confirmation back to the marketer's Web site for processing.
3. Mailto link: A link in the message automatically opens a new email message with the "to" field already filled in.

Over the last few years, there has been some debate as to which of the three mechanisms is most effective. Many email marketers prefer the reply or mailto method, both of which will also work when the user is offline. But as more and more consumers use broadband or work-based email accounts, the number of recipients working offline has steadily declined, and the need to address offline issues has diminished.

The reply method has its own downsides. Omnipresent spam filters can occasionally trip up your recipient's confirmation email, leaving the double opt-in incomplete. More challenging yet are the new "disposable email" addresses offered by Yahoo's AddressGuard and similar services (see Chapter 19). Users create an address specifically for the purpose of your opt-in, but when they attempt to reply to your confirmation, their email program sometimes resorts back to their primary address. The result is that the double opt-in confirmation does not match the address of the original opt-in, and your EMS mistakenly believes that it never received the confirmation.

Many of the organizations with which I consult use the embedded link because it ensures completion of the double opt-in confirmation. When a user clicks on an embedded link, it immediately opens a Web page. The Web page interaction is real time and is nearly impervious to human error. The EMS updates the double opt-in permission on the Web page and confirms it back to the user.

Until 2004, more and more companies were using embedded links. However, with the release of new versions of AOL, Hotmail, and Outlook in early 2004, the tide is likely to shift back to the double opt-in using reply-based confirmations. In an attempt to stop spam, these new email clients strip all links and images from messages whose senders are unknown to the user (this effectively disables Web beacons). But many of these email clients will automatically consider an email address a "known" or "friendly" entity once the recipient hits reply and sends back a message. When you ask a customer who has one of these new email clients to reply to your double opt-in confirmation, the client will automatically add your address to your customer's friend list or address book. The reply method will ensure that you have a high level of permission, and it will help your messages get delivered.

One hotel company takes its double opt-in a step higher to protect itself. As a recipient is responding to its confirmation, the company captures his *Internet Protocol address (IP address)*. If the recipient later contests the opt-in, the company can produce not only the date and time of the opt-in, but also the user's email IP address as further proof that the opt-in legitimately occurred. Just keep in mind that whenever you capture personally identifiable information (PII) such as an IP address, you need to respect privacy issues and inform the user of what you are doing.

Permission Requests

Many of my clients have found themselves with a list of unclear origin and permission status. The list may have been passed along during an acquisition or channeled from another division. Or, it may be so old that no one remembers how permission was gathered. Whatever the circumstances, marketers with such ambiguous lists face a tough trade-off. If they take a conservative stance and simply toss out the list, they lose a very valuable asset. If they send to the list, crossing their fingers that they have sufficient permission (CAN-SPAM does allow for messages to be sent without confirmed permission, provided that the messages are treated as CEMMs and filtered through the organization's opt-out list), they may be branded spammers.

I have seen virtually every approach to the "old list" problem, and I believe there is one simple best practice for brand-conscious companies. Marketers can *re-permission* their list by sending out a message requesting or confirming each recipient's permission. Re-permissioning occurs in one of two ways:

Customer Permission Assumed (CPA): Unless the recipient takes specific action to opt-out, his permission is automatically assumed. This method, the most common one used for confirming appended email addresses with third-party data providers, is similar to the opt-out approach to permission. Although CPA will generate larger lists than CPR-based approaches (see below), marketers need to be extremely careful to make sure that their assumption does not get them in trouble with customers and negatively affect their brand perception.

Customer Permission Request (CPR): Permission in this case requires a specific action on the part of the recipient, for example a reply or click. This practice is as vigorous as the double opt-in, and it is probably the most conservative way to confirm permission.

Remember, when you send a permission request message, treat it as a CEMM and label it according to CAN-SPAM stipulations. Also, absolutely make sure that you scrub your list against your organizational opt-out list to ensure that anyone who previously opted-out is not contacted again.

Offline Permission

Gathering permission offline can be every bit as sticky as it is online—perhaps even more so. I am often asked, "If I gather business cards during a trade show, does that constitute permission?" In some respects, the question isn't as open-ended as it might have been a few years ago. CAN-SPAM does allow for commercial messages to be sent without permission, provided that the sender includes the proper wording and honors all opt-outs. However, if the question is, "Can I add the addresses from the business cards to my 100 percent opt-in house list?" the answer is less clear.

A trade show attendee who hands you a card will probably expect to receive a follow-up call or email. But if you want to add that person to your newsletter list, the safest approach would be to ask for affirmative consent (by asking the recipient to check a box on a form). Whether you collect an email address at a trade show, point of sale, or call center, handle it the way you would a permission request message—gather affirmative consent and follow up with an email confirmation.

■　■　■　■

To have a successful email program you need permission. Permission is not only a matter of consideration, it is also now regulated by the U.S. government. Permission is the platform that elevates email from a mass media to a relationship tool.

In the end, permission is not about legalities. It is not even something you *obtain*. Permission is a *mindset*—it lives in the minds of your recipients. If your recipients anticipate your messages, and expect the frequency with which you are sending, you have their permission.

With regard to the actual permission request, the amount of permission required hinges upon relevancy and the CVE. The lower the relevancy of your messages to your customers, or the more skewed the CVE, the higher the level of permission you should seek. If you handle permission wisely, you'll simultaneously release many of the constraints imposed by CAN-SPAM, raise your EBV, and improve your overall customer satisfaction.

Chapter 11

CUSTOMER PREFERENCES

It is our choices…that show what we truly are.
—Professor Dumbledore, *Harry Potter and the Chamber of Secrets*

Give the Customers What They Want

Even though permission can exist at several different levels, by itself it is still a blunt tool—your customers either want to receive your emails or they don't. If your communications go beyond a simple newsletter or a stream of promotions, you'll need a more precise tool that enables your customers to fine-tune control over their own messages.

Many marketers operate under the rule of, "If I want to say it, they will listen." Recipients do *not* want to read everything they receive. Furthermore, not every recipient wants to read the same types of messages.

"Today's customers don't want to have *marketing* relationships with the businesses they patronize; they want *service* relationships," says Hans Peter Brondmo in his book, *The Engaged Customer*.[1] You want to make your customers feel as though *they* have the keys to your business and they're calling the shots.

For yesterday's mom-and-pop stores, delivering personalized service was intuitive. The clerk knew exactly what each customer wanted as soon as he stepped through the door. Even though an email does not afford the face time of a shopkeeper and his customer, you can make the communication personal the moment you ask your customers what they want to receive from you and how often they want to receive it. *Preferences* enable you to reach this higher level of personalization. Preferences are the ultimate way to steer your campaign from the sender side—to the recipient side—of the Campaign Value Exchange (CVE) spectrum, and to move your email program from the old marketer-centric system to the new customer-centric philosophy at the heart of CCM.

Research has proven that consumers want control over the emails they receive. Users polled by IMT Strategies said that the ability to control communications and to self-select content were their two favorite forms of personalization.[2]

With preferences, the recipient controls more of the communication than the sender does. Allowing recipients to dictate their own content and mix of messages ensures that they anticipate your emails, and it increases the likelihood that they will respond.

Preferences also enable marketers to consider customers' receptiveness, interests, and frequency needs. Some customers, for example, may be responsive to advertising messages; others may see them as annoyances. Some customers may want to receive messages once a week; others may not want to hear from a marketer more than once a month.

If your communications traverse one end of the CVE to the other (for example, some messages benefit you and others benefit your recipients), preferences let your recipients adjust the balance to a place where they feel comfortable. Customers set the level of advertising and promotion they receive from you to fit their personal taste.

But preferences do not only work in favor of the recipient—they also serve the sender. When recipients control what messages they get, their relevancy goes way up, and with it their open and click-through rates. Nearly 75 percent of people surveyed by DoubleClick said they were more likely to open emails that contained information based on interests they had specified to a company. A prespecified interest was an even more compelling reason to open email than relevant content (67 percent), according to consumers.[3]

In a world without preferences, the only option for recipients is to opt-out—the end of the line for all communications. Remember that story I told you back in Chapter 2 about my credit card company? If they had only offered me the chance to change my preferences, I wouldn't have had anything to write about.

Marketers are often engaged in intricate and costly endeavors to analyze customer behavior, yet they pass up the most obvious opportunity to learn about their customers' interests. If you ask the right questions of your customers via preferences, you'll learn more than you would from many forms of customer analytics. And if you handle your preferences correctly, your relevance and Email Brand Value (EBV) will go way up.

How Do Preferences Work?

Many marketers mistakenly believe that preferences are solely about defining the message format: HTML, AOL, or text. Although formatting is part of the customer choice process, preferences encompass far more message options.

Preferences may be referred to by different names, including "subscriptions," "profiles," and "preference center." Simply, each customer or recipient can select from a set of email options, sort of like an a-la-carte menu at a restaurant. On a preference page, a customer could ask to receive a weekly newsletter, for example, or set the frequency of promotional emails.

Profile is a related term used to describe the information a marketer may want to collect about a customer (such as gender, address, and date of birth). Preferences and profiles often work hand in hand to give the marketer a more three-dimensional view of each customer.

Profiles and preferences are most commonly gathered on Web pages, often called a *profile page* and a *preference page.* Typically, the profile and preference page are components of the *registration* process. When new customers visit a company's Web site, fill in personal information, and sign up for emails, they are registering themselves with that company.

American Airlines's preference page offers its customers a choice of four email options:

1. AAdvantage eSummary—A monthly email for AAdvantage members containing program information such as frequent flier mileage balance and account summaries

2. AAirmail—A monthly newsletter that targets content specifically to the individual customer

3. Net SAAver Fares—Weekly updates that highlight discounted fares and other special promotions

4. AAdvantage Promotions—Promotions from American Airlines's partners

American has given its customers several choices because, although it has a wide range of topics to communicate, the airline isn't presumptuous enough to assume that every customer wants to read every message. Preferences are also valuable to American's customers because its messages range from one end to the other of the CVE. For example, AAirmail is very customer focused and contains no advertising content, whereas AAdvantage Promotions is almost purely promotional. By letting recipients decide which messages best fit their interests, American avoids forcing a single average position on the CVE spectrum for all its customers. Instead, customers decide which types of messages work best for them, and they plot their own ideal spot on the CVE spectrum. The result is that the company's overall EBV goes up.

What Goes Into a Preference Page?

A preference page consists of two components: administrative options and content preferences. On the administrative side, marketers often include some subset of the following choices:

- Email format (HTML, text, or AOL)
- A clear and easy way to unsubscribe from all mailings
- Password change (if appropriate)
- Email change of address option

Content preferences are usually just a list of possible messages (e.g., news or sports) the recipient can choose to receive. The customer selects each preference by checking a box next to it. When you list your message choices, I recommend that you include a description of each option, and, wherever possible, a link to an example of the type of email the customer could expect to receive. Once the user has set his or her preferences, you'll also want to follow up with a confirmation email reiterating the updated choices.

What doesn't need to go into your preference page? You can leave off transactional and relationship messages (TRMs), receipts, and e-bills. These kinds of messages are usually an extension of the company-customer relationship. Under CAN-SPAM, companies are given a fair amount of leniency to send TRMs without explicit customer permission. Although you always want to ask for as much permission as possible, you risk creating a real problem for yourself if you give customers the preference of not receiving transactional messages. If they elect not to receive these messages, you may not be able to complete important business transactions. Generally speaking, don't request permission for transactional messages unless they are optional from a business process point of view and/or they are promotional in nature.

On the content side, you need to figure out how much control you can give your recipients without having to offer an unmanageable number of preferences. If you include more than eight to twelve options, you might bewilder your customers.

If your preference list is growing too long, you may need to group preferences together by category (news, cooking, or travel, for example). Category grouping makes sense if all your preferences fit neatly into groups. But if you have, for example, twenty-five different preferences and only eight themes to group them into, an effective alternative is to group them by the promotional level of each preference.

Think about the CVE when you're grouping items—the value of the message to you versus its value to your recipients. Customers are naturally sensitive about receiving promotional materials. They'll be more receptive to your message if you give them some control over the amount of promotional material they receive. For example, put all highly promotional messages together, and clearly label them as such. Then offer a group of promotion-free messages that benefit only the sender.

American Airlines has done a great job of letting its customers drive their own preference page. It has kept its number of subscriptions small and manageable, and it has clearly delineated its informational (AAdvantage eSummary) and promotional (AAdvantage Promotions) offers to let customers choose which message type they want to receive.

When designing your own preferences page, I recommend that you consider creating an "anchor" newsletter that is heavily skewed toward the recipient on the CVE. Let customers know that if they sign up for only one newsletter, this should be the one. Make the newsletter appealing by maximizing the amount of valuable content and minimizing the number of advertising and promotional messages. Once you have customers hooked on that one newsletter, you increase your chance of gaining their permission for other mailings and reduce the likelihood that they will opt-out altogether. The anchor newsletter is the ultimate way to (gently) cross-sell your other subscriptions.

American is so intent on increasing the value of its core newsletter, AAirmail, that it uses past transactional data to customize each recipient's version to be as relevant as possible. A customer who traveled to Miami in the past, for example, might receive an email promoting discount fares to Florida. Such high levels of personalization push American's EBV to even higher levels.

Frequency

I have saved the most intriguing and most complex preference for last: frequency. If you read industry white papers and articles, you'll find recommendations for frequency preferences repeated over and over (pun intended). Letting the recipient control the frequency of your communications is a great idea and it makes good business sense. When you let customers control how often they hear from you, they will respond more often and your EBV will go way up.

Consumers have made it very clear that they consider frequency to be a major issue. When asked what most concerned them about their inboxes, frequency of permission-based email (42 percent) came in second only to spam. People also said they prefer different frequencies for different types of communications. They want news and weather daily, but they would rather receive special offers weekly and billing statements monthly.[4]

Consumers are clear on how often they want to receive messages, yet few companies give their customers the opportunity to dictate their own frequency. If frequency is such a good idea, why is it so rarely available as a preference? Two reasons. First, frequency is tough to control from a process perspective. Building a campaign is difficult enough, but trying to set frequency to please each customer complicates the process even further. For example, if you've put together a weekly newsletter and some customers ask for monthly messages, do you send every fourth newsletter or consolidate all four into a single monthly newsletter? If some of your customers receive only one out of every four promotions, they will miss three-quarters of your offers. And trying to combine all of your weekly promotions into one monthly digest is difficult to accomplish without specialized technology systems or a significant amount of extra work.

Second, only certain types of messages lend themselves to recipient-controlled frequencies. Promotional messages benefit highly from frequency control, whereas transactional or administrative messages may not work at all. For example, a security software company that lets its customers control the frequency of security alerts is inviting a whole range of problems. If a customer misses a security alert on the latest virus, his system integrity could be compromised. Frequency control is both difficult to implement and not appropriate for every kind of communication.

How Many Preferences Are Too Many?

Preferences are good for your EBV, but if they aren't handled with great care, they can actually frustrate your customer. Some companies, for example, try to pack twenty or more options onto a single preference page. Choices are good, but if you give your customers too many, they'll tune out and click to another site before they finish filling out the preference form. I don't have any hard research numbers to back this up, but I tend to go by the rule of a dozen. Any more than twelve options are probably too many for your customers to process.

Also, as I mentioned in Chapter 4, don't try to ask for your customer's hand in marriage on your first meeting—date your customers. Remember that you are taking the first tentative steps toward building a customer relationship. Your preference page is like a first date—through it, your customers are meeting your email program for the first time. In the early stages of any relationship, especially one developed online, trust is often tenuous. Try to limit your questions at this early stage of the relationship to the most basic, and necessary. If you ask for only a name and email address at the first opt-in, you can always gather more information through surveys, polls, etc., as your relationship progresses. The less you ask from your customers up front, and the more of a reward you offer in return, the greater the likelihood that your next interaction will be more impactful, according to Seth Godin.[5]

MarketingSherpa presented a great case study on one company that decided to find out just how much information they should request at the initial opt-in stage. NetLine, an eMarketing solutions provider, decided to offer a free white paper to anyone who registered on their site. Marketing vice president Raechelle Drivon put together a compelling paper, but she wasn't sure how to present the sign-up form. It had to be long enough to gather the essential information, but not so long that it scared prospects away. Drivon came up with a novel solution: She devised two different versions of the form and tested one against the other. The short form requested only basic contact information: name, title, company, phone, email, and one question ("How does your email-based lead generation fit into your marketing mix?"). The long form was more in-depth and added three nonrequired questions that helped qualify the prospect.

When the results were tallied, the short form was the undeniable winner. Fifty percent of people filled out the long form but nearly 75 percent filled out the short form.[6]

The Pitfalls of Preferences

Preferences can get sticky when it comes to opting-out. If you encourage recipients to opt-out via an email reply, how do you handle the unsubscribes? Do you remove customers from just the one preference, or go all the way and remove them from all preferences? No right answer to these questions exists, so whenever possible, drive your customers to your Web site for opt-out or preference changes. Once there, customers can see exactly what options they are signed up for, and know exactly which messages they will no longer be receiving. I also advise that you send a confirmation whenever a customer changes his or her preferences. That way, if the removal was accidental (or malicious), the customer has the opportunity to get back on your list.

Pitfalls can also strike your preference page at the enterprise level. A preference page is often the first initiative undertaken when a company is moving toward an overall CCM strategy. The preference page is a well-intentioned place to start because it is visible and because it resides in the central point where all existing email efforts converge.

However, companies (especially large, multisender companies) run into problems when trying to merge multidepartmental communications into one program. Without an overarching strategy, the combined effort often ends up looking like a patchwork quilt—a mess of mismatched preferences and profile questions. And, if the groups within your organization haven't all agreed to use the same preference page, customers could change their preferences and continue to receive emails from a department that isn't tied in with the program. The brand impact of such a mistake can be very negative. In your customer's mind, not only are you spamming them, but your company also lacks the coordination to live up to its promises. For this reason, companies are wise to wait before rolling out their preference page until they have a strategy in place and an enterprise policy to manage it.

Case Study—The *New York Times*

If you're looking for a model preference page, visit http://www.nytimes.com/. The Web site of the *New York Times* has put its customers firmly in the driver's seat when it comes to designing their own communications experience. The renowned publication truly embodies the best practices in customer preference management that I've outlined in this chapter.

When customers enter the registration section of NYTimes.com, they are given access to their profile information (password, date of birth, etc.) and email preferences. The page is segmented very clearly into four sections: Email Delivery Options, Daily News, Newsletters, and Special Offers and Announcements. Each section contains a list of selectable preferences and a clearly worded explanation describing each product within that section and its delivery options. Promotional messages are plainly labeled with the word "advertiser" so customers cannot mistake their purpose.

Let's look at one section of the preference page—Daily News. Within this section are two options: Today's Headlines and "DealBook." The description next to Today's Headlines reads: "This email, delivered every morning, brings you the Top Stories, Quotation of the Day and as many sections from the list below as you like." A link takes customers to a Today's Headlines sample, where they can see what the message would look like if they selected it. Underneath the description is a list of eleven content options: National, Sports, Editorial, Washington, Op-Ed, Technology, Daily featured section, Business, NY Region, International, and Arts.

Despite the long list of possibilities, customers who sign up receive only one message per day. Using dynamic content (see Chapter 20), NYTimes.com assembles each customer's selections into a single message of varying length.

The *New York Times* also offers a paid email service called Times News Tracker. The presentation of this service is a best-in-class example of frequency preferences. Times News Tracker customers can select from a seemingly infinite variety of options. They can request alerts based on keywords, topics (from a predefined list), or stock ticker symbols. When they choose an option, they are shown recent articles that match their selection and asked to confirm that they really wanted that subscription option. Then they can pick one of three frequencies: instant alerts when news happens, a daily report summarizing the day's events, or a weekly news digest.

When customers want to change their preferences, NYTimes.com again provides several options, all of which are linked from the email:

- Edit your preferences. This option takes customers to their preference page to log in and make changes.
- Unsubscribe. This option takes customers to a Web page, where they can opt-out of one specific subscription.

- Opt-out of all email. This option is not actually included within the email, but it is available on the preference page.

NYTimes.com spent a lot of time crafting its preference page. Its email program treats each subscriber as a partner in its marketing venture. NYTimes.com makes registration as easy as possible for its customers by offering a wide range of options in a clear and easy-to-navigate format. Was the end product worth the effort? You bet. Today's Headlines alone has nearly 4 million registered subscribers to the daily email service.[7] Altogether, NYTimes.com sends out a whopping 1.5 billion messages per year.

■   ■   ■   ■

Preferences are the ultimate tool for achieving customer-centric communications. Rather than forcing content into a one-size-fits-all package, preferences let recipients custom design their communications with your company. Preferences take into account each customer's interests, receptiveness to promotional messages, and frequency appetite.

We may never return to the kind of one-to-one service that mom-and-pop businesses were famous for decades ago. We can, however, offer our customers an oasis from the teeming and impersonal world of mass commerce. Preferences bring individual choice back to email communications. They make the customer an equal partner in the transaction with a stake and an interest in the outcome. When the customer is involved in the communications, the messages become more relevant and the sender's EBV soars.

Chapter 12

OPT-OUTS

Don't come a hangin' around my door; don't wanna see
your face no more.
—"American Woman" by The Guess Who

Opt-Outs Are Simple, Right? Wrong

I am not a scientist. Let's make that clear up front. But for the edification of my readers, I have been engaging in a bit of experimentation. I've opted-in and opted-out of dozens of newsletters, sale updates, and other email lists, curious to see how companies handle their opt-outs.

Now, on the surface, opt-out seems like a simple process. But, based on the results of my little experiment, I discovered a surprising number of approaches. Some companies asked me to type my email address in a box; others asked me to reply to an email message with the word "unsubscribe" in the subject line. Some sent a confirmation message; others never contacted me again. One of my favorites instructed me to: "Go to www.xyz.com, log in with your username and password, then update your communication preferences." Three steps, just to opt-out.

Email users are already skittish about opting-out. Nearly 60 percent of them prefer to hit delete rather than opt-out, because Internet "urban legends" forebode that spammers will simply use their response as confirmation that they've nabbed a real live address and send even more junk mail.[1] But as my experiment proves, spammers aren't the only ones eroding consumer confidence in the opt-out process. Some legitimate marketers are creating their own brand of confusion when their customers attempt to opt-out.

The opt-out has always been a tricky issue for marketers. Even before CAN-SPAM, companies who handled their opt-outs poorly risked angering recipients and losing the right to market to them forever. In the new world of CAN-SPAM, the stakes are even higher. The new law mandates that marketers remove opt-out addresses from their lists within ten days, although this is subject to change by later FTC review. Companies that fail to comply with their opt-outs are now breaking the law and risking steep fines and lawsuits.

Third-Party Lists

Even as it simplifies the email marketing landscape in some respects, CAN-SPAM raises a new set of questions that had otherwise been clear to marketers for years—among them, how do you handle opt-outs when it comes to third-party lists? Several years ago, opt-outs to rented lists were captured and processed by the list owner. Now many legal experts (and list owners) are interpreting CAN-SPAM to mean that the company that *rented the list* should handle the opt-out. This means that you, the advertiser, now have to record any opt-outs generated when you mail to third-party lists. Worse yet, once you've captured opt-outs from your third-party sends, you need to add them to your organizational opt-out list. You can *never again* send to those people for any reason.

The complexities don't end there. Now that you have to maintain a master organizational opt-out list, most legal experts believe that it is your obligation to check that your opt-outs are not on your rented lists. The trouble is, few list owners will give you their lists to scrub against. And conversely, few companies I know are willing to share their organizational opt-out lists with a third-party list firm to scrub on their end. How can you manage opt-outs in a CAN-SPAM world when sender and list owner must share critical, private data, but neither is willing to make the first move?

Opting-In Again

The handling of return email customers is also somewhat vague. If a customer asks to be taken off your global opt-out list, should you restore them to every list they were on previously? If someone opts-out of all your lists, then signs up for a newsletter on your site, can you begin marketing to them again? What if they opt-out of a division that markets completely unrelated products? Can you still keep them on your list? Finally, how can companies with multiple lists and a variety of email delivery systems possibly coordinate opt-outs across their organizations within the CAN-SPAM specified ten-day timeframe?

The rest of this chapter provides some useful case studies and best practices that will hopefully help you develop your opt-out strategy. As you might imagine, there are no straight or easy answers to the questions I've outlined above. Some questions will be resolved as the FTC completes its rulemaking process. Others will have to wait until the courts battle out the fine points of the legislation. Until CAN-SPAM matures, each company (with the judicious advice of its legal counsel) must arrive at its own policies by considering its brand perception, its type of business, and the process by which it establishes affirmative consent.

Despite the unsettled questions mentioned previously, I can offer you a bit of immediate resolution. CAN-SPAM has at least clarified the name of the action. A few years ago marketers used a variety of terms, including *remove* and *unsubscribe*, interchangeably. For better or worse, CAN-SPAM has cemented opt-out as "the term" to describe address removal. In the interest of full compliance, we'll stick with opt-out in this book.

Managing an Organizational Opt-Out List: A Case Study

In the spring of 2000, nearly three years before CAN-SPAM, IBM decided to formalize their privacy and marketing communications practices. With their long heritage of personal information sensitivity, IBM knew that standardizing their practices and policies was the right course of action in the new electronic marketplace. IBM's goal was to ensure that their customers and other constituencies could easily understand their privacy practices, and that they were clear about their choices with regard to the company's information usage. IBM also wanted to ensure (as much as it could) that they presented a consistent face to their customers. Even though the company had traditionally sought out and honored customer preferences, the decision to create a consistent practice standard for personal information processing created a powerful wave as it swept across the organization.

Although many customers view IBM as one big corporation, they are actually a group of individual, and often very distinct, divisions. Each of these divisions has one or more of its own customer and marketing databases. The new policy dictated that opt-outs within each division be honored across the entire organization. The designers charged with this effort needed to create a solution in which customers could count on having their opt-out request honored, no matter where it originated. Fundamentally, the goal was to protect IBM's customers.

The Requirements: IBM needed to create an enterprise-wide system for communicating customers' opt-out instructions across all company communications. The system had to be available to every division across the globe, as well as to all third-party list owners or processors. It had to be large enough to screen millions of customers. And it had to interact with a wide array of existing business systems and applications.

The Challenges: The sheer size of IBM's organization had produced hundreds of email address databases. IBM needed to synchronize opt-outs across all of these databases on a regular basis. The solution also had to enable third-party list providers to screen their own lists prior to sending out messages on behalf of IBM. To complicate the effort further, all of this integration and synchronization had to be accomplished without compromising the privacy of IBM's customer information.

In addition to all of these requirements, the solution had to be compatible with the European Union's Data Protection Directive. As I mentioned in Chapter 8, this act created a very strict set of laws governing the storage and usage of personal information and customer data. IBM divisions in several European countries were concerned that exporting European customer data to the United States for consolidation might put them in conflict with the EU laws.

The Solution: Because no prebuilt global opt-out solutions existed when the project was launching, IBM produced their own—a single solution called Global Email Cleansing Service (GECS)—to manage their entire worldwide opt-out database. GECS acts as a clearinghouse for email databases across the company. The GECS database is continually updated with opt-out addresses gathered from customer service and from IBM's company-wide mailings. Users upload their address to GECS, which scrubs those lists against its opt-out database. Users get a list of matched addresses, which they can suppress from their lists on future mailings. To keep the system simple and highly responsive, IBM decided to use GECS as a list-cleansing solution only. GECS does not deliver email, nor does it offer real-time individual suppression checks.

To solve both the EU and third-party security issues, IBM hired a trusted intermediary—the international direct marketing services firm Harte-Hanks—to run the database. With Harte-Hanks hosting the master databases, list owners no longer needed to share their lists with IBM, and vice versa. To minimize EU privacy concerns, and to deal with any possible data-transfer issues from the EU to the United States, Harte-Hanks operates the system out of Brussels.

What makes the IBM solution even more unique is that it is fully accessible to IBM's list-processing vendors. IBM maintains a Web site to which both third-party vendors and IBM teams can submit their lists for screening.

Are You Going to Let Your Customers Just Walk Away?

When I conducted my opt-in/opt-out experiments, I discovered that nearly every opt-out confirmation I received acknowledged only that I had been removed from the list—nothing more. They had my attention—why didn't those companies use the opportunity to engage me one last time?

Whenever you're faced with an opt-out, make the most of it. Every opportunity you use to engage and communicate with your customers is another opportunity to learn more about them and to build greater customer value.

First, you can give your customers the chance to rescind their opt-out. Ask one last time whether they truly intended to opt-out, and include an easy link for opting back in. (But if they do nothing, remember that the opt-out stands.) Tread lightly here, however. If your plea is too aggressive, this approach can backfire. But if you ask appropriately and remind recipients of the value of being on your list, you may find that enough customers will stay to have made it worth asking.

Second, you can offer your customers the option of changing their subscription preferences. A customer can choose, for example, to receive your newsletter monthly, rather than weekly. Ecost.com, a consumer electronics e-commerce site, uses one of the best opt-out examples I've seen. When customers indicate that they want to opt-out, they are taken to a Web page. The page contains four options: confirm opt-out, receive messages weekly, receive messages twice a month, or receive messages monthly. Rather than just letting recipients exit their promotional mailings, Ecost.com makes it easy for them to change their message frequency. Providing more options often addresses the concerns that brought your recipients to your opt-out page, while giving them enough control over future messages to possibly change their minds and keep them on your list.

Third, you can survey your customers to find out why they want to leave. The idea is to get as much information as you can before a customer is gone for good. Were they receiving too many email messages? Are they no longer interested in your product or service? Was the content not relevant enough? You can even provide an empty text box in which they can add their own feedback. Once you've gathered the survey information, use it to improve your practices with the customers who remain on your list.

Surveys are easiest to set up when you use a Web site link for opting-out. When the customer arrives at the site to opt-out, the survey information is readily available (but not required). If you use a reply-based opt-out, you can include the survey in the confirmation email or link to it from the email. (Typically, confirmation emails are unnecessary when opt-outs occur via a Web link—the Web page itself is considered sufficient confirmation.)

When sending an opt-out confirmation, you should consider including one of the following:

- A friendly but professional thank-you message
- An acknowledgement that the opt-out has been recorded and that the customer will see a reduction (or cessation) of email within X days

- A link (or a survey on the page) requesting feedback on the rationale behind the opt-out
- A clarification of whether the recipient is opting-out of one list, or all of your messages. If the person is opting-out of only one subscription or preference, your confirmation should remind them which preferences they are still opted-into.
- A link to re-subscribe
- Your company's privacy information. Your opt-out message should make it clear that, once the customer has been removed from your global list, his email address will no longer be used in any way.

Even as I lay out a foundation for opt-out strategy, I should remind you that the world of organizational opt-outs is still in its infancy. There are many open issues still to be resolved before the industry settles in on best practices. If you're truly stuck, ask your ESP to help you navigate through some of the more complex issues.

Interpersonal Commercial Email

So far in this chapter, our discussion has focused on the most familiar permission territories—large-volume email marketing and communications. But according to many legal experts, CAN-SPAM encompasses a much broader range of messages. Many people feel that opt-out standards now apply to every single commercial message your company sends. Whether one of your salespeople is emailing a prospect more information about your company, or a call center representative is highlighting the value of a new product for a customer, some experts suggest that all commercially based messages must follow CAN-SPAM opt-out guidelines.

As companies set up comprehensive opt-out systems to govern their enterprise email programs, many are failing to include interpersonal messages as part of their overall strategies and policies. One-to-one, interpersonal commercial emails, whether sent to prospects or existing customers, *are* legal under CAN-SPAM. But when they fall under the category of CEMMs, they are subject to the same stringent legal requirements that apply to bulk emails, namely:

- Clear and conspicuous notice of their commercial nature
- An active opt-out processed within ten days
- Suppression if the recipient has added his or her name to the organization's global opt-out list

The challenge to CAN-SPAM compliance is the level of technology required to process interpersonal messaging. Most sales and service teams use desktop email programs such as Microsoft Outlook, which have limited or nonexistent opt-out and suppression management capabilities. Very few commercial solutions in existence today could manage organizational opt-outs for both high-volume marketing and interpersonal communications.

Even before CAN-SPAM, the vice president of sales at one of my client companies was prescient enough to recognize that he needed a way to regulate promotional (commercial) email originating from his sales force. He asked his IT department to develop a customized web-based email system that was entirely templated to keep the tone and language of each message consistent. It could also be modified to accommodate organizational opt-outs, to ensure that his organization was CAN-SPAM compliant. His sales and service teams still used their desktop email program for their day-to-day messaging, but they rely on the new system for sending promotional and prospecting emails.

Any time you solicit new business via email, whether in bulk or one prospect at a time, you risk creating a negative image and damaging your brand. As CCM matures across organizations, policies governing interpersonal communications should become a fundamental and integral part of any overall strategy.

The Right Way To Manage Opt-Outs...Is There One?

I wish I could share with you the single best method for capturing an opt-out. Unfortunately, there isn't one. There are five—each with its own set of pros and cons:

Figure 12.1 Pros and cons of the five opt-out methods

Opt-Out Method	Pros	Cons
Single click opt-out	Provided that the link is not buried in the message, this is the easiest and fastest opt-out method for the recipient.	The sender can get into trouble if messages are forwarded. If the new recipient tries to opt-out, he can unknowingly opt-out the original recipient.
Reply-based	This method, like the single click, is easy for the user, although some users will make mistakes when they attempt to re-type the specific wording required.	Because a reply is required, there is always a chance that the opt-out will never reach the sender. It may get stuck in a spam filter, or, because all email clients process replies differently, it may lose the specific information needed to process the request.
Web-based with prefilled address	The pretyped email address minimizes accidental opt-outs from forwarded recipients.	The sender is asking the recipient to take two steps to reach the desired outcome.
Web-based with no address	Requiring the user to type his email address eliminates accidental opt-outs from forwarded recipients.	The sender is asking the recipient to take three steps (click – type – submit) in order to opt-out. Plus, recipients who have multiple email addresses may be unsure which one to enter.
Password protected	The high level of security prevents any kind of accidental or malicious opt-out. It also protects the recipient's private profile information from anyone who might view the original message.	The multi-step process will immediately annoy many customers, especially since they will have to remember yet another username andpassword in order to be removed from mailings. This approach makes sense only in the context of a larger customer relationship, for example an online banking system or an airline frequent flier program.

When choosing an opt-out mechanism, you'll want to balance your risk of missing opt-outs (especially with reply-based solutions), against your risk of angering the recipient with a multistep opt-out process. Generally speaking, the more your CVE—see Chapter 9—tilts in your favor, the easier you should make it for your recipients to opt-out.

American Airlines has taken what former marketing manager Elaine O'Gorman calls the "hard to opt-in, easy to opt-out" approach. Each customer must log in with a valid username and password to opt-in, but they can easily opt-out without a password through almost every mechanism listed above.

On the other extreme is an online marketing company (name withheld to save them the embarrassment), which for a while was gracing my inbox with a large number of unsolicited messages. When I finally decided to opt-out, I discovered that I needed to have an account to do so. *I had to create a username and password—to opt-out.* After I had gone through the process and opted-out, I emailed the company and asked why they had set up such a convoluted opt-out system. Shockingly, I never heard back from them.

Technical Issues

Compared to accounting or CRM systems, the technology needed to build and manage an enterprise-wide opt-out list is relatively basic. The biggest challenge is how to manage the sheer number of interactions that occur between the organizational opt-out database and other systems within the organization.

The opt-out system must be set up for several functions: It must touch all outbound email marketing. It must capture opt-outs and filter outbound messages from salespeople and customer service personnel. And it must come equipped with secure external interfaces, against which third-party data providers can scrub their lists.

Unfortunately, most commercial email marketing systems run opt-outs against their outgoing email lists manually. As with any manual process, human error is unavoidable. One small slip-up and your opt-out list becomes the recipient list for your next promotion. Technology can and will come to the rescue, however. In the future, cutting-edge EMS solutions will be able to automatically check every single outgoing message against opt-out specific lists. Automating the process will remove the possibility of human error and ensure 100 percent CAN-SPAM compliance.

In the meantime, if you decide to use your existing internal systems to manage your organizational opt-out list, CRM systems are a likely candidate to handle the task. But keep in mind that this approach may raise several issues. If you gather opt-outs from people with whom you have no prior relationship, your CRM system may not be able to manage records that hold no customer information other than the suppression request itself. Many lightweight CRM systems are unable to manage suppressions at all—they simply tag customer entries with a do-not-send flag. Some CRM systems even lack the ability to perform basic list functions, such as merge and purge, which are needed to handle suppression data outside of the CRM system.

My company, Silverpop, was one of the first email service firms to develop a comprehensive opt-out solution (called "Permission Management"). Two of our technology products, Silverpop Marketer and Silverpop Messenger, provide the foundation of Permission Management. Our Marketer product is aimed at traditional email marketers who are managing targeting, delivery, and analytics across their marketing organizations. Our Messenger product allows sales and customer service center personnel to send interpersonal or small list messages. In addition to these two products, we've added an automated opt-out management system that can be augmented with additional interfaces for third-party list scrubbing and call center opt-out requests.

What makes Permission Management so advantageous is its level of automation. Human error is always possible, but the key is to minimize the number of places in which it can occur. Solutions like Silverpop's remove the highly manual suppress/purge process that is usually required for high-volume email opt-out management. It then applies the automatic opt-out suppression to interpersonal messages as well, to ensure that anyone who opts-out of company communications—bulk or individual—stays opted-out. This "email opt-out firewall" approach is likely to gain favor as companies increasingly rely on interpersonal email communications, while still striving to remain CAN-SPAM compliant.

The Pitfalls of Organizational Opt-Outs

As with any new technology or approach, there are the daring navigators who brave uncharted waters, and the circumspect who wait to move forward until they can be assured a safe journey. A few years from now, every major American company will likely have an enterprise-wide opt-out mechanism in place. But as companies ramp up their systems, they have much to learn from the mistakes of the intrepid few who braved the waters ahead of them.

Without a company-wide opt-out in place, the potential for error or misuse is high. During a promotion, one company sent their global opt-out list to their partner to make sure all of the addresses were suppressed from their partner's list. Somehow, the promotion was mistakenly sent to the company's global opt-out list. The fallout was less disastrous than it could have been, but both sides wound up doing quite a bit of tap dancing and apologizing.

Another company I know became engaged in an interdepartmental competition when one division used the organizational opt-out list to gain an advantage over other divisions. To prevent other divisions from encroaching on its business, this division added every single one of their customers to the company's global opt-out list.

With an organizational opt-out system in place, the stakes for one division's bad judgment suddenly become much higher. One poorly designed campaign can easily drive a spike in opt-outs company-wide. As CAN-SPAM drives large enterprises to implement organizational opt-outs, it will also drive them to adopt policies that regulate the way email is used across the enterprise.

■   ■   ■   ■

Managing opt-outs has always been a necessary (if not always properly executed) part of any email customer relationship. No company wants to close a route of customer communication, but failing to honor a customer's request will only dissatisfy and alienate that customer further. Under CAN-SPAM, the cost of mismanaging opt-outs has risen substantially. Now you'll not only damage your brand—you could get sued.

If the vision of CAN-SPAM's founding fathers comes to fruition, and the FTC begins actively prosecuting spammers, perhaps one day the urban legends that haunt the opt-out will be history. (Hey, I'm an optimist.)

The opt-out itself is undergoing a transformation. It is poised to become one of the more fruitful sources of customer information. In the future, each opt-out event will be seen as a critical customer touch point, managed and measured as stringently as any other touch point. No longer will a customer leave a list without being given an opportunity to state why. Every opt-out will be asked for a reason, presented with a variety of new options, and given a real incentive to stay.

Part IV

MANAGING EMAIL ACROSS AN ENTERPRISE

PART 4
MANAGING EMAIL ACROSS AN ENTERPRISE

British Sky Broadcasting (BSkyB or Sky) is the undisputed digital television leader in the United Kingdom. The broadcaster delivers nearly four hundred channels of news, entertainment, and sports programming to more than 17 million viewers.

In the summer of 2003, Sky was enjoying the benefits of a brisk email program. All of its divisions were individual players in what amounted to a substantial subscriber outreach effort. Each month, Sky was sending out millions of messages.

Sky had what appeared to be a very successful email program. But beneath the surface lay a number of potential snags: The company's opt-outs were poorly managed. If customers opted-out of the sports newsletter, for example, they would continue to receive third-party promotions. Also, its delivery technologies were inconsistent, and it had very little insight into its overall response rates, delivery rates, or frequency.

To make matters worse, the UK was preparing to enact its stringent Data Protection Act (see Chapter 8). As the DPA deadline loomed, Sky was already beginning to see one or two complaints *per day*. Not only was Sky facing internal pressure to rework its email program—but it was also about to face some serious penalties if it failed to comply with the new regulations. Its email problem needed a solution—quickly.

Sky is far from the only email program feeling the heat these days. Companies in the United States are also dealing with strict email regulations as a result of CAN-SPAM, and even many of the most well-intentioned of them are struggling to comply.

With CAN-SPAM, having a cohesive email strategy has become an absolute necessity. Yet most email programs are still independent initiatives run at the department level with very little coordination across departments and divisions, and very little oversight. Without a governance program in place, these independently run email programs have reacted sluggishly to the new anti-spam legislation. By comparison, the companies that have a governance model in place barely missed a beat when CAN-SPAM became law.

The next few chapters will show you how to manage your email program across your enterprise. Even if your company is small, you should be able to apply many of the case studies and best practices to your program. If your company is a multisender organization, the following chapters may save you a great deal of heartburn and might even deflect a few legal hassles down the road.

Chapter 13

GOVERNANCE

To tap the true power of email, companies must make permission email processes and strategies a priority of the executive agenda. In the short term, winning organizations will harness the power of these online marketing assets through better process management. In the long term, executive management needs to lay the groundwork for sustainable permission marketing programs that close the gap on customer expectations to attain competitive advantage.
—Stephen Diorio, author of *Beyond-E*

Moving Email to the Enterprise

In 1781, the thirteen original American colonies lived by a "firm league of friendship," which became known as the Articles of Confederation. Under the Articles of Confederation, the colonies operated as thirteen sovereign and independent states, each following its own set of rules. The weak central government had little jurisdiction over commerce; it could not raise taxes, and it had little power to resolve disputes between the states. With its treasury depleted and its military ineffective, the United States sat on the brink of anarchy.

A strong central government was needed if America was to survive. In the summer of 1787, representatives from each of the colonies came together in Philadelphia to draw up the country's first self-regulatory document—the Constitution.

The Constitution set up a set of checks and balances and laid out the framework for three branches of government: executive, legislative, and judicial. A Bill of Rights was added to protect the freedoms of speech, press, and religion. In 1789, the Constitution went into effect, and the United States at last had a strong government armed with a consistent set of rules.

In the 1990s and early 2000s, most corporate email programs were set up very much like the original thirteen colonies. They were nothing more than grassroots efforts run independently at the departmental level. A study by IMT Strategies found that email policy enforcement was scattered all over most organizations. Forty percent of the surveyed companies said their marketing department directed their email program; but at other companies, IT, Internet marketing, or other groups were in charge of email.[1] Executive management rarely saw the need to oversee email because it was so new, and because it represented only a minute portion of the overall marketing budget.

Ironically, most corporate divisions would never dream of sending out a postal direct mail campaign without at least consulting their marketing department. They know instinctively that they can't tackle logistics, list management, and negotiations with third-party providers on their own. But companies rarely feel the same compunction when it comes to email. Perhaps they are less rigorous with email because of its low cost. Maybe they are so accustomed to the process of sending messages from their desktops that it has become second nature. Whatever the reason, email is often decentralized and run at the departmental level.

In the mid 1990s, companies treated their Web sites in the same manner. A Web page was always a side project—a cheap and easy afterthought. Today, I can't think of a single company that doesn't centralize the design and deployment (not to mention the branding) of its corporate and product Web sites. Management has realized the importance of having a strong online brand presence, and it has no intention of corrupting such a powerful resource.

Companies are now coming to a similar realization about their email efforts. Now that CAN-SPAM has made poor email practices a punishable offense, the stakes are too high to let departments continue to play by their own rules.

The Steps to Making Email an Enterprise Initiative

You can move your email program to the enterprise level in a number of ways. The following are the steps I generally recommend that my clients take:

1. Conduct an *Enterprise Email Assessment (EEA).*
2. Get executives to buy into the necessity of an enterprise initiative.
3. Establish an individual (or group) to be in charge of the email program.
4. Formalize a *policy* or best practices guidelines.
5. Continually manage and police the enterprise email effort.

Enterprise Email Assessment (EEA)

The word "audit" is often used to describe the email assessment process, but to avoid dredging up unpleasant memories of tax season, I'm going to use the term "Enterprise Email Assessment," or EEA. Regardless of what words you use to describe it, the action is the same—reviewing your current email program, department by department, to find out what all of your groups are doing.

Ask two questions before embarking upon an EEA. First, should you use a third party to assist with the process? Outsiders often bypass some of the internal politics, and they can bring a much higher degree of experience and "best practices" knowledge. Second, do you have sufficient internal support from senior management? Without your senior management team on board, your coordination efforts can stall within the ranks.

Once you have enlisted your senior management team, keep in mind that they may not look kindly upon the various programs once all of their blemishes have been fully revealed. I was recently involved in a particularly painful EEA. As details of the company's past email flaws came to light, the CEO put the brakes on all marketing email. He refused to let a single message go out until the EEA was complete and the new policy was in place.

As you begin your EEA process, keep the following questions in mind:

- Which groups are sending email?
- What kinds of emails are being sent, and in what volume?
- What kinds of response rates have groups seen historically?
- How is permission being handled? Is there any coordination between groups?
- Which third parties are being used for delivery and data services?
- Are data collection, usage, and customer notification consistent with the company's privacy policy?
- By comparison, how are the best-in-class email marketers (particularly competitors) managing their programs?

A service provider can help ease you through the EEA process and give you a clearer perspective on where your email program stands. For example, one EEA with which I was personally involved was tasked with finding and reporting on every single email marketing initiative across a large multinational organization. We pulled together all of the company's lists and sent back a report highlighting potential snags, such as customer overlaps, deliverability issues, and overlooked opt-outs. The last step was to survey our client's customers directly—both email recipients and non-recipients. I've found that such surveys help companies understand their customers' receptivity to email; it also provides them with valuable feedback about past campaigns.

Getting Buy-In

After years of running their email programs autonomously, departments grew accustomed to the freedom and tended to greet even the suggestion of corporate oversight with some resistance. When you embark upon a centralization effort, the last thing you want to do is get into a game of tug-of-war with a resistant department. Though you must institute corporate governance to remain CAN-SPAM compliant (and to execute your CCM strategy), the process doesn't need to be a painful one.

Simply educating current senders on the penalties associated with CAN-SPAM noncompliance can illustrate the value of an enterprise initiative enough to avoid a lot of arm-twisting. But if your corporate culture is such that various departments are firmly against any sort of centralized control, you can take one of several steps to drive buy-in:

1. Get support from the top. As I mentioned earlier, the best first step you can take is to enlist the support of your CMO or CEO. You'll have a much easier time convincing employees to follow your plan if the direction comes straight from the top. If you're struggling to get high-level support, see items 2 through 5 below.

2. Shed light on your email program. Use the EEA to show reluctant managers how your email really looks to your recipients. Put together a presentation of email screen shots, as well as statistics on permission policies or opt-out handling. If your company is inconsistent or varied in its use of the medium, the EEA can be a real eye opener and a powerful tool to drive home your point about making email an enterprise initiative.

3. Establish a global opt-out policy. If your departments are already aware of CAN-SPAM and its implications, you'll have a relatively easy time selling them on the importance of managing opt-outs across your enterprise. But if they persist in their old ways, keeping their fingers crossed that they'll get away with it, you can always ask them if they want to be responsible for sending their own CEO to jail.

4. Promise them list access. Marketers love data, especially customer data. Email marketers want to collect as many valid email addresses as they can find. They probably already know that a rich house list will help them better target and reach potential customers. Offering the promise of a master list that pulls together the breadth of names collected across the organization is a powerful incentive for departments to get on the enterprise bandwagon.

175

5. "Show them the money." I've never met a marketing department that boasted about having an abundance of funds. The promise of additional resources can entice even the most cynical groups to join a project. The best approach is to pool all email budgets and then use the increased purchasing power to negotiate better rates from vendors. If money isn't enough of an enticement, try drawing in disparate groups with the promise of personnel sharing.

Who Is in Charge?

For smaller companies, email governance is simple. One group, usually within the marketing department, handles all email campaigns. Companies with a single product line or division lend themselves to a natural centralization.

Asking "who is in charge" at a larger company is trickier. Often, the answer is everyone—and no one. When various internal groups have a history of working independently, introducing coordination and accountability can be tough, especially if the governance body decides to respect all or part of the independent efforts. The act of compromise itself can be as difficult (if not more difficult) as starting from scratch.

I've seen two methods by which large companies grant authority at the enterprise level. The first I call "top down" or the "rightful heir." Someone, usually in the marketing department, declares himself or is anointed the company's email czar. The "czar" has the authority (and often the budget) to centralize all email functions and exert unilateral control over the enterprise-wide email program. Having one person in charge is an effective—and fast—way to move email from a grass-roots campaign to an organizational endeavor.

The second method is via committee. One or more employees champions the crusade to move email to the enterprise level. The initiator can then either seek backing at the executive level, or dig up support within the ranks of the organization. Surprisingly, this approach works as well as, and more consistently than, the "top down" method, perhaps because most groups tend to agree on the importance of email.

Managing the Enterprise

A policy is one of the pivotal facets of enterprise email governance. When a policy is well executed, it can bring disparate efforts together into a cohesive enterprise strategy. Creating and adopting a policy takes quite a bit of orchestration, which we'll get into in Chapter 14.

But even the best policy and governance model can do little without systems in place to facilitate the necessary cooperation and coordination across a company. Effective management requires processes, and it requires technology, especially when email programs grow to millions of addresses and hundreds of campaigns a year. Chapter 15 is devoted to managing customer information (including lists) across an enterprise.

The Governance Planning Pyramid

Management of an enterprise email initiative can take several forms. I've researched many corporate governance plans, and I've found some surprisingly consistent approaches.

But before I jump in and discuss the various models, I'd like to take a step back and give you a perspective on how email intersects with your company. Several of my colleagues illustrate their enterprise email initiatives with this three-level hierarchy:

Figure 13.1 The governance planning pyramid

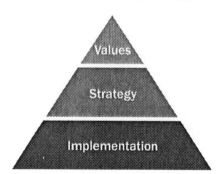

This three-level approach, with values driving strategy and strategy driving implementation, is helpful for both governance models and policy creation.

Values: Your company is run by certain core principles, or values, that likely influence every part of your business. When you sit down to put a governance plan in place, you should always start by writing down these principles in five to ten clear statements. Ideally, the formulation of these principles should be driven by groups within your organization that have a strong stake in furthering and protecting your brand, because these principles will ultimately steer your email program.

Once you have your principles down on paper, ask yourself the following three questions:

1. How will your email program intersect with your company's core values as they relate to your customers?
2. Will your email program help achieve your company's missions and objectives? If the answer is yes, how exactly will it do so?
3. How might email potentially conflict with your company's values?

Strategy: You undertake an enterprise email initiative with the understanding that, in return for the resource investment, you will create value for your company, and hopefully, for your customers. The incremental value you intend to gain through your email program can be captured and presented as a strategy.

When formulating your email strategy, consider the following questions:

- How can email give your company a competitive advantage?
- How does your email program fit within your overall customer relationships?
- Are there synergies with existing initiatives (e.g., multichannel marketing) that will prove mutually beneficial?

Your organization should have a deep understanding not only of its principles, but also of its own internal structure and politics. For example, some companies are very decentralized, whereas others adhere to a strict "top down" structure. When considering governance models for your email program, you need to consider the solution that will work best in your corporate environment.

Implementation: When it finally comes time to put your governance plan in motion, think about your company's culture and general approach to managing enterprise initiatives. Work out the requirements from your IT or service vendors in terms of accommodating those established company norms.

- How much should you rely on technology as opposed to manual processes?
- Would it be easier to purchase your own equipment and software, or rely upon outside vendors?
- Will your email campaigns be fairly regular, or will they come in bursts? Depending upon the answer, do you have the staff necessary to run your email program, or will you need to outsource?

Email Governance Models

For our discussion of governance models, I turned to Stephen Diorio, the author of *Beyond-E*, and one of the leading authorities on email marketing and next-generation channel models. Diorio has conducted extensive research over the years, and he has participated with me on several best practices governance projects.

Stephen defines three kinds of governance models: *decentralized, centralized*, and *federated*.

Decentralized governance is the easiest kind of enterprise governance. A decentralized email program is executed locally, within each department or division, with little or no intervention at the enterprise level. The benefit of a decentralized approach is that each initiative is managed by those who understand the product or service best. Because there is little influence from above, decentralized programs allow for the greatest amount of creativity. The downside is that, without a centralized authority, potential cost savings and revenue-generating opportunities may remain unrealized. Even more crucial, compliance with organizational opt-outs and other CAN-SPAM requirements may be overlooked, putting the entire company in jeopardy of breaking the law.

In a *centralized governance* model, all execution falls under a single point of control. Having one individual in charge provides the highest degree of enterprise email jurisdiction. It's a bit like living under a benevolent dictatorship, albeit one focused solely on email.

By incorporating the efforts of previously autonomous groups, a centralized model saves time and money and presents one cohesive brand message for the company. The trouble is, any form of bureaucracy has a tendency to stifle individual initiative and creativity. It can also mire the entire process in so much red tape that the inherent time and cost savings of email are never realized. Because email ends up being treated like a cost center, it can easily become underresourced and drag the entire initiative to its knees. And even the most well-intentioned authority occasionally creates too many approval and regulation processes, which slow the once rapid email process to a crawl.

A *federated* model is much like a democratic government: It runs underneath a strong central policy, yet it still allows a certain amount of autonomy at the local level. To achieve this process-oriented approach, you need a fully evolved policy, as well as cross-divisional representation from various levels of the organization (including high-level management). The leadership must (1) agree on an approach to policy, strategy, and implementation; (2) strike the right balance between regulation and autonomy; and (3) be empowered to make changes across the organization.

Although it lacks the tight control of the centralized model, the federal approach allows for a higher degree of individuality and creativity. Plus, it fully utilizes the budgets and expertise of divisions throughout the company. When executed properly, the federal approach is by far the preferred governance method for most companies.[2]

The Microwaved Potato Theory

When putting a policy in place, your organization has to ask itself, "How much is enough? How much is too much?"

Having no centralized control over an email program can lead to problems, but exerting extreme control can likewise cause issues. If you lock your policies and systems down too tightly, your marketers may either ignore them or find ways to work around them. For example, a frustrated department could subtly steer around your rules by hiring an outside service provider that offers email as a service (but perhaps not as a specialty). The provider might look the other way when email campaigns stray from your organization's policy.

My American Airlines friend, Elaine O'Gorman, explains it best: "Locking down email policies and enforcement too tightly is like cooking a potato in the microwave. If you don't poke some holes in the potato before turning on the microwave, you'll be doing a lot of cleaning up afterwards."[3]

If you don't give your marketers enough flexibility, they may circumvent the processes you've carefully established and put your entire email program at risk.

Risk Management

When talking to my clients about governance, the subject of risk management often comes up. For the sake of brevity, I'll only touch on the subject in this book. But I do need to mention that risk management is always a key goal of any enterprise initiative. CAN-SPAM raises the bar somewhat, because the consequences are far more serious than before the law went into effect, but governance and policy can go a long way toward mitigating your organization's risk.

As I mentioned in Chapter 8, the FTC draws spam under the larger umbrella of privacy issues. As with any privacy issue, marketers can take precautionary measures to avoid running afoul of the law. In its report, "Privacy Online: Fair Information Practices in the Electronic Marketplace: A Federal Trade Commission Report to Congress," the FTC focuses on four principles: Notice, Choice, Access, and Security:

(1) Notice—Web sites would be required to provide consumers clear and conspicuous notice of their information practices, including what information they collect, how they collect it (e.g., directly or through non-obvious means such as cookies), how they use it, how they provide Choice, Access, and Security to consumers, whether they disclose the information collected to other entities, and whether other entities are collecting information through the site.

(2) Choice—Web sites would be required to offer consumers choices as to how their personal identifying information is used beyond the use for which the information was provided (e.g., to consummate a transaction). Such choice would encompass both internal secondary uses (such as marketing back to consumers) and external secondary uses(such as disclosing data to other entities).

(3) Access—Web sites would be required to offer consumers reasonable access to the information a Web site has collected about them, including a reasonable opportunity to review information and to correct inaccuracies or delete information.

(4) Security—Web sites would be required to take reasonable steps to protect the security of the information they collect from consumers.[4]

In addition to abiding by the four principles outlined in the FTC's report, you can take any of the following steps to reduce your risk:

1. Establish a privacy body (a chief privacy officer or cross-divisional board).

2. Put a written security policy in place.

3. Have third parties (e.g., your financial auditors) conduct annual privacy audits.

4. Post clear online policy guidelines.

5. Compare your published policy to that of your competitors'.

6. Ensure that your policies are consistent across all of your marketing channels and divisions.

BSkyB Case Study Part I: Governance

As you'll recall from the introduction to this section, Sky's email program was inconsistent and poorly managed. The company was facing potential penalties from the recently enacted UK anti-spam legislation, and coming under increasing pressure from its customers. So how did it get a handle on its email problem?

Sky's solution was to set up a federated model. It established a clear set of policies to govern how email was to be used throughout its enterprise. And it created a cross-divisional group, known as the "Sky Email Stakeholder Committee," to govern email policy across the organization. This group comprises members from marketing, legal, Sky.com, the various channel groups (Sports, News, Movies), IT, as well as a member of the Silverpop team who is there to assist in the long-term evolution of the company's email strategy and policy. The committee is empowered to make policy changes and assess overall policy effectiveness.

As I was writing this book, Sky was easing into its governance model. Although it was still working from separate lists, it had already coordinated delivery and suppression, and it had charted a clear path toward a single, centralized email list.

■　■　■　■

Many corporate departments have been operating much like the original thirteen American colonies—blissfully independent. Operating an email program without central coordination is like trying to govern an entire nation with a chaotic jumble of independent legislative bodies.

The beauty of a *federated governance* approach is that, like our own federal government, it focuses control in a strong central body, yet it still allows a reasonable amount of autonomy at the local level. With an empowered governance group in place, a company can coordinate cross-department email efforts, facilitate resource sharing, and respond quickly and effectively to any change (legislative or otherwise) in the email landscape.

Chapter 14

ENTERPRISE POLICY

A policy is a temporary creed liable to be changed, but while it holds good it has got to be pursued with apostolic zeal.
—Mohandas Gandhi

Up to this point, I've discussed a lot of interconnected elements that need to go into your email program. Policy is where all of these elements finally come together and begin to resemble something coherent.

A company's policy is often the first tangible manifestation of the architecture behind its CCM strategy.

The "P" Word

The legal counsel for one of my clients once said to the company's email team, "If you hadn't used the word 'policy,' this would have been a lot simpler." The very word "policy" makes many corporate lawyers—and leaders—squirm. Even at its most benign, policy can represent one of the most intractable and fearsome aspects of the corporate world. More cynical interpretations invoke images of Orwellian corporate governance, every move dictated down to the letter by an omnipresent Big Brother.

Although many corporations assign the term "policy" a very specific meaning, this chapter could just as easily have been called *guidelines* or *guiding principles*. For email marketers, a policy defines a consistent set of processes and treatments that promote the responsible use of email. It reduces the risks to both a company's brand and its bottom line.

Like the client I mentioned at the beginning of this chapter, some large companies have very clear, if not Orwellian, processes by which they publish and distribute guidelines. Fortunately, for smaller companies, a policy (or whatever name you apply to it) is relatively easy to set up.

No matter what level of review and oversight your company requires, once a policy is in place, it will prove an invaluable asset that will help unleash the promise of CCM.

What Is a Policy?

As I've already mentioned, a policy is a set of rules or guiding principals that define how a company uses email for the purposes of marketing and communications.

Why do you need a policy? First, because email rides atop the dynamic Internet marketplace. Navigating the constantly shifting tides of government regulation and technological progress requires a company-wide commitment to best practices and consistency.

Without a policy, even the brightest minds within an organization would probably arrive at a diverse set of opinions on how email should be performed. A policy or guideline cuts through personal preferences, creating a unified action plan that can be applied to the entire organization.

For larger, multidivisional, multisender companies, a policy is essential. It enables the necessary coordination between disparate departments on such critical issues as global opt-out and CAN-SPAM compliance. Customers already see most large corporations as one entity; a policy ensures that that entity speaks with one unified voice.

What Are the Benefits of Having a Policy?

Email technologies, best practices for customer communications, and legislation are all changing at a rocket's pace. To keep up, companies must be willing to invest the time and resources to understand the potential impacts of their email program and implement a clear set of guidelines to mediate those impacts. Formalizing a set of guidelines or policies, rather than relying on spoken assurances, makes it far easier for companies to update their practices, and then distribute those updates whenever changes arise.

In particular, large companies are regular targets for lawsuits. Documenting established processes is a good defense against legal actions. If you can show that you have a written set of guidelines that are widely distributed and reasonably enforced, you may be able to diffuse some of the more baseless suits if they are ever brought against you.

Policy Challenges

One of the great challenges of policy development is finding just the right level of control. If a policy is too strict, it will be ignored. One of my college professors used to say, "The more policies and procedures you put in place, the more people will try to get around them and the less responsibility they will accept themselves." Conversely, if a policy is too loose, it probably wasn't worth creating in the first place. I've found that the right degree of control varies tremendously by company—no single approach works for everyone.

The same professor also said, "The harder a discretion is to catch, the harsher the punishment should be." In other words, for a policy to make a difference, it has to be policed and enforced. Unfortunately, enforcement can not only be intrusive, but it can also be extremely difficult to put in place. Chapter 15 presents a range of enforcement approaches, including some simple solutions that won't risk the microwaved potato problem.

Creating a Policy

Your policy is the manifestation of every customer-facing aspect of your company as it relates to email. It should cover everything from your marketing guidelines and permission strategies, to list-management processes, delivery methods, and privacy issues. It should capture your intended tone, your desired level of assertiveness, and your commitment to quality.

Your policy should launch from the same starting points as your governance model, looking hard at your company's values, strategies, and implementation plan. It should address not only positive attributes, but also potential sticking points. A good example is frequency. You'll need to consider how often your customers should hear from you. Too little contact and you will fail to achieve the full benefits of your email program. Too much contact and you will diminish your response rates and drive down your EBV.

The relatively low cost of email makes frequency an especially sticky point. Marketers have a longstanding rule of thumb—the more I pay, the more people I can influence. Email, because of its low cost, defies that rule. Before email became popular, companies would ask, "How often can we *afford* to communicate with our customers?" Now they should ask, "How often is *too often* to contact our customers?"

Frequency is proof alone that email initiatives need to be scrutinized and documented to ensure that they hold up to your company's values and strategies. But frequency is by no means the only justification for careful policy analysis. All of the policy components in the next section deserve varying degrees of review.

Components of a Policy

I've reviewed dozens of policies and have been involved in the creation of many policy initiatives. Over time, I've compiled a list of the most common policy elements I have come across. For the sake of convenience, I've grouped them into seven areas:

1. Strategy
2. Process and Execution
3. Marketing Objectives
4. Managing Permission
5. Message Content
6. Infrastructure
7. Third-Party Data

Strategy

Strategy is where a policy starts. As the first, and often the most important, part of a policy, strategy sets the tone for every component that comes after it. Specifically, it:

- Establishes email's place within the enterprise, particularly in relation to other initiatives such as privacy, information technology, and multichannel marketing.
- Describes the company's values with regard to the email channel.
- Establishes the governance body and outlines the mechanisms by which it will manage and make changes to the policy.
- Defines an internal language of email terms that will be used consistently throughout the organization. It also establishes a uniform system of measurement for the entire company.
- Determines the types of email governed by the policy. A policy might determine, for example, whether it will cover interpersonal messages and internal broadcast messages to employees.
- Sets up rules governing how Personally Identifiable Information (PII) can be gathered and used within the email program.

Process and Execution

The policy defines the enterprise email process, from approvals to quality controls. It:

- Delineates the email "owner"—the individual or department that will take responsibility for a portion of, or the entire, email program. To give you an example, within a single company, the IT department might own receipts, the finance department might own e-bills, and the marketing department might own newsletters.

- Establishes the legal, brand, and content-approval process. (Who needs to approve messages before they are sent?)
- Sets up a consistent quality assurance process to make certain that each email adheres to the company's standards.
- Designates the visual layout of the preference page.
- Identifies a list of third-party service providers who have been prescreened and who meet the company's qualifications. This list might include advertising agencies, ESPs, and consulting firms.

Marketing Objectives

The policy establishes clear rules for customer contact and campaign testing. It:

- Defines frequency (how often each customer may be contacted).
- Determines what types of customer information can and should be collected for later use in profiling and analysis.
- Sets targets for opens, click-throughs, conversions, and other response rates.
- Determines whether viral messaging should be promoted, and, if so, what privacy and CAN-SPAM guidelines should be applied.
- Establishes methods for testing email campaigns to determine optimal content or offers.
- Specifies how and where recipients should reply to messages— via email, or directed through the company's Web site.

Managing Permission

A policy establishes the levels of permission required for various email types (commercial versus transactional, for example). It also:

- Sets a standard practice for opt-ins, clearly defining privacy policies and email address usage.

- Specifies the types of permission data that need to be captured at the opt-in (for example, date, opt-in Web page URL, IP address, etc.).

- Defines the mechanisms by which customers can opt-out (via a reply or on the company's Web site), sets the content of the opt-out response, and determines the turnaround time for removal. (CAN-SPAM specifies fewer than ten days, but some enterprises will adhere to even stricter deadlines).

- Sets policies for submitting and applying opt-outs across the enterprise.

- Specifies how and when email lists can be shared among separate divisions within the company, as well as with outside companies (list vendors or co-marketing partners, for example). This is particularly important for organizational opt-out lists.

- Defines specific target groups that require restricted or limited communication (for example the media or shareholders).

Message Content

The policy identifies acceptable content, and it sets a consistent look and feel for all messages across the organization. Specifically, it:

- Defines what content goes into the all-important "from" field.
- Establishes the look of the message—the fonts, colors, logo usage, and layout.
- Sets the tone and writing style of the message (for example, addressing the customer as "Dear Sir," or less formally as "Dear Adam,"), and it establishes the legal boilerplate language that must be included in every message (privacy policy and opt-outs).
- Addresses the types of personal customer information that can be included in a message body (email becomes inherently insecure after it leaves the sender's servers), and it defines the types of email content that require the user to visit the company's Web site for authentication.

- Defines which kinds of advanced content (JavaScript, cascading style sheets, embedded forms, and rich media), can be used in various message types.

- Addresses global email issues, for example the use of foreign languages within boilerplate text, design, and navigation.

- Considers what message body types (HTML or text) will be available.

- Determines whether delivery testing is needed and decides which email clients should be tested against before delivery.

Infrastructure

The policy will outline such issues as security, response management, and delivery as they apply across the organization. For example, it:

- Sets security requirements with regard to handling data and capturing customer responses from forms.

- Defines the technical specifications for capturing and handling replies/responses.

- Provides a list of approved products and/or vendors that can deliver large-volume campaigns.

- Aligns the global opt-out process so that it is consistent across the organization.

- Lays out the requirements for automatic data extraction from master customer lists, and the mechanisms by which customer information (such as opt-outs and preference changes) is updated (see Chapter 16 on data integration).

Third-Party Data

A policy lays out the company's specifications for working with third-party data providers. It:

- Establishes list rental, append, and co-registration guidelines at the enterprise level.

- Creates a list of approved service providers.
- Sets requirements for all third-party data providers with regard to liabilities and service guarantees.

Pulling Together a Complete Policy

Now you have a (quite extensive) list of ingredients. How do you mix them together to make an integrated policy recipe?

When writing your policy, you don't need to include every item on my list. Use it instead as a starting point. Choose only the areas that apply to your organization. You can simplify the policy-writing process by breaking the list into pieces and working on one set of questions at a time. Each piece of the policy can exist as its own separate entity. For example, if you create a narrower guideline focused solely on message content, you can later give it to the agencies or the individuals within your organization who are responsible for content development.

The key to creating an effective policy is not only *having* the right elements, but also *formalizing* them. Don't rely on notes and memory, which are evasive—write everything down in a formal document and circulate it for comments. That said, given the fluid nature of email, your policy will never be set in stone. Look at it as a work in progress: a consistently updated source to which members of your organization should regularly return to keep abreast of the latest best practices and potential risks.

And no matter how effective your policy appears on paper, without a governing body to oversee implementation and ensure compliance, it will quickly become meaningless and unenforceable. Every good email policy has either an executive or a governance body behind it. This group (or individual) authors the policy, keeps it updated, and ensures that the entire organization complies with it.

CHANNELS AND YOUR POLICY

When email was still in its infancy, nearly all large-volume outbound communications were either advertising or promotional messages. With only two types of emails going out, companies did not need a complex (if any) governing policy.

Today, companies use email for a wide range of communications, from newsletters, to press releases, e-bills, and e-receipts. Even with a comprehensive policy in place, companies are now finding that their broad email initiatives don't fit neatly into one category.

Channels can help companies organize their email efforts into a more manageable framework by grouping similar message types. Channels can be applied in many different ways, but the general idea is to simplify one large policy into several subpolicies, each of which refers to a different type of email. For example, third-party promotions and product promotions might each be assigned their own channel.

Each channel would have its own distinct set of attributes and policy requirements. A third-party promotions channel might require a high level of permission and a low frequency threshold, for example. A product updates channel, on the other hand, might have no frequency controls yet require careful scrutiny and regular approvals. A large organization might have a single policy governing Strategy and Infrastructure, but have multiple channels within that one policy, each with its own requirements for Process and Execution, Marketing Objectives, Managing Permission, Message Content, and Third-Party Data.

Preference Pages and Channels

Preference pages and channels are both means of segmenting content into various brackets. But they are not the same animal. Whereas a channel is inward facing and administrative on the company side, preferences are external and customer driven.

Going back to the *New York Times* preference page I illustrated in Chapter 11, each type of content (e.g., National, Sports, Editorial) would constitute a different preference, although they would likely have similar channel attributes. On the other hand, advertising and marketing communication (for example, the *New York Times* Get-Aways), might be better managed as a separate channel.

BSkyB Case Study Part II: Policy

When Sky set out to write its policy, its primary focus was on coordinating email lists among its many divisions. The company's very first policy, therefore, leaned heavily in the areas of content consistency, permission, and list sharing.

The policy Sky created recommended a consistent boilerplate language for all company messages: general terms and conditions, specific opt-in and opt-out language, and a link pointing customers to the company's privacy statement. To manage opt-outs globally, Sky's policy authors built a company-wide list, then asked all list managers to begin tracking email permission status (they call it the "Direct Marketing Flag") and third-party message permissions (they call it the "Third-Party Marketing Flag" or the "DPA Flag").

With a working governance body to oversee its efforts, and the first critical pieces of a policy in place, Sky kicked off its new enterprise-wide email effort in mid-December 2003, just as the UK's Data Protection Act (DPA) was being put into place. I'll share the end of the Sky story with you, and show you how its enterprise initiative fell into place, in the next two chapters.

■　■　■　■

When it comes to email, no department is an island. Even though each group may be focused on different priorities, the end product must present a consistent face to customers. A policy ties disparate units within an organization into a coherent whole that manifests itself internally and externally.

A solid policy requires an investment both of time and of money. But once properly executed, your policy will form the backbone of your email program. It will ensure that your brand—and your message—are represented appropriately and consistently on all occasions. Furthermore, it will support your email program as it rides through the inevitable sea of changes within your organization and throughout the industry.

Chapter 15

MANAGING LISTS ACROSS A COMPANY

If you guys can't share, I'm taking it away and then nobody will have any.
—the author's mother, when the author was eight

We've already discussed several approaches for integrating multiple email programs into a cohesive enterprise initiative. The next point to consider is how to manage the logistics of running an enterprise email program on a day-to-day basis. At the highest level, managing email in a multisender organization requires attention to three distinct yet interrelated issues: (1) policy and governance (which we've already covered); (2) list sharing (which will be covered in this chapter); and (3) data management (which will be covered in Chapter 16). If you're part of a multisender organization, you should find the next two chapters helpful in easing you through the transition from autonomy to a working CCM initiative.

As I mentioned in Chapter 13, most email initiatives were born deep in the inner recesses of corporations, far from the scrutiny of senior management. In the early days of email, there was little reason for management to pay attention. After all, the technology was new, it was cheap, and it had little impact on a company's overall business.

For years, individual departments essentially ran their own show with little or no oversight from the top and with very limited interference from other departments. But in 2003, with CAN-SPAM looming, the days of the independent email program became numbered. Senior management at large corporations found themselves face to face with an email program they knew little about, and which they suddenly had to consolidate and coordinate into an enterprise-wide effort.

Coordination also introduced a new range of challenges at the departmental level. Previously satisfied departments often began acting like petulant children when they were asked to relinquish control over their lists and mailing procedures. Even groups that wholeheartedly supported consolidation sometimes had trouble adapting their established routines to fit the new email program structure.

The Challenge

When the majority of email initiatives were still decentralized, each group within an organization cultivated—and enjoyed exclusive and unrestricted use of—their own list. Soon, mailing lists were everywhere. A 2001 IMT study found that nearly a third of companies had twenty or more email lists.[1] While I am not aware of any recent studies on the subject, the average number of lists per company has probably grown since then. Imagine trying to tell a dozen or more list owners that not only do they have to share their data with other divisions, but that they also must now adhere to company policy every time they use the customer information they collected.

The fundamental problem with list sharing is that marketers want to talk to customers far more often than customers want to hear from them. In a single-sender organization, the sender feels firsthand the consequences of the customers' dissatisfaction: responses decrease and opt-outs increase. But with multiple departments simultaneously launching email campaigns to the same customers, the enterprise-wide implications are less visible. Customer response becomes hard to gauge because any negative reaction is diluted by the sheer number of departments in the mix. Without clear results to work from, departments find that their ad hoc frequency management efforts are rendered virtually ineffective.

Individual senders know how often they want to reach their customers, but they are reluctant to coordinate and prioritize their needs with those of other divisions. I'll give you an example. Consider the case of a large, multidivisional bank. The bank offers its customers a number of services, from loans, to mortgages, to credit cards. In the bank's credit card department, John is getting ready to send out an email campaign promoting a new frequent flyer rewards card.

Meanwhile, Bob in the mortgage department is planning to send customers news of a lower interest rate, followed by a direct mortgage offer. The more credit cards John sells, the higher his bonus. The more mortgages Bob sells, the bigger his bonus. Both John and Bob have put together compelling campaigns. Both are also sending to the same list. And neither wants to give up or delay a valuable promotional opportunity.

But what happens when customers are bombarded by credit card offers and mortgage ads from the same bank at the same time? They click "unsubscribe" and disappear from the bank's list forever. When recipients opt-out, not only do John and Bob lose customers, but the bank as a whole appears uncoordinated and overly aggressive.

The problem of interdepartmental resource sharing is far from new. Long before email and email lists existed, departments sparred over another scarce resource—money. To vie for a piece of a limited budget, each department would present their case to management, declare what wondrous results they could achieve with additional funding, and then cross their fingers that management would agree. But budgets are finite resources. If the bank I mentioned has a $100,000 budget, and it spends that $100,000 on marketing mortgages, the money will simply not be available for a credit card promotion. End of story. Email list access, on the other hand, is neither limited nor mutually exclusive. Therefore, marketers are continually tempted to overuse and abuse it.

The term "management" in Customer Communication Management speaks directly to this challenge. Without the natural cost and expertise hurdles, an ad hoc approach to customer communication will simply not work for long. A new level of oversight and management must be applied to ensure that the customers' interests are protected in the new world of low-cost communications.

In the remainder of the chapter, we look at the many ways in which an enterprise can allocate lists across divisions and manage enforcement processes without compromising the needs of its individual departments.

Mechanisms for Sharing Lists

When companies get ready to initiate a list-sharing process, they must consider two questions: "How do we allocate list access so that our company's ultimate goals are met?" and "How do we control and enforce that allocation?"

Allocation can be accomplished in one of several ways. Here are the four methods that have worked well for my clients and colleagues:

Marketing calendar: Most marketing departments already use a calendar to plan and budget their activities. That same calendar can easily be applied to manage list access across several groups. The benefit of this approach is that the allocation is plotted out (and can therefore be modified) up front. When one group is scheduled to send out a newsletter, for example, that time block is closed off to other groups to avoid overlap.

Frequency: Frequency allocation specifies how many messages a particular address can receive (ideally, based on that recipient's stated preferences). Once an address has reached its message threshold, it is either excluded from the current campaign, or the mailing is delayed until the next cycle. This approach requires sophisticated technology that may not be available to every company.

Pay-based: This capitalist approach awards the greatest email list allocation to the highest bidder. Departments pay (either in real dollars or in some internal transfer costs) for the privilege of emailing to the company's list. The pay-based allocation method fits nicely into the advertising model (the more money you spend, the more audience you reach), but it can backfire if departments are willing to pay for more allocation than the organization is willing or able to provide. One way to get around limited allocation is by having an auction. The search engine Google, for example, has only a finite inventory of ads for certain keywords. To be fair to its advertisers, and to bring in the most revenue for itself, Google auctions off ads to the highest bidders. Companies can similarly determine a finite number of messages they'll let reach their customers, then award those messages to the groups that are willing to pay the most for them.

Merit-based: Merit-based allocation systems reward departments for past campaign success by granting them additional access to the shared lists. Success can be measured by click-throughs, opens, and/or opt-outs. Higher opens and click-throughs in past campaigns move a department higher up on the queue for list allocation. High opt-out rates drop a department's next list request lower on the priority scale.

Remember that list sharing can take many forms. If every group wants to send to the whole list with each mailing, for example, calendaring is the best and fairest approach. But if marketers are sending to only small segments of the overall list at one time, other allocation methods may be more effective.

Even if you have the best allocation plan in place, be prepared to review and occasionally override your system. Regular review meetings by an email governance group can help keep track of your allocation system, and easily enable you to make changes when necessary. The governance group may want to appoint an arbitration subgroup to deal with the conflicts and issues that will inevitably arise. Having to make periodic changes does not in any way imply that the allocation approach has failed; but neglecting to resolve problems that do arise can cause the entire governance model to fail.

Enforcement

It is the rare company that can execute any business initiative without a single hitch or hiccup. The subtleties and complexities of marketing pretty much ensure that at least one department will inadvertently go beyond the bounds of its allocation. Unless you're working in one of the rare corporate marketing utopias, you will need to apply some method of enforcement to your allocation plan.

In a centralized governance model (see Chapter 13), enforcement is relatively easy. There is, by definition, only one group of individuals with access to the systems and vendors needed to deliver campaigns. This group has already vowed to adhere to the company's overall email requirements (they probably wrote them). And, because they see the "big picture" in terms of responses, opt-outs, and overall satisfaction issues, they willingly hold the organization's needs above the needs of any single division or department. But, as I mentioned in Chapter 13, the centralized approach tends to be bureaucratic, and most companies eventually replace it with a more flexible governance model.

Federated and decentralized models are more democratic and less restrictive than the centralized model, but they require more active enforcement. Generally speaking, the more dispersed the email initiative, the more stringent the enforcement required.

Enforcement can be accomplished in a myriad of ways, but I like to divide it into three categories: Access, Approval, and Audit. A solid enforcement approach will always use at least one, and sometimes two or three, of these categories.

Access: This approach works as a sort of gatekeeper, granting only certain employees access to data and campaign execution systems. Access can take one of several forms: providing access to the underlying data, allowing use of the email campaign tool (Email System (EMS) or distribution system), or educating staff on the importance of using the data appropriately and the implications of using it inappropriately. Nearly 87 percent of best-in-class companies used database access to enforce their policies, according to an IMT Strategies study. Also popular were distribution systems (63 percent), rules (53 percent), and education/training (47 percent).[2]

A commonly sought-after form of access control is address usage regulation or frequency control. Rather than giving senders unfettered access to the entire list, the EMS controls frequency based upon the organization's preset definitions. If too many messages are sent to a block of recipients within a specified period of time, the system will automatically block any further message attempts to those addresses.

A complementary approach allows enterprises to control access at the message content level. With their EMS, companies create a "template" that is then used by all departments. Some fields in the template are left open for the user to add a marketing message; other fields are already filled in. The subject line and message body may be modifiable, for example, whereas the "from" field and boilerplate CAN-SPAM message remain the same for every message. The template solution becomes increasingly important as more departments within a company are given email sending privileges. Sales organizations and call centers in particular are becoming increasingly interested in using email tools to control templates and address books so that every department is automatically CAN-SPAM compliant and brand sensitive.

Although access control gives the governance body or management more control over message content and frequency, be wary when using it for enforcement. Some companies get so carried away with access control that they lock down their system to the extent that their marketers find it unusable. Rigid access control not only risks the exploding potato metaphor I described in Chapter 13, but it can be an administrative nightmare. In most cases, simply educating your users and asking them to act responsibly is enough to prevent most sending mishaps. (Call me an eternal optimist.)

Approval: As with any other approval process, marketers must gain permission from a managing body before sending out campaigns. Approval is the most intuitive approach to enforcement, and the method most companies leap to first (especially in industries such as financial services, where email communications are heavily regulated).

But keep in mind that approval-based enforcement can add a lot of time and administrative overhead to a campaign. If you're trying to release a message on Monday about a one-day sale happening on Tuesday, you can't afford to let your message sit on a manager's desk for two days.

If you're looking to use the approval process, weigh the benefits against the risks. Consider whether the consequences of a typo or other mistake are worth slowing down your email marketing to the point that your colleagues become frustrated and seek other marketing solutions.

Audit: One of the most effective ways to enforce email policies and list allocation is by conducting regular audits. The audit approach has been used for decades for other forms of marketing. It tends to work most effectively in organizations that are already inclined to follow best practices. The main difference between audits and approvals is that audits catch bad behavior *after* it has occurred; approvals catch it before it happens.

Some industries (for example, financial services) are required by law to keep copies when they send out certain types of messages. Email audits are similarly little more than paper trails—a helpful way of checking up on campaigns to ensure that they are following corporate policies and are staying within the bounds of branding practices and corporate culture.

One simple approach to the audit is to seed your house list with one or more in-house addresses. That way, at lest one person in your organization receives a copy, and therefore keeps a record, of every message sent. Your governance group can periodically review sent messages, and take action if compliance slips.

What's the Right Frequency?

You already know that if you email recipients too frequently, your EBV will plummet. So before allocating list data among your senders, you naturally want to come up with a finite number of messages each customer should receive. But then the natural question arises: What *is* the magic number of messages to send each customer?

As I mentioned in Chapter 2, marketers have come up with the Rule of 24 to dictate message frequency. The rule stipulates that companies limit their correspondence to twenty-four messages per customer per year (or two messages per month). But this blanket approach doesn't take into account the customer's anticipation of—and receptiveness to—messages. The Rule of 24 also doesn't account for the message content: Are these unwelcome promotional messages or crucial product security alerts?

For instance, if an airline were to send frequent fliers free lifetime upgrade coupons every day for a month, I doubt that any of the recipients would complain. But if a mortgage company sent teenagers an offer for discounted rates, the sheer irrelevancy of the message would make even one email too frequent. As these examples illustrate, sophisticated marketers should be less focused on *frequency*, and more focused on *relevancy*.

Despite the greater subtlety relevancy affords, many organizations tend to fall back on frequency, simply because relevancy is difficult to measure without undertaking a great deal of sophisticated and expensive testing. If you must use frequency as a guide, at the very least manage it with channels so that some types of messages are sent less often than other types based on their position along the CVE (see Chapter 11).

When determining your optimal frequency caps, you might want to use these research results as a guide. Figure 15.1 shows the frequencies that retail marketers prefer:

Figure 15.1 Email Marketing Frequency Used by Retailers in the U.S. Source: the e-tailing Group, April 2003[3]

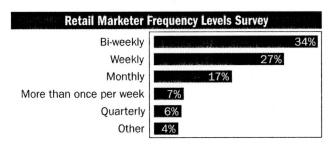

In contrast, Figure 15.2 shows the frequencies that consumers prefer:

Figure 15.2 Frequency with Which Online Consumers in North America Would Like to Receive Permission Email Promotions and Advertisements (as a % of respondents) Source: Forrester Research, April 2002[4]

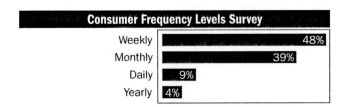

Clearly, the best frequency approach is to ask your customers how often they want to hear from you when they fill out or update their preference pages. If you lack the processes or technology to manage frequency, the next best solution is testing. Try varying frequency levels over a month or two among a random subset of your list. You can then analyze the relative response rates, opt-outs, and conversions to see if there is an "optimal" frequency level that can be applied to the entire group. If none of these approaches works or is appropriate for your company, refer to the two figures above as a frequency guide.

The Future

Nearly every emailer I know (including myself) falls prey to the same limiting email management tactic. We force our campaign thinking into one of two neat buckets: a single specific message that appeals to a subset of our audience, or a broad set of topics that applies to most or all of our audience (e.g., a newsletter). The result of this narrow approach is that we fall back on managing frequency in order to ensure that our EBV remains high.

But what if you could combine the best of both approaches and eliminate the frequency issue altogether? What if you could create a single communication vehicle that was both highly targeted and widely appealing? It may sound paradoxical, but one company has already done it.

Every week, the email marketing group at American Airlines gathers dozens of email requests from its various divisions. Each request contains a target audience and proposed content. Some communications are meant for all American Airlines customers; others target a specific demographic or geographic subset. Some content is promotional; some is informational. American's email group analyzes all departments' requests, and it prioritizes (scores) each communication based on its perceived benefit to every customer on American's mailing list.

The results: Every single American Airlines email customer receives a newsletter filled with individual content segments targeted specifically to them. For any given mailing, there might be hundreds or even thousands of different newsletters sent out. Although this approach requires the technology to mix and match content with customer interests, it is the ultimate win-win solution. Marketers at American can send out as much content as they want with any given mailing, and are assured that their messages will always reach the most receptive audience. Meanwhile, customers receive one periodic newsletter from American, rather than a hodgepodge of messages. That single newsletter is so perfectly targeted that American's click-through rates are some of the highest in the industry.

American's approach is, to put it simply—ingenious. It uses dynamic content to strike a balance between the company's desire to send multiple messages to the same customers, and the customers' desire to receive consistent and relevant communications. American's program shows how email can be used to deliver the kind of personalized customer communication that would be impossible (or at least, impractical) via any other mechanism. Its approach hints at the kinds of communications channels we can expect to see in the future—communications that combine ultra-precise targeting with superior relevancy, all wrapped up in a manageable customer communication framework.

Sky Case Study Part III: Allocation

As the Sky Stakeholder Committee rolled out its enterprise CCM effort, its IT department was simultaneously developing a single, backend customer management system. Meanwhile, each of Sky's divisions continued to maintain its own lists. Without the centralized technical infrastructure in place, Sky's policy and governance group was the primary control point for customer communications.

In its early meetings, Sky's Stakeholder Committee set a broad goal that the company would send no more than two promotional messages to each customer per month. Using a calendar allocation, the governance committee worked with each division to coordinate communication types and frequencies that would achieve each department's objectives while supporting the overall enterprise goals. Sky decided not to "lock down" its allocation too tightly. The company wanted to make sure that each division had the flexibility to operate autonomously as promotional opportunities arose.

The Stakeholder Committee kept tabs on all of its divisions by placing a few internal seed addresses on each group's lists. Any misstep was immediately apparent and relatively easy to fix.

Sam Fay, operations manager for Sky Online, spearheaded most of the company's CCM initiatives. As of this writing, Sky's enterprise-wide email program was still evolving, but "our early efforts allowed us to get everyone on the same page. And, frankly, the results have been impressive," says Fay.[5]

■　■　■　■

Managing lists among multiple senders is one of the toughest email challenges that large organizations face. The actions of a few overzealous emailers can threaten a company's brand and legal standing, and compromise its entire email effort. The challenge is finding the right managerial balance: implementing enough control to regulate activities among disparate departments, without restricting marketers so much that the entire program grinds to a halt.

The most successful email programs are able to find a comfortable balance between risk management and creativity and flexibility. The key is finding the techniques that have worked in the past for other aspects of your business and fine-tuning those processes to fit the technological and operational nuances of your email communications.

Chapter 16

EMAIL DATA INTEGRATION

Technology doesn't make you less stupid; it just makes you stupid faster.
—Jerry Gregoire, former CIO, Dell
as quoted in *FastCompany*, March 2002

Up to this point in the book, we have focused on the processes and models needed to manage email in a large enterprise. The challenges so far have all been somewhat familiar to marketers: organizing information, communicating between groups, and creating policies. The last part of this section, however, takes marketers one step outside their comfort zone—smack into the world of technology. Many marketers I know would rather spend the afternoon at an IRS audit than tackle a joint project with their IT department. If you are among the technology averse, know that you are not alone.

As we discussed in Chapter 7, email marketing is deeply rooted in technology. Just managing opt-outs across an enterprise requires a sophisticated exchange of customer data between the EMS and a company's operational databases. The EMS needs access to the most updated customer data, just as the corporate database needs opt-out and preference information from the email system.

Most of the critical customer data that marketers need for email, or for any other kind of marketing, is locked away in back office business systems. Marketers rarely have access to this data; and, even if they were granted access, the business systems managing the data would be unlikely to provide marketers with the functionality (e.g., testing, reporting, and analytics) they need to carry out necessary marketing functions.

Rather than trying to squeeze marketing functionality out of, say, an accounting or billing system, most companies take a different approach—they extract the data from various business systems and aggregate it into a database built primarily for marketing's needs (often referred to as a *marketing data warehouse*). There are many ways to build a data warehouse: packaged CRM solutions, specialized data warehouse and analytic products, or solutions developed internally by a company's IT department.

Regardless of how the marketing database is built, its flow should resemble the diagram in Figure 16.1. Information is pulled from various operational databases and business systems and pooled into a single, high-performance data warehouse whose primary purpose is to provide marketing functionality.

Figure 16.1 The typical flow of several internal systems into a marketing database

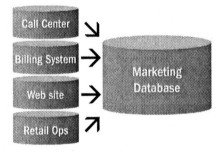

INTEGRATING EMAIL INTO THE MARKETING DATABASE

Regardless of whether marketing information is stored in a single shared database, or scattered among several distinct databases owned by individual departments, the email system needs to pull certain customer information from wherever it is stored to execute campaigns.

The primary issue for senders is how their email system will interact and share data with existing customer databases. Essentially, only three choices exist:

1. Ignore the existing databases.
2. Integrate with the existing databases.

3. Establish the email database as the principal database with which all other marketing initiatives are integrated.

Although many marketing departments start by ignoring existing databases, they can rarely survive this approach for the long term. The ultimate desire to achieve multichannel marketing, coupled with the necessity of maintaining customer data integrity, eventually pressures marketers to stop ignoring and begin integrating. In fact, managing global opt-outs for CAN-SPAM compliance is one of the most pressing reasons why marketers ultimately put the necessary integration in place.

I added the third option because many email-centric marketers have successfully used the email database as the primary database approach. Unfortunately, most current EMS solutions are not advanced enough to handle a centralized customer database. But in the future, EMS systems may have progressed to the point where email marketers can use them for online *and* offline marketing solutions.

For the time being, the majority of large, sophisticated emailers will continue to go with approach number two. The rest of this section will address the various ways in which to integrate the marketing database(s) with the email system.

Marketing Database Integration

Figure 16.2 The diagram shows the major steps (or "engines") to integrating an email marketing and communications technology solution with a traditional marketing database

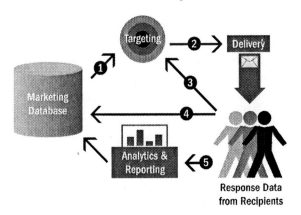

209

The diagram in Figure 16.2 might appear complex, but if you break it into its individual components, database integration becomes relatively intuitive for most marketers. To simplify, let's first isolate and describe each area of functionality:

Marketing database: A consolidated data warehouse built either internally or with an off-the-shelf marketing database package or CRM product.

Targeting: Testing, identifying segments, incorporating past email behavior (and behavior with regard to other marketing mediums) into new segments, managing frequency, controlling list access, managing automated campaigns and life cycle marketing, accepting and acting on external event triggers.

Delivery: Deliverability, bounce handling, recipient-facing actions such as capturing opens and click-throughs, delivering rich media, dynamic content assembly, opt-outs, and other basic list hygiene (essentially the basics we covered in Chapter 6).

Analytics and reporting: Capturing email-specific data and presenting real-time reports, translating massive amounts of email-generated data into usable marketing information (i.e., simplifying all message opens into aggregate and unique opens), generating behavior data and feeding it back real-time into the targeting engine.

Now that we've laid out the major components of an integration plan, let's see how information moves between each component, then discuss the factors marketers need to keep in mind when designing their integration. Each of the information flows is designated by an arrow and identified by a circled number.

From Marketing Database to Targeting (Circle 1): The first step is to move basic customer records, including email addresses, en masse to the targeting engine. The targeting engine must receive and process large amounts of customer data in order to perform the kinds of selections that sophisticated marketers demand. Because of the sheer volume of data exchanged, some emailers, especially those at Level 2 (see Chapter 3), design their integration so that the targeting engine runs on the same database (and sometimes on the same software) as their customer data warehouse. It would seem a logical choice because many marketing databases come already equipped with powerful targeting tools.

However, as companies move to Level 3 and begin implementing more advanced personalization and targeting techniques, the marketing database becomes a less effective targeting engine. Many marketing data warehouses have difficulty handling several essential targeting capabilities:

- Event triggers and targeting one recipient at a time,
- Automating sequences and internal time-based triggers, and
- Incorporating real-time email responses and recipient behavior into automated campaigns

Traditional marketing databases also struggle when it comes to dynamic content, which requires that segmenting be performed as part of the delivery process. Having two separate systems—one for targeting and one for delivery—can lead to awkward or missing functionality in key areas like life cycle automation. So as companies move toward Level 3, they tend to pass over more generic marketing database targeting tools for more specialized solutions, such as dedicated EMS or all-encompassing CRM packages.

The timing of data movement from the marketing database to the targeting engine is also crucial. Timing can be handled in one of three ways:

1. Manually, whenever the marketer requests it
2. On an automated, periodic basis (provided that the mailings themselves are periodic)
3. Fully synchronized, in which changes made in the marketing database are instantly updated in the targeting system

From Targeting to Delivery (Circle 2): Similar to the process in Circle 1, moving the targeted data into the delivery system can be accomplished in one of three ways:

1. Manually
2. On an automated, periodic basis

3. Fully synchronized, in which completed targeting tasks generate recipient lists that are then pushed to the targeting system

When targeting is complete, only the customer information that will be used for personalization or dynamic content logic needs to be sent to the delivery system. For example, you might target a campaign based on recent purchases or other customer information, but once the targeting engine identifies particular groups of customers, their buying history is probably not needed for delivery. First and last name might be the only information required at this stage of the process. The point here is that the data transfer between targeting and delivery (Circle 2) is often much simpler, smaller, and faster than the data transfer between the marketing data warehouse and the targeting engine (Circle 1). Note that if targeting and delivery run on the same system, data transfers are seamless.

Customer Response and Analytics (Circles 3, 4, and 5): As soon as the message has been delivered, the delivery system will begin generating massive amounts of raw data (click-throughs, opens, bounces, opt-outs, conversions, Web page visits, etc.). To get an idea of just how much data can be generated by a single mailing, let's consider a single newsletter sent to five hundred thousand recipients. With a 40 percent open rate, a 10 percent click-through rate, a 5 percent viral rate, and a 10 percent bounce rate, that newsletter could easily generate five hundred thousand individual response records (assuming multiple opens per person) within just a few hours. If you track specific data on dynamic content, the number of records could exceed 1 million. It is not unheard of for response data to generate 2 to 5 *gigabytes* of information *per mailing*. All of that data must be processed and analyzed.

Most marketers use their EMS as a basic analytic tool. The EMS not only provides real-time reports on campaigns as they go live, but it can also aggregate and distill large amounts of data into a manageable form so that they can be sent back to the marketing database. The EMS is also adept at feeding response and behavior data to the targeting engine in real time, making it a compelling choice for both targeting and first-stage analytics.

Although the EMS is effective for basic analytics, its use is limited to email data. If your company's non-email data is insignificant compared to its email data, your EMS should be sufficient. But most companies turn to their marketing data warehouse for advanced analytic requirements, because high-end marketing data warehouse tools have a richer set of analytic features than most EMSs, plus they can also integrate with *non-email* data.

My diagram and information flows are by no means the only possible integration approaches. I've seen integration accomplished in every imaginable way. The best practice is not what everyone else is doing, but rather, what best fits your company. When determining how to architect the right integration solution for your company, take into account which technology, product, or vendor is best suited to provide each function. Also consider which approach best matches your company's IT capabilities and established marketing practices.

Email Marketing Database Integration in the Real World

The model I discussed above could be used to integrate EMSs and marketing data warehouses in literally hundreds of different ways. But after working with a wide variety of marketers, I've found that large companies tend to take one of three approaches when it comes to integrating their EMS with their marketing database. All of these methods assume that an operational marketing database or data warehouse is already in place.

Direct marketing: The direct marketing integration approach borrows the same techniques used for years by offline marketing programs. Emailers perform selects of their primary database and transfer those subsets intact to their email delivery system. The email system collects tracking data, which is then transferred back to the marketing database. The sheer size of the data moving back and forth between the email system and marketing database makes this method somewhat unwieldy, but many marketers choose the direct marketing approach because it requires the least amount of technical sophistication. The turnaround time for this approach also fits well with the email cycle. Traditional direct marketing cycles are often measured in weeks, which makes this approach easily accomplished without forcing the data transfer cycles into an unnaturally narrow time window. When related to my integration diagram, this approach involves bulk transfers of data between components, often initiated manually by the marketing department.

Hybrid: The hybrid approach launches with the direct marketing model, but it also allows marketers to take advantage of more advanced delivery techniques such as dynamic content. After initial targeting is complete and data is prepared for delivery, the hybrid approach sends along "prescored" data to be acted on by the delivery engine. For example, rather than just personalizing the message with a first name, the targeting engine could select which recipients should receive each of four different offers based on a predictive model or analytic score. The scoring information is sent along with the customer's first name, enabling the delivery engine to send out more customized campaigns. The hybrid approach is popular because it allows traditional marketers to use some Level 3 techniques without requiring the technical sophistication of the fully synchronized approach.

Fully synchronized: The previous two approaches have their merit. But to achieve the highest levels of sophistication and take advantage of all Level 3 techniques, the fully synchronized model is the ideal choice. Synchronizing records among the marketing database, the targeting engine, and the email delivery system enables the delivery engine to automatically generate event-triggered messages based on date, threshold, and other triggering rules. A bank, for example, could send a customer a deposit reminder the moment the customer's account balance dropped below a predefined level.

The main difference between this last approach and the previous two is that data is no longer moved in bulk or on weekly cycles. When the data is synchronized between each component, only the updated information about each recipient is typically sent. As a result, the marketing database, targeting engine, and email delivery system each maintain a full and updated copy of the customer database. The actual amount of data transferred is lower with the synchronized model than with other approaches, but the technical sophistication is generally much higher. The fully synchronized approach enables companies to move their communications from "batch and blast" to individually timed and highly customized campaigns.

Setting Your Solution in Motion

Chapter 17 will cover insourcing versus outsourcing in greater depth, but I want to at least glance over the resource implications of implementing an integrated solution. Regardless of how your solution is built, one of the most important aspects to consider is how your marketing department will actually operate the solution on a daily basis.

Although the basic operations of most integration solutions will require little assistance from IT, challenges can quickly arise when the marketing department wants to set up complex targeting or specialized reports. I would advise that you consider the capabilities of your IT department (as well as their availability and other priorities) when choosing your integration strategy and the software products for each component. If the tools are functionally rich but require high levels of ongoing IT involvement, you may find that the longer IT cycle times keep you from realizing the full benefit of the solution you spent so much time building.

A few companies have managed to automate their solution to the point where their marketing departments can operate autonomously. One of my clients, a financial services company, needed a system that could juggle multiple automated mailings for their huge and diverse customer base. Promotions, follow-ups, reminders, and surveys needed to be timed precisely to fit each customer's product purchase dates and billing cycles. That kind of automation required literally hundreds of different automated campaigns running simultaneously. Silverpop helped this company set up a data management model that automatically synchronized their customer database with our EMS. With all of their most recent customer data available in Silverpop's EMS, the company's marketing department is able to set up, change, report on, and cancel automated life cycle campaigns with virtually no outside assistance from Silverpop or their IT department.

Alternatives to Integration

In many companies, marketers do not always have the option of choosing the ideal integration approach. IT resources or budgets may be limited. More pressing projects may take priority. Corporate executives may have mandated the use of certain applications that already include some degree of email functionality. Regardless of the reasons for choosing a particular integration approach, two methods can help avoid the complexities (discussed earlier in this chapter) that may arise: CRM applications and full outsourcing. Although both of these alternative approaches require serious compromises, they can each be made to work to varying degrees.

CRM Applications for Email Marketing

On the surface, your average CRM application's email marketing feature set seems an appealing option. It offers a single solution with a single interface from a single vendor. The data is already in the CRM system, and it therefore moves seamlessly between the various engines.

But delve a bit deeper into the CRM solution and complexities emerge. Rarely can a CRM application rise to meet the needs of sophisticated email marketers. CRM vendors are typically experts in CRM, not email marketing. Few CRM tools are set up to provide the advanced features most marketers require, and even fewer have the email services depth to augment their technology with specialized consulting on issues such as deliverability, new marketing techniques, and legislative frameworks.

Rarely will you find a CRM package that is considered "best-of-breed" for each component in the integration solution in Figure 16.2 (especially the delivery component). Some packages have trouble handling deliverability; others aren't set up to process email specific reports. Most packages are so broad in scope that they provide far more intricate functions than most marketers need, and they are too complex to scale back without significant IT support. And, most CRM systems are not engineered like specialized EMSs. Whereas most CRM products comprise a limited number of customer records packed with complex attributes, EMSs tend to have a much larger number of records with very few attributes each. The difference becomes appreciable when the system tries to handle real-time recipient-based actions or manage complex automated customer life cycle communications for hundreds of thousands or even millions of customers. Costs can rise significantly when a CRM solution tries to tackle the high transaction volumes and detailed analysis required by most email marketing solutions.

Bottom line—most CRM tools are poorly equipped to meet the needs of sophisticated email marketers. First, they lack the deep, specialized features that marketers require. Second, deliverability has become such a dynamic issue that few CRM software providers can keep up, and even fewer IT departments are prepared to roll out the updates as quickly as marketers demand. Although many companies have undoubtedly benefited from the wealth of CRM tools out there, CRM alone is not a sufficient platform on which to build a world-class email marketing and communications program.

Outsourcing the Customer Database

Years ago, marketers had little choice but to farm out their technology solutions to specialized marketing services firms. The databases needed to run advanced marketing analytics relied on huge data centers filled with mainframes and staffed by teams of technicians in long white coats.

Today, plummeting hardware prices and powerful enterprise software packages have brought high-level solutions within the reach of nontechnical marketers. Nonetheless, many marketers stick to their old outsourcing habits, and with good reason. Even though most companies have solid IT departments, they are not set up to provide the hourly turnaround and highly flexible services marketers demand. Specialized outsourcers, on the other hand, can turn around a development project quickly, and they can handle all of the technical work so that marketers need not have any interaction with the technology systems. Plus, large service firms have enough marketing expertise to bridge the culture gap that separates most marketing and IT departments. They have both the technical savvy to handle the nuts-and-bolts setup, and the marketing proficiency to understand and deliver the right solution.

But for all of its benefits, outsourcing is not without its disadvantages. Complete outsourcing can be cost prohibitive, especially when a marketing department is struggling with a limited budget. Outsourcing can drag down the overall project completion time, especially in comparison with rapid turnaround self-help systems such as large CRM solutions or specialized ESPs. Outsourcing can raise security issues, because marketers regularly process and handle sensitive customer data. And finally, most large marketing services firms simply don't have the depth to handle the email component of database integration. Although they can call in the services of a specialized ESP, the nuances and best practices of email delivery are often lost in the process.

Sky Case Study Part IV: Integration

Even after Sky rolled out its policy and governance model, each of its divisions continued to maintain its own list. Some divisions use a hybrid approach to integrate with Silverpop's EMS; others keep their lists completely within our EMS. But all of Sky's lists are integrated with a single, global opt-out list. The company is set up to honor all opt-outs, regardless of which division they come through. As Sky rolls out its enterprise email initiatives, its IT department is finalizing a single, large-scale customer management system. Each one of Sky's lists has been designed to quickly transition to the new master CRM system once it has been completed.

Sky's departments also remain individual in the management of their day-to-day email efforts. Some groups outsource everything under the full-service model (see Chapter 17); others use a self-service or service bureau model. Sky's governance model is truly federated in that each group operates autonomously, depending on its IT, budget, and personnel requirements, but all groups operate under a single, enterprise-wide governance and policy model.

I chose to highlight Sky's enterprise email efforts because I found them to be one of the best representations of an email program in progress. Although Sky has made great strides with its email initiative, like most forward-thinking emailers, its CCM initiatives will never be "complete."

Another reason for choosing Sky was to highlight one of the most important issues in creating world-class enterprise email programs: the customer. Although the mechanical and architectural aspects of CCM that I have laid out in this book are undeniably important to any email program, companies like Sky are gaining the greatest benefit by taking a strategic view of their email programs and shifting their thinking from internal processes to customer-centric philosophies.

Sky's CCM strategy will invariably continue to unfold over the next few years, but its early results clearly indicate the value of leading an email initiative with a strategic approach and placing the greatest emphasis on the customer. You may recall from the introduction to Part 4 that, prior to Sky's enterprise initiatives, it was receiving one or two customer complaints *each day*. With its governance model in place and its policy enforcement under way, Sky's efforts have already begun to pay off. In the first half of 2004, the company's complaint count dropped from a few a day to *a few over an entire six-month period*. Sky's early CCM efforts have put it in the ranks of world-class emailers.

■　■　■　■

As much as marketers would like to avoid it, technology is an omnipresent and growing aspect of their world. Savvy marketers who not only accept but also embrace technology will gain a formidable competitive advantage for their companies.

How to structure the technology components so that they fit together into a world-class marketing initiative is among the most important technology decisions any company will make. Simply choosing the right elements is not enough. The long-term flexibility and responsiveness of the enterprise email initiative depends upon the clean integration of various components, the accessibility of the technology, and the availability of crucial customer data. A well-designed integration solution will not only streamline marketing's day-to-day tasks, but it will also bolster the governance efforts that underlie the entire enterprise email program.

Part V

EXECUTION

PART 5
EXECUTION

The final section of the book is where CCM goes from theory into action. Parts 2, 3, and 4 laid the foundation for an effective enterprise-wide, multisender email program. In Part 5, you'll learn how to pull all of the elements together and set up your day-to-day execution.

When implementing an email program, the first question marketers inevitably ask is: "Should I outsource my email technology and services or handle them internally?" Chapter 17 addresses this question. Chapter 18 offers some answers to another popular question: "How do I build my lists so that my email programs become more impactful?" Chapter 19 overviews day-to-day deliverability and renderability challenges and Chapter 20 illustrates advanced techniques, such as life cycle automation, that bring email marketers fully into the realm of Level 3.

The final chapter in the book looks toward the future of CCM. Once your company has put a solid CCM strategy into daily use, Chapter 21 will help you map out the next set of challenges and take advantage of opportunities down the road.

Chapter 17

INSOURCE VERSUS OUTSOURCE

The secret to creativity is knowing how to hide your sources.
—Albert Einstein

You can have all the pieces to a great sports car—a 400 horsepower V8 engine, double wishbone suspension, and high-performance tires— but unless you can find someone who knows how to put them together, you won't get your car out of the garage. Likewise, you can have all the elements of a great email program—a comprehensive policy, solid governance model, extensive and highly permissioned list, and perfectly targeted content—but your messages will go nowhere unless you have the resources to help you execute your campaigns. Choosing the right service provider who will treat your email program with the same care and respect you'd give it is one of the toughest decisions you'll have to make with regard to your email campaign.

In the early years when email was just ramping up as a communication medium, many companies found that they could easily implement their email program internally. But as the technology gained momentum, and marketers jumped on its huge potential for attracting and retaining customers, an exponentially higher number of messages started pouring through internal servers. The demand by marketers for new and more sophisticated features, coupled with the rise in email deliverability challenges, strained technological infrastructure and manpower resources. Soon companies were forced to make a critical decision: Should they continue to handle email development and execution in-house and possibly overtax their IT department, or should they set aside a portion of their budget to farm the work to an outside vendor?

An increasing number of companies are choosing the latter approach and turning to outside providers for their email services. But in doing so, many companies 'put the cart before the horse.' They focus exclusively on picking a vendor without considering their technology and budgetary needs. In the end, they find themselves at the wrong end of a poor decision, with an email solution that can't even come close to meeting their organization's requirements.

First Things First

Before we talk about how to choose the right sourcing option, I need to clarify the terms we'll be using. Although their intentions appear obvious, the terms insource and outsource are imprecise and often misleading. First, they may refer to either a *technology* or a *service*. Second, not all solutions are purely one or the other. Some outsourced solutions, for example, still require the day-to-day involvement of internal staff.

For the sake of clarity, I've divided technologies and services into their respective options. First, let's look at the list of technology service options that exist today:

Internally developed: Your IT staff develops and runs your EMS. If you recall from Chapter 7, the EMS is a set of tools that handles high-volume email delivery, management, and reporting. An internally developed solution requires dedicated hardware, software, and personnel.

Commercial software: With the assistance of your IT department, you choose and purchase commercial EMS software from a third-party software vendor and install and run it in your data center. Although the initial purchase may appear cost effective in comparison to the other two solutions, costs can grow over the long term as the technology requires upgrades, new servers, and occasional hands-on assistance.

Application Service Provider (ASP): You turn to an outside technology vendor, which hosts and runs the software in its own data center, eliminating any need for you to resource hardware, software, bandwidth, or personnel. With a full-service option, the ASP runs the entire application invisibly to you. With a self-service option, you operate the email marketing delivery engine through a Web-based interface.

225

Next, let's look at the range of professional services and expertise that are available:

Email strategy: Establishing a governance model, developing a policy, and setting up list allocation processes

Email best practices: Putting techniques in place to ensure CAN-SPAM compliance or improve response rates

Fulfillment: Preparing the message for delivery by loading and tweaking HTML code, configuring campaigns, and performing quality assurance

Creative design: Designing a visually appealing message format through the use of graphics and various layout techniques

Marketing strategy: Selecting target audiences and creating promotional offers

You don't have to limit your outsourcing to one choice. Similar to an a-la-carte restaurant menu, outsourcing offers a choice between one or more options from column A and one or more options from column B. Which options you choose depend upon your internal manpower, your program needs, and your budget. If you have a strong internal creative and marketing team and a limited budget, for example, you could outsource hosting and fulfillment and handle creative design and marketing strategy internally. Or, if your staff is more limited than your budget, you could hire an advertising agency to do your creative and marketing strategy and call upon a technology vendor to set up and host your application, then simply sit back and keep an eye on the entire operation to make sure it's running smoothly.

WEIGHING TECHNOLOGY AND SERVICE APPROACHES

When determining which technology and/or service approach is best for your company, there are five key issues to consider:

Expertise

The dynamic nature of email makes expertise increasingly critical, even for day-to-day tasks such as email delivery. But how much expertise does your email program need? That depends on your program's current level of sophistication, and the capabilities you want it to eventually deliver. It also varies based on how email fits into your marketing strategy. If email is primarily an extension of your existing Web systems (e.g., electronic receipts), you'll need little more than technology expertise from your vendor. If your email initiative is as straightforward as a few simple newsletters and occasional promotions, you can easily hand it off to your agency. However, if you want to make email a central component of your customer communications strategy, you'll want to make sure your outsourcer has specific depth in three areas: email marketing, technology, and strategy.

Even if you know that you need certain expertise, how can you be sure that the provider you've chosen can deliver it? Discerning a vendor's expertise can be tricky. If you're flying to Florida and you ask your pilot how he'll use the cockpit controls to get you there, his answer will have little meaning to you if you've never taken flying lessons. You'll have to sit back and trust that he knows which gauges to read and which levers to move. Similarly, without any personal experience in the area, you may have difficulty determining whether your service provider is truly capable of following through on their claims.

That said, I can give you a list of questions to ask that can help you infer a provider's level of expertise, regardless of your own knowledge base:

Company focus: Although imprecise, asking what services the company offers is one good way to assess their depth. Do they provide email services only, or will they wash and wax your car for an extra charge? Even if they only focus on email, how many different services and technologies are their staff members trying to juggle? Also check the company's Web site. Are you scrolling down for several minutes to get through all of their varied offerings? Does the site even mention that the company offers email? If not, I wouldn't count on a high level of expertise.

Publications and conference presentations: Those who can, do, and those who can do really well, write about it. Leaders in their subject area like to share their knowledge with other professionals in the form of white papers and other publications. The number and quality of white papers under a provider's belt can speak volumes about the expertise of their staff. A well-versed company will also have a substantial podium presence at industry conferences.

Client list: How far have their clients' email programs progressed? How many have reached Levels 2 and 3 (see Chapter 3)? If you aspire to Level 3 status, and all of your provider's clients are at Level 1, you'd better be prepared to climb the learning curve alongside your provider.

Data Security and Integration

The number one reason I've heard companies use to justify the choice to insource their EMS is data security. In our increasingly privacy-concerned world, companies understandably shy away from entrusting even the tiniest morsels of sensitive customer data to a third party. Security is especially important to regulated companies (financial institutions, for example), or those that use highly personal customer purchase information for segmenting or targeting.

A number of companies also choose to handle their integration in-house, but not just because of security. In some cases, integrating your email with existing business systems is somewhat easier if you run email in your own data center (see my CNN case study on page 139). Even though many ASP solutions are perfectly capable of moving and even synchronizing data with your company's operational databases, running the EMS internally is sometimes the best solution for achieving the highest levels of integration.

Your Relationship with IT

When making the decision on insource versus outsource, think about how much you are prepared to rely on your IT department. After all, you might be working with Nick Burns: Computer Guy, from the Saturday Night Live sketch, who orders you to "Move!" from your computer, then mocks you with a "There, was that so hard?" (I'm allowed to make fun of IT people because I used to be one.)

Even if you have a great relationship with your IT department, don't forget that you don't always share the same project approach. Most IT projects are large and time intensive. Whereas a marketer might run campaigns on a weekly, or even on a daily, basis, the average

IT project can take months or even years to complete. It's not that IT can't handle short-cycle projects; it's just that they've earned their technology badge by being better at larger, long-term projects. But the difference in timing can lead to frustrating expectation gaps. Additionally, IT departments are not always as able to jump on new opportunities as quickly as marketers, because they are subject to different priorities and processes. For example, if your latest email campaign requires big changes to the EMS configuration, you need to know whether your IT department will give it priority over the latest virus outbreak.

Before you embark on a joint venture with your IT colleagues, find out how much help you need and ask IT how long they expect the project to take. The more you can handle without IT's help, the more control you will have over your cycle times and the faster you can respond to last-minute opportunities or problems that require quick solutions. In situations that absolutely require IT's involvement, you'll help yourself if you anticipate your needs and calendar them in advance. That way, IT builds the project into its long-term cycles, you achieve your goal on deadline, and everyone ends up happy.

Deliverability

I've seen even the most determined in-house efforts finally cave in and concede their project to outsourcers. Why? The internal technology team just couldn't handle the barrage of deliverability issues that inevitably complicate otherwise smooth email campaigns. In my experience, deliverability has become the number one factor that drives companies to outsource email technology and use an ASP solution. Chapter 19 covers the issues on deliverability in greater depth.

Handling deliverability requires a multitiered approach. ASPs who do it well must:

- Have the technology to properly send messages and manage bounces.
- Establish and maintain relationships with ISPs.

- Continually adjust their systems to accommodate the ever-evolving challenges presented by ISPs and corporate spam filters.
- Have the expertise to understand every potential deliverability hurdle, and work with their customers to soar above those hurdles so that every message is delivered.
- Be active in industry groups that identify solutions to spam and deliverability challenges.
- Monitor complaints and replies.

Because deliverability requires a complex combination of technology and expertise, I expect that most companies will continue to outsource their delivery for the next few years. Always the optimist, though, I think delivery challenges will become more manageable in the future, and deliverability will no longer be the primary determinant in the choice between insourcing or outsourcing.

Features

Years ago it was relatively easy for a company to develop their email system in-house. But today, most internal IT departments would be hard pressed to match the levels of sophistication and scalability, and the sheer number of features, offered by the best commercial EMSs.

Presenting a comprehensive list of features to look for in an EMS would be beyond the scope of this book, but I can point out some of the basic features and technologies you'll need to take into consideration when you set up your system. First, remember that email technology goes far deeper than delivery engines. Even the most basic EMS must be able to handle complex tasks such as segmenting; reporting on opens, click-throughs, and conversions; processing bounces; and importing and exporting data.

A full email initiative requires even more advanced features, such as:

- Web-facing servers—image hosting, forms
- List management—selects/targeting, list cleansing, easy integration with external systems

- Delivery—bounce management, throttling (changing the rate of delivery to prevent click-throughs from overloading your Web site), specialized reporting (e.g., delivery by domain)
- Reporting and analytics—real-time feedback on results, slice-and-dice response data
- Reply handling—opt-outs, complaint monitoring
- Level 3 email features—automation, sophisticated content customization

Rather than burden their IT departments, the majority of companies still find it easier to outsource some, if not all, of their email marketing technology. High-end ESPs offer more comprehensive, and cost-effective, capabilities than most companies could replicate internally. That said, I also see a trend toward internalized email marketing expertise. The new high-end EMSs are so easy to use that marketers no longer need to be technicians. Plus, marketers already know the basic email principles and practices. They are beginning to find that they can save money and be more responsive if they bring more of the campaign strategy and execution in-house.

A Case Study of an Insourcer

The company: CNN, a division of Time Warner, Inc.
The rationale: To control its own email destiny
The email manager: Ken Craig, vice president of Internet Operations

CNN kicked off a sophisticated email initiative several years ago, well before most companies had realized the potential of the new medium. Even at that early stage, CNN's email initiative had reached an unusually grand scale: It sent millions and millions of messages each week from an equally substantial email list. If CNN were launching its email program today, it would find a number of third-party solutions available to match its scale. But at the time, most of the third-party solutions available were relatively immature and nowhere near being up to the task.

On top of its scalability issues, CNN wanted control over data usage. CNN is one of the most widely recognized, and most trusted, brands in the world. The slightest misuse of sensitive subscriber data, whether malicious or unintentional, could severely and irrevocably damage its brand.

Another pivotal outsourcing determinant was integration. When news breaks, CNN's editors use both the Web and email to immediately get the word out to customers. Because the two media are so tightly integrated, editors can type news items into a single interface, which automatically speeds the information to countless affiliates, subscribers, Web site locations, and email recipients all over the globe. CNN needed this unusual degree of integration to ensure that news hit the marketplace within minutes or seconds, rather than hours.

Insourcing has served CNN well for many reasons. First, because CNN launched its online strategy unusually early, its technology and marketing teams have worked together for years, and have therefore reached an exceptionally high level of alignment. Second, CNN's Web presence is so large that the incremental costs of adding email bandwidth, servers, and even IT personnel were relatively small.

CNN's broad technology investments, and the unique nature of its online presence, really tipped the scale in favor of insourcing. But not all companies have the same advantages.

A Case Study of an Outsourcer

The company: Sallie Mae
The rationale: Lower costs and reduce turnaround times
The email manager: Kaenan Hertz, Ph.D., director of Customer Relationship Management and Market Intelligence

Many years ago, Sallie Mae, the nation's largest provider of education funding, decided to build its email solution internally with the help of its IT department, using off-the-shelf software tools. Even though its early solution worked, Sallie Mae soon found that the cost of operating an internal email program was higher than the price of hiring an outsourcer. Also, the marketing department's rapid turnaround expectations were putting stress on its normally long-term-focused IT department.

After about a year of handling its systems and support internally, Sallie Mae decided to take some of the work outside. "The real question we had to ask ourselves was, 'What is our core business? Is it IT and email marketing, or is it creating and selling our products?'" Hertz explains. "Clearly, our business is financial services, and that's where we chose to invest the energies of our internal team."[1]

The first outsourcing phase split efforts between internal resources and an outsourcing partner. To speed turnaround times, Sallie Mae handled the areas in which it had already developed internal competencies. "I can turn multichannel analytics around faster than my outsource partner because I have internal resources that I can reprioritize immediately as the situation demands," says Hertz. Meanwhile, Sallie Mae's outsourcing partner took over the more complex campaigns that required greater sophistication and technological expertise.

When making the decision to insource or outsource your email system, consider your current workload and budget, advises Hertz. Find out whether IT resources are available, and whether senior management is willing to assign those resources to the project. Then compare the cost of an outside vendor to the cost of purchasing equipment and hiring personnel. Which is more cost effective: building or buying?

As the tools available to Sallie Mae improve and its internal expertise grows, Hertz plans to begin handling more of his own campaign execution. But for now, relying on an outsourced partner for expertise and top-quality tools—and handling the bulk of the execution internally—is proving just the right balance.

Available Outsourcing Solutions

If you are reading this book, it is likely that email is, or will soon be, a strategic marketing channel for you. Most neophyte email marketers are mystified by the bewildering array of costs, service levels, and features available to them. To help you make sense of your options, I've simplified email solutions into four broad categories. The first two, entry level and midlevel, are not necessarily applicable to sophisticated marketers but are nonetheless worth exploring. The third category, CRM, is applicable to companies that already have a large-scale in-house CRM solution. And the final category, high-end solutions, is the most popular among sophisticated marketers. Let's start by looking at the lowest cost offerings.

Entry-level Email Solutions

Their Web sites boast "30-day free trial," "free download," and "pay online." For as little as $99, they promise "a complete email marketing solution you can run from your PC or Web browser." Entry-level email solutions are a relatively cheap (anywhere from $25 to $2,000 per year) and easy-to-use option. They can either stand alone or come as part of a broader solution, for example, the email module of a larger CRM, sales management application, or small business marketing suite.

Broader-based tools can be helpful if you don't need your email program to do much more than augment your sales communications. You'll run into trouble, though, if you try using them to perform more complex, email-specific tasks like merging and purging multiple lists. You'll also find that most low-end packages won't be able to do such basic functions as conversion tracking, field customization, viral messages, list export, and interactive reporting. And don't expect your provider to help you out if you are struggling. Most basic solutions don't offer email strategy or best practices advisory services.

Although it almost goes without saying, companies that offer credit card sign ups or "free trial downloads" are targeting a very different audience than the well-branded midmarket companies or the Global 2000 set. Because these low-end solutions attract a wider set of emailers, you might find yourself sharing the same delivery systems (and often the same IP address) as "Katie's Kozy Krafts," "José's Pineapple Juice Emporium," and other online merchants who aren't likely to follow the most conservative list-building practices. (José is too busy squeezing pineapples to gather affirmative consent from his customers.) Your deliverability may suffer by association.

Midlevel Solutions

For a higher, but still relatively inexpensive, price tag (yearly costs start at around $2,500, and can reach $10,000 or more), you can get access to more sophisticated features and more comprehensive services. Midlevel solutions range from simple installable software to focused ASP offerings. Although few midrange solutions have the marketing expertise to provide full service, some offer a level of service beyond basic tech support. For those marketers who don't need cutting-edge solutions, midlevel solutions are more than sufficient.

Provided that your email volume is still relatively low (less than fifty thousand or one hundred thousand per month), midlevel systems provide good solutions for the money. But when you get beyond the range of one hundred thousand messages per month, the scalability demands can bring many midlevel solutions to their knees.

These solutions also tend to be weak in sophisticated email features. Few solutions in this price range support test cells or dynamic content, and almost none can support life cycle automation. Midlevel solutions may also lack valuable features, such as Application Programming Interfaces (APIs) and sophisticated reporting. And, although many midlevel solutions appear to have simple, intuitive interfaces, they are not always as effective as they seem. Some quickly slip into "geek speak," requiring highly technical SQL, HTML, or scripting expertise to execute even moderately complex campaigns. Others lock you into "wizard whiplash," forcing you to step through four, five, or six screens to execute even the most basic functions.

CRM Solutions

Most marketers have long realized that you get what you pay for. Unless their needs are modest and are likely to remain modest, highly evolved marketers bypass most of the lower and midlevel offerings and head straight for more advanced solutions.

One possible high-end approach is the "email module" associated with popular CRM systems. In Chapter 15, I talked about the viability of using large-scale CRM systems as EMS solutions. High-end CRM solutions can be appealing because the email component is built in and is often "thrown in for free" with a big software purchase. But even though some of these packages offer Level 2 and even some Level 3 features, email is not their focus. CRM companies rarely offer any email expertise, and they are far from the cutting edge when it comes to deliverability or other technical best practices.

I did a fair amount of research on the subject, and I was unable to find any company that was successfully executing an enterprise-class email program on its in-house CRM solution. Not a single one. I am sure that companies like that exist somewhere, but I can honestly say that the majority of CRM solutions are unable to meet the needs of high-level email marketers.

Sophisticated Outsourced Solutions for Sophisticated Emailers

The last part of this section will focus on the most common, and highest-level approaches, to outsourced solutions. These approaches have worked time and time again for large, sophisticated emailers, and they've been backed up by extensive analyst research.

You could potentially mix and match the three technology approaches and five service categories on page 136 into dozens of different service combinations, but most outsourcers fall into one of four categories:

- Full service
- Service bureau ESP—a specialized ESP offering a-la-carte services
- Self-service ESP—a specialized ESP providing technology only
- Installed software

Figure 17.1 compares some of the benefits of each model.

Figure 17.1 A simplified view presenting the trade-offs of the four most popular models for running large corporate email initiatives
Note: These comparisons are anecdotal, not scientific.

	Full Service	Self-Service	Service Bureau	Install
Upfront costs	Varies	Low	Low	High
Cost per message	Varies	Low	Medium	Lowest
Overall costs	Highest	Lowest	Medium	Medium
Level of email expertise required	Lowest	High	Medium	Highest
Marketing value-added services	Highest	Low	Medium	Lowest
Email expertise available	Highest	Low	High	Lowest
Pricing is based on	Campaign + per message	Per message	Per message + services	Per server or list size

Full Service

Companies with limited staff or limited email expertise benefit most from a full-service model. Full service is also useful to companies that need a broader range of services (such as search engine optimization or direct mail).

Advertising agencies, direct marketing agencies, and a few ESPs are able to offer the soup-to-nuts solutions required for full service. They will not only deliver your messages and report on the results, but they will also help you with your marketing strategy, creative design, analytic modeling, and almost everything else you'll need to launch your email program (although I doubt they'll wash and wax your car).

Obviously, the cost of such a comprehensive solution will be much higher than it would be with a self-service offering. However, the benefits are compelling: You define your marketing and business goals in broad terms, then turn over the keys to your full service outsource partner. They'll do the rest.

One note: When you outsource to an advertising or direct mail agency, they're likely to turn around and outsource many of the email-specific initiatives to a more focused email expert, such as a specialized ESP. With the increasing complexity of EMS technology, it's simply become more cost effective for agencies to farm out the technical stuff to a specialist ESP. The agency handles the marketing aspects of the project, and the specialist ESP handles the technology end.

Self-Service ESP

If your budget is scarcer than your time, self-service may be the way to go. A good self-service ESP will offer some level of guidance in the form of technology support and white papers, but the rest is up to you. You'll perform all of the services, from strategy to execution. Many marketers prefer this approach because they control the cost and the timing of virtually every aspect of their campaigns.

When going the self-service route, make sure your ESP's technology is easy to use. Screen shots and quick demos are not sufficient to determine real ease of use. Whenever possible, try out the system yourself on one of the campaigns you intend to use it for. Pretty screens are a plus, but you'll quickly tire of looking at them if it takes twenty-five of them to set up and execute a simple campaign.

Service Bureau ESP

A service bureau ESP offers an a-la-carte menu of services that you can mix and match as you need them. This model is among the most common and fastest-growing in the industry because it enables marketers to build and run the simpler elements of their program themselves, but still lean on their ESP whenever they require additional technical support and email expertise.

The service bureau ESP approach is ideal for companies that have unpredictable or sporadic workloads. Having a team of people on call who already know your business lets you quickly add resources whenever you need them. And, because you pay for only the services you need, you always know what you're spending and can keep your costs under control. Most marketers are getting comfortable enough with the technology that they prefer to handle most of the work themselves, but don't be afraid to rely on your ESP. A good ESP can set up the most sophisticated features of your program and light your way through the first campaign or two.

Install

Installing the EMS in your own data center was popular a few years ago, but the method has come under pressure in the last year, primarily because of deliverability issues. Deliverability will undoubtedly improve, however, and if you ever intend to use the install option in the future, you'll need to understand the basic ideas behind it.

If you were to choose the install method, your vendor would deliver software to your IT department on a disk or over the Internet. Your IT department would then install and configure the software on your company's servers and databases. You would access the software via an Internet browser, in much the same way that you access your corporate intranet system.

Install is, on the surface, the cheapest and most secure approach. It can also be the most cost-effective approach when sending large volumes of email. (Estimates for the break-even range from five million to twenty million messages per month.) Install gives marketers the greatest amount of control over their own data, which is a plus to security-conscious emailers who hyperventilate whenever their sensitive customer data get into the hands of an outside vendor. But if you choose this method, be warned that you're going to be seeing a lot of your IT department. You'll have to rely on IT for any technical setup, and they will likely have an ongoing involvement in deliverability management, customer data attribute changes, and custom reports.

EVALUATING VENDORS

The term "author" next to my name may be a bit of a misnomer. The truth is, I don't write books for a living. I have a day job as the CEO of a top email service provider, Silverpop. In my "real job," the issue of vendor evaluation comes up in conversation at least twenty times a day. I am admittedly biased, but I have seen some general truisms that may benefit you if you ever find yourself having to select a vendor. I've listed a few items below that you should consider when talking to companies like mine.

Analysts

If you're not an expert and you're not sure which of your prospective vendors to trust, look to the unbiased experts for guidance. Major analysts such as Forrester and Jupiter regularly generate Top 10 vendor lists. Any company that can make it into the ranks of an analyst's list (especially a company whose name appears on multiple lists) is pretty much guaranteed to be respectable and trustworthy. Most recommended vendors are worthy of consideration.

But as you read through the lists, keep in mind that every organization's needs are different. No two analysts can agree on rankings for the same reason that no two companies will have the same experience with a single vendor. Analyst rankings are a great tool, but the number one vendor on an analyst's list is not necessarily the best vendor for you. Use Top 10 lists only as a means of identifying potential vendors. Then re-evaluate each vendor based on your company's needs.

Features

The first thing I tell prospective buyers is that a vendor is more than just the sum of its features. Features are important, but they are not the only drivers of long-term email success. Although it's wonderful that your vendor offers drill-down click-through reporting or life cycle automation, these features alone won't make or break a successful email program. One vendor will always brag about offering features that no other vendor possesses. Rather than focusing on a particular feature, try and get a broader sense of how quickly the vendor grows their product and how responsive that growth is to their customers' needs.

Start asking the big-picture questions: What level of sophistication do I need now (email Level 1, 2, or 3)? What level will I need in the future? And will my vendor's current (or anticipated) product give me the appropriate capabilities when those needs arise? If you are looking for the most advanced capabilities, ask to use the product yourself. Also ask for the vendor's references, not only to confirm that other customers are satisfied, but also to ensure that they are satisfied with the advanced features you plan to use. Finally, look deeper than the "major feature list" (e.g., dynamic content and triggered campaigns). From a day-to-day productivity point of view, it's the hundreds of smaller features that will enable you to achieve your goals as much as, if not more than, the bigger features.

Usability

If you're going with the ASP model, don't simply go through the demo and write a check. Ask the vendor to give you a startup account and some basic training, and try out the program yourself. You may be disappointed at how difficult some features are to use in the real world.

In the early days of email marketing, I was shocked at how often buyers simply looked at the feature checklist without carefully reviewing the usability of those features. Having behavior-based segmentation is nice, but not if its setup requires four hours worth of effort by a team of high-priced specialists. When using technology, marketers often forget that their time is as valuable as their money. According to a mid-2004 JupiterResearch report, "Less than one-half (43 percent) of marketers said they perform a proof of concept or demonstration to assess applications' usability when selecting and evaluating email marketing applications and service providers. Usability must measure email marketing solutions and features because usable applications can radically decrease per-campaign salary costs."[2]

Pricing

Ask your prospective vendors to lay all costs on the table up front and make sure you understand them. Consider all potential hidden charges, such as image hosting, form hosting, database changes, viral messages, customized reporting, access to APIs, and deliverability monitoring. Also, factor in your scalability needs. It's not uncommon for early email marketers to see their volumes go up tenfold as their programs grow. If your future volume or service needs escalate, is your vendor going to kill you on overages and other charges?

Support

Don't wait until that first midnight problem arises to find out if your provider's support services live up to their promise. To test their responsiveness, call the support line or contact your designated account manager before you sign up.

Data Security and Uptime

You know the customer information and mailing history database you've carefully grown over the years? Imagine losing it in an instant. Not a pretty picture, is it? Because you never want to lose important data, you need to know up front if your ASP's data center is sufficiently secure and backed up. (Your IT staff can check and confirm this for you.) Be particularly wary of very small or underfunded ESPs. Creating a robust data center is expensive, and many small companies underinvest in this behind-the-scenes but otherwise critical aspect of their business. Lastly, ask your prospective ESPs for the last year's worth of reports on their system uptime. Remember, even 99 percent uptime means that their servers were down for more than 3.5 days during the year.

Financial Stability

The dot-com bust is over, but it continues to leave casualties in its wake; make sure your ESP isn't about to become one of them. Having been a venture capitalist for several years, I've gained a few insights on how to evaluate a company's (especially a young company's) financial stability.

First, is the company growing? More than 25 percent growth per year is a good sign. Second, if the company isn't profitable, how long can they survive on its current cash? Being unprofitable is not necessarily a bad thing, especially for young venture-backed companies. But any company that is working with less than six months worth of funding can easily go out of business, especially if they aren't backed by "name brand" venture capitalists. Third, even if the ESP is currently profitable, consider what would happen if they lost one or two of their largest customers. Assuming that it takes between six and nine months to replace a key client, how long could they survive on their cash on hand?

Don't assume that an email vendor's viability is guaranteed simply because they are owned by a larger organization. Although the email portion of the business is not likely to drive a large corporate parent to bankruptcy, I can remember at least a handful of young email companies that were bought by large corporations, only to disappear within a year or two. It's very hard to predict how a large company will deal with a small division such as email marketing. The constant profit drive and strict allocation of R&D funding can quickly undermine even the best email vendor if a lack of resources chokes them into mediocrity or death. Size is by no means an assurance of long-term viability.

Long Term View

Look at your vendor as you would look at a potential partner. Can you see yourself sitting in a rocking chair gazing across at your vendor in five years? You want a vendor you can grow old with, a company that can not only support your needs now, but one that can also accommodate the higher service levels and increased message volume you're likely to need in the future. And, talking about the future, if you think you'll want to bring the software in-house at some point, find out if your vendor has or can develop a software version that will run in your data center.

Also, look at your vendor's other clients. How carefully has your vendor selected their clients? Is the company willing to work with anyone that will pay them, or are the majority of their clients respectable businesses like your own? Ask the vendor how many clients they have fired for reasons other than nonpayment.

Lastly, look at the vendor's strategy, vision, and history of innovation. Is the vendor leading or following their peers? How often do they update their product, and how significant are those updates? What was the last innovation the vendor introduced to the industry?

■　■　■　■

I wish I could point you to the one universal or perfect solution to all of your email sourcing needs. Unfortunately, there isn't one. In the end, the number of potential choices is almost limitless. Each insourcing and outsourcing option comes with its own set of benefits, trade-offs, and compromises.

Every company will have a different answer when trying to justify service levels versus cost; cutting-edge technology versus tight integration; and external support versus internal headcount. What solution should you choose? That ultimately depends on your company's unique budgetary, service, technology, and integration needs and constraints.

One of my clients has a large, sophisticated, and responsive IT department. I asked her why she chose to outsource to Silverpop rather than handling her email internally. Her answer: "It's easier to torture you guys." There you have it.

Chapter 18

BUILDING YOUR LISTS

I started my career early in direct marketing, long before email marketing. Sometime after I had told my grandmother what I did for a living, I overheard her explaining my profession to someone else. She told them that I stole information from phone books and then used it to bother people.
—John Ripa, head of e-products at Acxiom

Beefing up Your House Lists

As an email marketer, your house list is one of the most valuable assets you possess. Campaigns sent to your house list will regularly outperform almost any list you can rent or buy. Carefully cultivate your house list, and it will reward your investment—in spades—over the long run.

A house list simply makes good marketing sense. Starting out with existing customers and opt-ins who already have a familiarity—and an affinity—with your products gives you the perfect gateway through which to build long-term relationships. Having a strong and viable house list will give you the power to fully unleash the potential of your email marketing program.

Great lists aren't built in a day. There are no shortcuts. List building takes time, and it requires integration with every one of your endeavors, both online and offline. Consider this—as you gather names and ask for permission, you not only add to your list—you preserve it. Email addresses change every year. As soon as you stop building, your list will begin to shrink.

Lists can grow in many different ways, but they should all start in the same place: at every significant touch point with your customers. Here are just a few potential ways to build your list:

1. Gather opt-ins on your Web site: Ask for opt-in during an e-commerce transaction or offer the incentive of an email newsletter, white paper, sweepstakes, or other valued content.

2. Rent lists: Rent third-party lists, then ask the recipients if they would like to opt-in to your house list.

3. Appends: Append email addresses to your list of mailing addresses with the help of a third-party service provider.

4. Co-registration: Allow customers to opt-in via a partner's site.

5. Cross promotions: Combine efforts with other divisions or partners to drive additional opt-ins.

6. Viral marketing: Encourage your existing subscribers to share your messages with their friends and co-workers.

7. Email Change of Address (ECOA): Keep your list of email addresses up to date as customers change ISPs or companies. (Many firms will scan your bounced customer records and provide you with updated email addresses.)

8. Direct marketing: Make sure to include your email registration Web page URL on all of your traditional direct marketing campaigns (the same goes for TV and print advertising).

9. Point of sale: Capture addresses via a sign-up form at cash registers and at other visible locations in your stores.

10. Customer service representatives: Have your salespeople and customer service representatives ask for email addresses in the course of customer communications.

11. Product registration: Ask for email addresses on your standard product registration mail-in card or Web page.

Let's look at a few of these options in greater depth, using case studies to illustrate which techniques work and which methods are best to avoid.

Gathering Opt-ins on Your Web Site

Every day, potential email recipients visit your site. They may find your Web address through a search engine, link to it from another site, or type in a URL they've discovered in one of your marketing materials. The method by which they arrive at your site is less important, however, than the fact that they are there. They've come to your site because they believe your company has something to offer them.

What happens if customers can't find the one thing they were looking for? They will probably leave, and possibly never return. But with email and house lists, you can turn a one-time visit into a long-term relationship that may eventually elevate that prospect into a customer. You simply need to ask for an opt-in.

This is such an obvious point, yet I can't tell you how many companies bury their email opt-in forms deep within their site. You need to make the opt-in process as easy as possible for your customers by prominently featuring the sign-up on your home page, as well as on every other page of your site. The Home Depot Web site is one of the best examples of a well-designed opt-in. Visitors can easily find a mini email opt-in form on *every single page* of the site.

My clients have consistently found that their opt-in rates are dependent not only on the location of their email address field, but also on the content they surround it with. Providing a link to your privacy policy and clearly describing how you intend to use the email address will increase consumer trust and potentially add more names to your list.

Renting Lists

Are rented lists still valuable, or are they more trouble than they're worth? The industry is locked in a heated debate on the subject. The general perception is that response rates on rented lists are slipping. In a 2002 survey, close to 40 percent of marketers reported that their response rates for third-party lists had declined in the previous year.[1]

To really understand the value of list rentals, marketers must be able to distinguish between the two different types of firms offering lists. First are the third-party list owners. These firms build large lists of email addresses through a variety of mechanisms. Second are the *list brokers*, which are like agencies for lists. They offer services and expertise, and they are proficient at choosing just the right list for a particular campaign from a wide variety of third-party list owners.

Third-party list firms come in two varieties. The first, *co-branded list* owners, rent the names of recipients with whom they *already have an active relationship*. Examples of co-branded list owners include magazines or Web sites that provide their users' information to marketers. The second type is the more common *list aggregators*. These firms build their lists from one or more sources into a single *masterfile*. Although they have no relationship with the majority of their list addresses, they are usually able to offer a larger selection of names and recipient attributes than co-branded list owners. Pay attention to the difference between the two types of list owners. Because co-branded firms have an existing relationship to protect, they not only send your messages under their brand (in the "from" field), but they also tend to be far pickier about the content they send and the frequency with which they send it. The masterfile owners generally don't have any other asset or relationship to protect aside from their list database, so they tend to attract a wider range of advertisers and, as a result, often get caught up in deliverability issues and spam filters.

The real difference between the co-branded and masterfile approach lies in the eyes of their recipients. Masterfile list rentals appear to come from the advertiser who, in most cases, has no current relationship with the recipients. (The masterfile owner is generally an aggregator who is unknown to recipients.) With their inboxes filling up, and their time ever more constrained, recipients are responding by *not* responding to messages they have not specifically opted-in to receive, from companies they don't recognize. At best, unexpected messages are deleted. At worst, their senders are labeled as spammers.

Co-branded messages, on the other hand, appear to come from a company with whom the recipient has an existing relationship. Consumers are more likely to open a message from a familiar name, and less likely to perceive the advertiser as a spammer. Because of their inherent familiarity with consumers, and resulting higher open rates, co-branded list rentals are likely to remain a viable acquisition tool for marketers.

Case Study

The following is a transcript of a conversation I overheard between a well-known list aggregator and a potential customer:

List Exec: (grandly) We have one of the biggest lists in the business. We've got more demographic data than any other list company out there.

List Buyer: How did you build your list?

List Exec: It's 100 percent opt-in. In fact, we instantly remove anyone who no longer wants to receive messages from our customers.

List Buyer: Yes, but where did your original names come from? How do you build your lists?

List Exec: We acquire lists from partners who gather email addresses on their Web sites. Each recipient has granted his or her permission. They've *asked* to be contacted by our client companies.

List Buyer: What kind of Web sites are you talking about?

List Exec: (pause) Oh, sweepstakes sites—that sort of thing. But every recipient grants his or her permission. We have permission for every single name we get.

List Buyer: But how do you confirm permission? What does the recipient have to do to confirm permission?

List Exec: (clears throat) We send each person on the list an email. They can always click on a link to be permanently removed from the list.

List Buyer: You mean, if they do nothing, they are automatically added to the list?

List Exec: Yee-ees…but very few people click on the link. Obviously, the majority of folks out there want to be on our list.

At this point, I was dying to jump in and ask, "Did you ever consider the possibility that they aren't opting-out because they're *afraid* to click on the link? Afraid that if they do, they will be confirming their address to a spammer and will subsequently be inundated by unwanted messages?"

The point of this story is that not every list firm is as conservative in building their lists as you would be when putting together your own house list.

Things to Ask When Renting a List

A number of marketing professionals will warn you right off the bat to avoid renting lists. I'm not going to give you advice either way, but if you do want to pursue this option, I'll tell you how to do it smartly. First, make sure you're ready to handle the new CAN-SPAM opt-out requirements. Second, don't forget that recipients may resent receiving unsolicited messages from you, which could negatively impact their impression of your company.

Remember that your list company is not just any vendor. They are going to prospect your product or service on your behalf, and give your recipients the impression that you sent the message yourself. Before you put your list company in the driver's seat, you need to make sure that they will handle your campaign with the same care and attention you would give it yourself.

You'll save yourself a lot of aggravation and potential brand damage in the long run if you ask the right questions of your list company up front:

- Where do they get their names? "Recipients have opted-in" is not a sufficient response. You should be assured that all recipients have not only opted-in, but that they are also *anticipating* solicitations from partnered companies.
- Are there any hidden charges? For example, is HTML extra? Is there a charge for image hosting?
- How are campaigns tracked and reported? Make sure you get a clear explanation of how opens and click-throughs are measured. (For example, are they measured uniquely, or in aggregate?)
- What are the list owner's frequency rules? How many times will they send a given message to recipients within a month? Excessive or undermanaged frequency should be warning signs of potential trouble.

- What name will appear in the "from" field? Your company address? The list owner's company address?

- Does the list owner require specific wording (for example, a disclaimer or administrative notice) at the top and bottom of the message? If so, make sure you're comfortable with the wording *before* the first mailing, because it will shape your recipients' impression of your offer.

- Will the message contain a header informing the recipient why they are getting the message and from whom the message is being sent (e.g., "You are receiving this email because you opted in for third-party messages from list ABC")?

- How is the pay rate structured? Will you pay by the message (*cost-per-message*, or *CPM*), by the acquisition (*cost-per-acquisition*, or *CPA*), or by the click (*cost-per-click*, or *CPC*)? The industry has been shifting away from CPM deals to "pay for performance" approaches such as CPA or CPC. The latter approaches often save money because marketers have to pay only when a customer responds to their message. But be warned—CPA still carries a potential danger. If the list is truly junk, your brand will be thrust in front of countless recipients who will view your message as unadulterated spam.

- What are the average deliverability rates? If you have a cost-per-message (CPM) agreement, will you be expected to pay for undelivered email?

- Does the list owner review your content before it goes out? If not, ask yourself how carefully the owner is policing communications their list recipients are getting.

- Will the list owner let you run tests up front to get a sense for your potential response rates, complaint rates, and undeliverables?

- Will the owner share opted-out addresses with you for your suppression list? The general interpretation is that CAN-SPAM requires marketers to handle opt-outs themselves, so you'll need those addresses.

- Will you get full approval rights before the email is sent? All lists should send you a test message so that you can confirm working links, content, grammar, and spelling. Any list that does not include you in the testing process should be avoided.

- Can you get your own copy of the list? If the list owner offers to give you your own copy (as opposed to renting it and sending it on your behalf), you have only one option. Run. Screaming. Legitimate list owners will ALWAYS send on your behalf. They will not want to give you any portion of their list because it is their only asset. If you do purchase a list from an owner, call me. I have some stereo equipment in the back of my truck I'd like to sell you.

Appends

One of the biggest challenges facing marketers is finding a responsive audience. The good news is, you already have a receptive audience—your existing customers. The bad news is, you may not have an email address for each customer. Trying to collect email addresses manually via direct mail or customer service representative calls can be as costly and time consuming as scouting for new customers, especially since 31 percent of email addresses are changed each year,[2] and many people use multiple email addresses.

But a host of service firms out there will take your offline or postal customer list and *append* email addresses to it from their customer data records. Appends are in a different class from list rentals because you start off with existing customers and existing relationships.

Here's how the append works: You give the service provider your list of postal mailing addresses. The provider compares your list against its massive database of consumers and businesses. When it finds a match to the name and postal address, it *appends* your customer's record with the email address. Before the append is final, the provider sends a confirmation message to customers asking if they'd like to be added to your list. Nearly all append requests are "Customer Permission Assumed" (CPA), which means that if customers do nothing, they are automatically appended to your list. When the process has been completed, your service provider hands you a list with (hopefully) thousands of new email addresses to add to your database.

Match rates range anywhere from 5 percent to 40 percent (but beware of providers who claim higher rates). The percentage you match depends upon two variables: the quality and size of the append service's list, and the matching logic it uses. Matching logic is an extremely important part of the equation. Poor matching techniques can actually harm your brand. For example, in 2003, one large bank appended email addresses to its long list of offline customer records. It then proceeded to send each of the addresses an invitation to sign up for its online banking service. The message it sent included the customer's account number and other personal banking information. The problem was—some of the matches were incorrect. Several recipients wound up with another customer's sensitive account information. In cases such as this, lower match rates actually work in your favor. If the match is never made in the first place, you avoid delivering to the wrong addresses.

Appending allows companies to save a great deal of money by moving some of their traditional, postal-based customer communications over to email. To put the costs in perspective, imagine that an average company sends four postal mailings to each of its customers per year. Each package costs the marketer about $.50 to send. Since email delivery costs only a fraction of postal mail delivery, you could pay as much as $2 for each appended name (that's a $2,000 CPM) and still break even in the first year after converting your communications to email. Luckily, append match rates aren't anywhere near $2 apiece. You can expect to see a ROI within a matter of months or even weeks.

Despite the considerable cost savings, just 4.8 percent of marketers surveyed by MarketingSherpa said they used append to gather email addresses.[3] Why haven't more companies adopted the technology? There are several reasons. First, not everyone understands the append process. Second, the append and list rental business is a bit like the Wild West: Not all append companies abide by the same set of rules. Companies who go with the wrong append service can easily get burned. Third, and perhaps most important, consumers remain so skittish about unsolicited email that many companies, even those who have worked with legitimate vendors, have had a bad experience with appends. My own experiences with list appends have been positive, but I always advise my clients to 1) make their expectations clear up front, and 2) always work with a reputable firm.

Finding the Right Append Service Provider

The key to making appends work is finding a trustworthy service provider. Just as with any potential service provider, you can make the process easier on yourself by asking the right questions up front. Because many append services rely on the same sort of large, proprietary lists used by third-party list services, you can refer back to the questions on page 150. Additional questions to ask are:

- Does the service match to prospects, or just to customers? Matching customers only is usually a sign of a more conservative append firm.
- What types of match rates are their customers getting?
- Will you be able to control or influence the confirmation message the append firm uses after a match occurs?

Case Study

Acxiom, one of the world's largest providers of third-party data, is also one of the world's most conservative list data providers. For example, Acxiom will append only "active customers"—that is, customers who have completed a transaction with one of Acxiom's clients within the last two years. According to John Ripa, who heads up the company's e-products and data enhancement services, everyone on Acxiom's master lists must be absolutely aware that they have agreed to be contacted. Acxiom audits every one of its list sources every month to confirm that its list-gathering techniques have remained consistent. Any change—no matter how slight—and all names from that source are reviewed and, in many cases, removed from the company's database.

Acxiom has not one—but two—levels of opt-out. The first level removes the recipient from the append requestor's list. The second opts them out of all future append requests. (Essentially, they are taken off of Acxiom's master list.) The two levels give Acxiom's recipients a great deal of control over how they are contacted. As a result, Acxiom's complaint and opt-out levels are considerably lower than the industry average.

Acxiom's matching techniques are equally rigorous. For example, most append companies match email addresses at the household level. If a husband and wife have two different email addresses, those companies will provide their clients with either address. Acxiom, however, matches each address to a single person.

Conforming to such strict standards isn't without a downside. Acxiom often sees lower-than-average match rates. But Ripa contends that match rates are not the real measure of success. Instead, he says, success is measured in the quality of the final list and in the number of opt-outs. If that is the case, Acxiom must be doing something right. It reports first-year opt-out rates after append matches of less than 1 percent.

Co-registration

Co-registration is one of fastest-growing areas for list development in the email marketing industry. With co-registration, marketers can place their opt-in request or other promotion on the registration page of a heavily trafficked Web site. This increased visibility allows marketers to reach a broader audience than they would have had access to on their own site. When users register for the web site's email list, they will see your offer and, by merely checking the box next to it, *co-register* for your opt-in list along with the site's list. Advanced co-registration systems can target the most relevant offers to each visitor based on information the site has already gathered about that person. For example, a thirty-five-year-old professional man might be presented with offers for investment services or a financial newsletter, whereas a forty-five-year-old woman might see offers for home and family products.

Consider the following issues with co-registration:

- Opt-in: Ask for real-time confirmation, and make sure you have final approval on the look and feel of the follow-up message. If you are going to handle the confirmation on your end, ask the co-registration vendor to send you the opt-in data in real time, to ensure that the message is sent immediately following the opt-in.

- Address quality: Co-registration services charge anywhere from $.05 to $2 for each referred subscriber. But the price of co-registration data is less important than the quality of the email addresses you'll receive. The only way to measure quality is to track conversions and revenues over time. Different co-registration sites will generate different quality leads, so shop around and try out several before making your final decision.

- Offer testing: Ask whether your co-registration vendor targets different offers to different demographics or will allow you to test the strength of various offers over time.

- Offer location: Purchase date only from single sites or networks that will tell you exactly where on the site your offer will be run.

- Experts: Co-registration is taking off so quickly that a host of expert brokers and networks are emerging. If you are new to this area of marketing, you might be best served to find a partner that can represent your interests across a wide range of networks and co-registration opportunities.

How One Popular Site Uses Co-Registration

Weather.com is the tenth-most-visited Internet site in the world. It is regarded as "the" source for everything weather on the Web. But despite its huge site volume, weather.com has always been focused on broadening its customer communications through other platforms such as email, desktop applications, PDAs and alerts. By extending its Web-based registration process to these new platforms, weather.com has been able to create a significant new revenue stream: co-registration.

The weather.com site's co-registration system uses Silverpop's core technology platform to deliver a unique set of co-registration ads for each visitor, manage the ads they are shown, and automatically send each of the site's advertising customers leads and daily reports.

As users go through the process of signing up for one of weather.com's many services, they are taken to a registration page. On the page is a list of offers from which they can choose.

Offers are presented dynamically, and are targeted to each user's interests, so that each user never sees the same offer twice. When a user clicks on a box next to an offer, weather.com treats the action as permission or consent, and sends the user's contact information to that advertiser for fulfillment. The benefit of co-registration with such a highly trafficked site is obvious. Marketers who partner with weather.com can build their lists very rapidly by placing their offer in front of a wide, and already receptive, audience. "Although advertisers generally buy weather.com to build their brand and drive awareness, co-registration has enabled us to add a lead-generation component and introduce this model to many traditional companies," says Jay Freshwater, sales director of database marketing at The Weather Channel Interactive, the parent of weather.com.[4]

How has the weather.com site's co-registration page fared? Within its first twelve months, it delivered more than 1 million co-registrations. That's an astounding twenty-five hundred to thirty-five hundred leads *per day*.

Point of Sale

Bricks-and-mortar companies have another opportunity to build their lists by capturing email addresses as part of the point of sale process. When customers make a purchase at your store, they are already interested in your brand. What's more, you have their undivided attention. They are presenting you with a perfect opportunity to get them on your list.

If you ask for the purchaser's email address at the point of sale, you may want to either send a follow-up message requesting affirmative consent, or ask for written acknowledgement of permission at the point of sale. CAN-SPAM isn't clear on offline permission, so ask your legal counsel if you want to be sure. Alternately, you can encourage purchasers to visit your Web site and have them perform the opt-in process there.

Although gathering permission at the point of sale sounds intuitive, it is not without issues. Asking your retail sales staff to assist with your list building is not always as straightforward as it sounds. A friend of mine discovered this recently as he waited in an extremely long line at a do-it-yourself retailer. When he finally reached the checkout counter, he peeked over the shoulder of the harried-looking cashier. He noticed that her computer required her to either enter an email address or note that the customer did not want to be added to the company's database. The retailer had obviously set up its system to accommodate opt-ins at the point of sale. But in her haste, the cashier neglected to ask my friend for his preference. She simply checked "does not want email."

Although the company was well intentioned, it failed to anticipate the actions of a pressured salesperson. If this retailer rigorously follows CAN-SPAM, the result of this seemingly benign action is to permanently bar itself from any and all future email communications with a customer. Multiply this transaction by the thousands of frenzied check-outs in all of the company's stores each day, and you'll see how quickly this company's point-of-sale list-building efforts will backfire.

Case Study 1: The Bombay Company

For years, home furnishings retailer The Bombay Company used its email program solely to promote its e-commerce site. Its early email program, though well intentioned, had several flaws that kept it from taking off. First, the company used a one-registration-for-all approach that fused opt-in with one-click checkout on its Web site. To opt-in, customers had to also provide their credit card number—obviously a significant barrier for many users. Second, the company had only a limited email strategy. Messaging was sporadic and lacked integration with Bombay's stores and catalogs. The company's approach, though original, was negatively impacting its registration rates.

In 2002, Bombay hired senior marketer Matt Corey to oversee its Web and email programs. One of Corey's early goals was to use email to drive both online and in-store sales. After a year of building the email program, he and his team rigorously tested it to see how well it was working. They quickly discovered just how powerful a cross-channel tool their email program had become. Not only was email driving offline sales—it was driving *ten times* more sales in The Bombay Company's stores than on its site. Having proven the cross-channel opportunities, Corey reset the strategy and kicked off an entirely new email program. "Email is not just about online sales anymore," he told me. "It's now about driving total company sales."[5]

The Bombay Company's new strategy uses a multichannel approach to drive sales across its more than four hundred stores, as well as on its Web site. In Bombay's stores, customers are given "bag stuffers" that encourage them to visit the Web site and sign up for email. Specially trained sales associates drive the point home by extolling the many benefits of site registration. Call center personnel similarly promote the site's many features and benefits. And Bombay's magazines and mailings are packed with endorsements for its site.

Bombay's email program plays a key role in its integrated approach. Customers who sign up to receive email promotions are privy to advanced sales notices, new product information, and coupons that can be used either on the company's site or in its stores. Corey stresses that the company's unusually high opt-in rates are the result of a very high value proposition, which they emphasize to their customers every chance they get. People aren't just signing up for a list, they're asking to receive valuable information and discounts as well.

So how well has the multichannel approach worked? In less than two years, Bombay has taken its list from twenty thousand names to six hundred thousand names, and has made its email program a crucial part of its overall marketing mix. Corey hasn't done too badly either. He was originally hired to run email marketing and Bombay's Internet operations. Today, he oversees the entire corporate marketing effort.

Case Study 2: GSG Entertainment

Bombay's experience is not unique. GSG Entertainment, a young company that handles direct marketing for the music industry, exemplifies another successful integrative approach. GSG came up with an unconventional, and ultimately lucrative, promotion to drive traffic to its site and fans onto its house list. When putting together a CD for a popular American band, GSG inserted a "backstage pass" promotion. The pass encouraged purchasers to visit the company's web site. Once there, it promised, they would hear previously unreleased songs by the band, and be able to enter a contest for a chance to win a real backstage pass.

The response was overwhelming. In the first two weeks, one hundred thousand people (about 30 percent of overall CD purchasers up to that point) visited the site and signed up for the email list. Ultimately, the promotion enticed about one out of every ten CD buyers to visit the site and register. Even more significant than response rates, the promotion illuminated some key audience metrics, according to GSG president Elizabeth Leahy. Before the CD was released, the band's label was sure that its audience demographic was ages eighteen to twenty-five, and 75 percent male. The Web site registrations painted a far different picture: purchasers were twenty-five to thirty-five, and equally split male and female.[6]

Both GSG and Bombay learned that the power of CCM extends beyond the email channel. By integrating their opt-in at every touch point, they did more than build a great email list; they increased the effectiveness of their overall marketing efforts.

■　■　■　■

Your house list is a powerful tool to help you increase the effectiveness of your communications and improve your overall return on investment. With a robust list, you can achieve the promise of email marketing—lower costs, speed, and higher response rates. But you must carefully cultivate and nurture that list.

Not every method I've outlined here will work for your company. Try several different approaches, or elements from various approaches, until you find the list-building technique that best complements your brand strategy. Building a list is not a one-time effort—it has to be part of everything you do. The moment you stop investing in your list is the moment your list starts to shrink.

Chapter 19

DELIVERABILITY

The PC Weenies®

"Don't get your hopes up, Ivor.
We're being spammed."

Waitress:	[We have] egg and bacon; egg sausage and bacon; egg and spam; egg bacon and spam; egg bacon sausage and spam; spam bacon sausage and spam; spam egg spam spam bacon and spam; spam sausage spam spam bacon spam tomato and spam…
Wife:	Have you got anything without spam?
Waitress:	Well, there's spam egg sausage and spam, that's not got much spam in it.
Wife:	I don't want any spam!

—Python (Monty) Pictures Ltd., Spam skit, 1970

A long, long time ago (in the mid-90s, to be exact), pressing the "send" button was assurance enough that your messages would reach their desired recipients. Not so anymore. Today, ISPs are in full spam-avoidance mode, and the casualty is your carefully targeted—precisely worded—and completely permissioned message.

Until the spring of 1994, the word "spam" meant nothing more than a somewhat ambiguous lunchmeat. Then the Arizona law firm of Canter & Siegel blasted out this message across the Internet:

Green Card Lottery 1994 May Be the Last One!!

THE DEADLINE HAS BEEN ANNOUNCED.

A few thousand newsgroup users found themselves face to face with an absolutely irrelevant message they hadn't requested, and didn't want. For better or (mostly) worse, spam was born.

As of this writing, spam is hitting its ten-year anniversary. Not a momentous occasion for most of us, I can assure you. In its short lifetime, spam has done greater damage to the email process than any other entity that has come before or since. Just as lunchmeat spam was an inescapable ingredient of every dish in the infamous *Monty Python* skit, email spam has become an inescapable reality in every one of our inboxes. No matter how much we try to avoid it, there it is, taking up our time and messing with our productivity. According to Ferris Research, the spam glut cost American businesses $10 billion in 2003.[1] Americans are already receiving about twenty-six hundred spam messages a year, and that number is expected to grow to thirty-nine hundred a year by 2007, says JupiterResearch.[2] Spammers didn't get that kind of market share by being honest and up front. They work in the shadows, never staying in one place for too long. "Spam king" Scott Richter, who runs a multimillion-dollar business hawking Viagra, porn, and diet pills, once boasted to *Newsweek,* "We can set up in another country within an hour."[3]

To evade the ISPs, spammers are constantly changing their identities. They use viruses and Trojan horses to commandeer unsuspecting users' machines and give the impression that messages were sent from the victims' computers instead of from their own. They constantly switch their IP addresses so ISPs cannot pinpoint where messages are originating. The faster the spammers move and the more identities they adopt, the harder it is for customer complaints—and the law—to catch up with them.

Because ISPs have had little luck pursuing spammers offensively, they have gone on the defensive. They block and filter messages that contain certain keywords, or ditch messages entirely if the sending email server is on a "blacklisted" server.

Unfortunately, blocking and filtering are still imprecise sciences. For example, by filtering out a message with the words "young girls love it," your ISP could be stopping a legitimate message about a boy band's new CD release from reaching your teenage daughter.

Filters often incorrectly tag legitimate, anticipated, and even critical email messages as spam. The result: Your opt-in message is treated with the same care as an email pitching Viagra or low-cost mortgages. Your message is either blocked from reaching its destination or tossed into a bulk mail folder.

The problem of incorrectly discarded permission-based emails, or "false positives," is rising. Nearly 19 percent of opt-in email is blocked by major ISPs, according to ReturnPath, Inc., and that number is expected to rise.[4]

Deliverability is a key concern among marketers, and with good reason. According to JupiterResearch, 60 percent of companies say that erroneous spam filtering has hurt their campaigns.[5] Mistakenly blocked permission email cost marketers $230 million in 2003. That number is expected to reach $410 million by 2008.[6]

Companies that aren't concerned about deliverability should be. One of my Fortune 100 clients, who was new to email marketing, once assured me that his company was so well known that no ISP would mistake *his* messages for spam.

I shared with him the following story: "Back in 2003, a number of Yahoo customers signed up for the FTC's new "Do Not Call" list. But when the FTC emailed them back a confirmation, Yahoo's spam filter blocked the messages and sent them into the users' bulk-mail folders. Many customers who missed the confirmation message were unable to respond to the FTC within the required 72 hours, and therefore did not get their names added to the "Do Not Call list."[7]

The point of the story is that if ISPs can mistakenly block email from the FTC, the guardians of spam legislation, *no marketer, no matter how legitimate and well respected they are, is immune to deliverability problems.*

In this chapter, I'm going to try to break through some of the shadows that tend to obscure the real deliverability issues. I'll also discuss renderability—the technical problems that prevent your recipients from viewing your messages even if they reach their inbox.

But first, let's separate the deliverability myths from the facts.

Myth Versus Reality

Myth #1: I'm complying with CAN-SPAM, so the ISPs *can't* prevent my messages from reaching my recipients.

Reality: The ISPs don't care about you, and they have no interest in whether or not you're following the new anti-spam legislation. They have only one concern—their subscribers. Unlike telephone companies, which are considered "common carriers" and are required by law to facilitate communications between their constituents, ISPs control their own network. Therefore, they can stop any messages they feel even remotely resemble spam. Even if they make a mistake, there's very little the law can do to reprimand them.

Myth #2: Every name on my list has opted-in and I can prove it, so my messages will always get through.

Reality: Again, ISPs work for their customers, not for you. They are more concerned about complaints from their customers than your opt-in status. And the truth of the matter is, your recipients are only human. All of us humans tend to forget things. If a customer can't remember where he put his car keys yesterday, do you really expect him to remember that he opted-in to your newsletter three months ago? Customers who forget are more likely to use the "report spam" button than the "unsubscribe" link. Too much spam reporting will nearly always cause ISPs to block your messages.

Myth #3: To avoid getting blocked or filtered, I simply need to have my company "white listed" with ISPs.

Reality: A few ISPs do maintain *white lists*—lists of legitimate senders they'll let through some of their spam filters. But getting on the list is a bit like gaining entry into a hot new LA nightclub. Only a chosen few make it through the door—the rest get stuck behind the velvet rope. If getting your company on the list were as simple as calling a few ISPs, don't you think all of the spammers would have already done it? At best, a couple of ISPs might turn off **some** of their filters if they believe you're legitimate. But if they receive even a handful of complaints from their customers, those ISPs will kick you off their white lists faster than an LA nightclub will throw out a drunken brawler.

Myth #4: My ESP has great relationships with all of the big ISPs. My emails will get through.

Reality: Having an ESP with well-placed friends at the ISPs can definitely be an asset. If your messages are *accidentally* blocked, your ESP can plead your case and perhaps get your messages unblocked...the first time. But the only thing unblocking does is give you a second chance. If you do not address the underlying problem, your messages will get blocked again and even weekly golf outings with the ISP president won't get them delivered. ISP customers will never tolerate poor emailing practices, no matter how many friends your ESP has within their ranks. Those customers are paying the ISP managers' salaries, and their wishes are gospel as far as those managers are concerned.

Myth #5: If I do run into delivery trouble, the ISP will alert me so that I can correct the problem.

Reality: ISPs are busy organizations. Billions of messages pass through their servers every day. From my experience, most ISPs won't even begin to address issues with emailers until their volume gets into the range of 50 million messages a month, and until the ISP can ensure the sender's legitimacy. ISPs simply don't have time to alert the smaller-volume senders when their messages are being filtered as spam. They don't call, they don't send polite email messages, and they don't have a Web site where senders can continually check their email delivery status.

Sometimes ISPs don't even bounce undelivered messages. They simply delete any messages suspected of being spam, and the only sure way to know if your messages have been delivered is to seed your lists with your own email addresses at that ISP and see if *you* get your messages.

DELIVERABILITY 101

Once your message leaves your ESP's server, its path is not necessarily direct to your recipient. Let's look at some of the hurdles your message may encounter along the way.

First, here are a few basic deliverability concepts:

IP Address: Every computer on the Internet has been assigned a unique set of numbers, called its IP address. A typical IP address looks something like this:

69.2.200.183

Every email server has a unique IP address. When ISPs filter messages, they're not looking at the "from" field, which spammers can doctor in hundreds of different ways. They're looking at the unchangeable IP address.

Most ISPs maintain multiple lists to help them classify the IP addresses of the servers that send mail to them. The two most common types are white lists (explained earlier) and *black lists*. You definitely don't want to be on the latter.

Black Lists: A number of email watchdog groups publish black lists containing the addresses of email servers that they believe are used to send spam. Some of the better-known public lists are SpamCop (http://www.spamcop.net), Spamhaus (http://www.spamhaus.org), and MAPS (http://www.mail-abuse.org). Many of these organizations have an admittedly anti-commercial email bias, and will aggressively blacklist addresses—even those of legitimate marketers. The good news is that most large ISPs maintain their own black lists. Only the smaller ISPs and a few corporate email filters subscribe to public lists.

How you get on a black list differs by list owner. SpamCop, for example, asks a subset of its users to "vote" on incoming messages. If you get too many spam votes or you get caught in a *spam trap* (an email address posted publicly for the sole purpose of snagging harvesters), your address will wind up on SpamCop's list faster than you can say "Lower your mortgage!"

White Lists: White lists are helpful but they are no panacea. Only a few of the large ISPs actually maintain white lists, and the ones that do have them often have vague submission mechanisms. Having your address added to an ISP white list is no guarantee that your messages will get delivered. Depending on the list, your status will probably do nothing more than help you bypass a few spam filters. And with just a few customer complaints, you'll be kicked off the list and right back to where you started. Restoring your address to a white list after you've been ejected is harder than getting added in the first place.

Corporate white lists can be more effective than their ISP counterparts, because they provide more sweeping admission. Email messages from whitelisted addresses are often allowed to bypass *all* filters.Unfortunately, literally tens of thousands of companies maintain their own lists. Very few senders can hope to get on even a fraction of the lists.

ABC's of Filtering

ISPs aren't the only ones playing gatekeeper to your messages. Emails can be snagged by corporate filters, as well as by personal filters on your recipient's desktop or email client.

Filters have several different methods for dealing with unwanted mail. ISPs and filter technology companies don't want to divulge their filtration methods, because if they did, spammers would just use that information to work around the filters.

But as a sender, you'll typically see your message processed in one of five ways:

1. It will get delivered to the recipient's inbox.
2. It will get sent to a "junk mail" folder.

3. You'll receive a response from the receiving server indicating that it believes your message to be spam (in which case your message will be "bounced" back to you).

4. The ISP will bounce back your message with an indication that there was some kind of delivery error (e.g., "invalid address" or "mailbox full").

5. Your message will simply be discarded, never to be heard from again.

Of course, to really confuse the process, the ISP will sometimes *tell* you that your message wasn't delivered, but deliver it anyway. Your poor message has no idea what it's up against. As it leaves your EMS, it embarks on a perilous trip to your recipient. Along the way, it faces challenges from countless filters, each of which try to knock it into the bulk folder or send it careening into a cyber black hole. In the following section, I'll show you some of the more common filtering technologies.

Network Configuration

One of the first challenges your message will face comes from the receiving server, which will scrutinize the way your EMS is configured. Network and EMS configuration gets into the deep gooey technical stuff. It may be tough to understand, so I'll stick to the basics. Most spammers don't have very deep pockets. Because they're operating on the cheap, they tend to cut corners in consistent ways. Because most ISPs *do* have deep pockets, they've invested in high-tech filters that are designed to spot the spammers' patterns.

Speed: One red flag for spam filters is the speed of incoming messages. Spammers tend to blast out a bunch of messages quickly. The idea is to get as many messages into the ISP as possible before the ISP's systems can detect a pattern or tally up their users' "spam button" votes. How quickly is too quickly to send messages, you may ask? It's tough to tell. No two ISPs use the same thresholds, and each ISP regularly changes its own threshold to keep the spammers guessing. Suffice it to say that if you send out large numbers of messages too quickly, those messages may be flagged as spam.

Email header: Spammers are like chameleons, always changing their IP addresses to disguise their origins. So spam filters are trained to scrutinize the email header for potentially false information. Legitimate mailers typically list their IP addresses in a directory called the *Domain Name System (DNS)*. The DNS converts domain names into IP addresses. A filter might raise a red flag if it finds an IP address that doesn't trace back to a legitimate domain name.

Bounce Handling

Lists need regular cleaning. For example, when messages are bounced because they can't be delivered, a good emailer will always follow up. If the recipient's server is busy or their mailbox is full, an emailer will try again later. More importantly, if the receiving server says the recipient's address does not exist, a responsible emailer will remove that address from their list. Spammers, on the other hand, are notorious for their poor list hygiene. They won't go through the trouble of checking up on bounces. So when a high number of bounces from the same server go unanswered, ISPs get suspicious.

Many ISPs have even more sophisticated bounce systems in place to thwart spammers. When a server rejects an email, it sends back a bounce message that explains why the email was rejected. The way the sender handles these messages helps ISPs measure the speed of bounce processing, the timing of bounce responses, and the frequency of bounces per address. If your email service does not handle bounces quickly and accurately, you will look just like a spammer to the ISP.

Content Filters

The English humorist and writer Douglas Adams once said, "If it looks like a duck, and quacks like a duck, we have at least to consider the possibility that we have a small aquatic bird of the family anatidae on our hands." The same theory holds for spam filtering. Certain types of content, no matter how benign their intention, will always get their sender labeled as a spammer.

Spam Assassin and other message content filters are programmed to assign spam scores based on certain message characteristics. These include:

Text: Filters look for words that spammers love to use, like "Viagra" and "cheap mortgages." Spammers have devised a number of tricks to get around the text filter, most commonly using letter substitutes or spaces ("Viáøgra" or "m-o-r-t-g-a-g-e"). Filters, in turn, have been programmed to look for larger-than-normal proportions of nonstandard characters and other text tricks.

Graphics: A few enterprising spammers, realizing that filters were picking up on their word choices, decided to "hide" their message in a graphic. Anti-spam filters have responded by giving high spam scores to messages with a disproportionate ratio of graphics to text.

Address: Spam filters often look to the address line when trying to nab spammers. They can now pick out techniques such as *batching* (putting large numbers of related addresses in the To: or Bcc: line) and *dictionary attacks* (automatically generated sequential addresses, such as lisa@aol.com, lisaa@aol.com, lisab@aol.com).

Bayesian filters: One of the newest and most sophisticated filters gets its name from the eighteenth-century mathematician Thomas Bayes, known for his probability theory. *Bayesian filters* use probabilities to predict whether incoming messages are spam. These filters actually learn how to distinguish spam from legitimate email. The user trains the filter by showing it a group of legitimate messages and a group of spam messages. The filter then calculates the probability of certain characteristics appearing in "good" email versus spam.

Although content filtering technology is improving every day, it remains a very rough approach, and one that is prone to error. Content filters will always be inexact, if for no other reason than one person's spam is another person's fantastic deal. Regardless, I wouldn't focus too heavily on content filtering. If you avoid sticky words (like "free" and "hot") and spamlike formatting (all caps and an abundance of exclamation points), and you choose an email service provider that will give you feedback *before* your messages go out, content filtering shouldn't be among your top deliverability challenges.

Reputation and Voting

I mentioned earlier that Spamcop uses a voting system to assign messages to its black list. Most of the major ISPs use a similar system. Rather than letting software determine what is and isn't spam, they let their users decide. If too many people vote that a message is spam, the corresponding IP address will be put on an internal black list.

For ISPs, this system works well, because their customers are determining which messages they want to receive. But the voting system can lead to a large proportion of false positives, especially if the filter in question uses a third-party voting system (such as the ones used by Spamcop), whose users are likely to view any sort of commercial message as spam.

Unknown Senders

Your friends, family, and coworkers would never spam you, right? At least, that's the assumption many ISPs and email systems follow when they practice the *unknown senders* filtering method. When a message arrives in a customer's inbox, the address in the "from" field is matched against the recipient's address book. If the sender's name is in the address book, the message automatically gains entry. If the name is not in the recipient's address book, the message has to go through at least one checkpoint before being allowed through.

One checkpoint approach is called *challenge-response*. This "guilty until proven innocent" method stops and holds a message until the incoming ISP can verify that it is legitimate. When the email is received, the ISP sends out a challenge, requiring the sender to perform some authenticating action, for example typing in a code and hitting "reply." Spammers and bulk emailers send high volumes of messages automatically via computer, and therefore would be unable to respond to a large number of challenges.

Once the ISP has verified that the sender is a real person, the sender's name is added to the recipient's address book, and no future messages from the sender's email address are blocked. If the challenge receives no response, the message remains undelivered.

The good news is that challenge-response is not widely used. And many of the large ISPs that do use this method will whitelist any address that is added to a large number of personal address books.

Another unknown sender challenge is called *image and link suppression*. If a message comes from an unknown sender, the ISP will disable all images and links. Even though this method does not stop spammers, it thwarts Web beacons and trackable URLs so that spammers can never confirm that they've reached a live recipient.

Disposable Addresses

One of the newest spam avoidance techniques, disposable addresses, lets users create temporary email addresses to use expressly when they opt-in to an e-mail list. Messages sent to these addresses are forwarded to the recipient's real email address. Users benefit because they can "hide" their primary email address. And, if they start receiving spam on the disposable address, they can just throw out that address and immediately put an end to the spam.

As a consumer, the disposable address is one of my favorite spam tools, and services such as Yahoo's AddressGuard make it easy to use. But as a marketer, I find the technique challenging. Disposable addresses will only increase the already existing address churn problem. When users disable any overly spammed addresses, your messages will suffer even if you are not the source of the problem. Additionally, many of these disposable address systems will only *receive* email from the disposable addresses but will *send* from the user's primary address. Even the most advanced EMS can get confused when a reply message for a double opt-in confirmation, or an inbound email message for an opt-out request doesn't match the disposable address in their databases.

IMPROVING YOUR EMAIL DELIVERABILITY

Acquiring new customers is an expensive business proposition. As I mentioned earlier in the book, scouting for a new customer is five to ten times more expensive than marketing to an existing customer. When emails get bounced back to you or disappear in cyberspace, you lose established customer value.

A January 2004 JupiterResearch study polled hundreds of marketers to find out what levels of deliverability they were getting on their house lists. Only one-third (33 percent) of marketers were getting delivery rates above 90 percent.

Figure 19.1 Deliverability rates on marketers' house lists
Source: JupiterResearch[8]

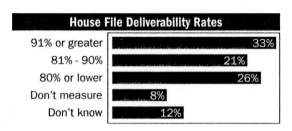

Even if you have low delivery rates, you can do a lot to make sure most of your messages get through. Some of the best deliverability approaches include the following techniques:

Authentication Schemes

Spammers are the ultimate chameleons, changing identities more often than most of us change clothes. With very little technical know-how, a spammer can make the name in the "from" field say just about anything. Thus anyone can pose as your bank, your ISP—even your mother. If a four-hundred-pound wrestler from Minnesota wants to bill himself as "Luscious Livvy" to sell sexy co-ed photos, no one will be the wiser. Without an effective way to trace a message back to its sender, there is no accountability for spammers who misrepresent or constantly change their identity.

But new *authentication schemes* such as Sender Policy Framework (SPF—supported by AOL), DomainKeys (proposed by Yahoo!), and CallerID (supported by Microsoft) are finally yanking spammers out of the shadows and throwing off their masks. (AOL and Microsoft have recently proposed combining their authentication schemes into a single new approach called SenderID.) Authentication schemes check that the origin of a message is what it appears to be. Some use special encryption that can be produced only by the purported author; others match the name in the "from" field or IP address to the public DNS record of the individual claiming to send the message. If a spammer attempts to send email from a fake address, these authentication schemes will catch them and flag their emails as spam.

Most of the spammer's power thus far has stemmed from his anonymity. When authentication schemes finally shine the spotlight on spammers and lift the rocks they've been hiding under, I think we'll start to see the first truly effective assault on the spam deluge. It won't happen overnight, but as these easily implemented approaches become more widespread, I'm confident that they'll begin to root out the spammers where they hide—or at least make them run faster.

Monitoring

No matter how many precautions you take, at least some of your messages are going to get bounced, erased, or otherwise misrouted away from their intended destination. The only way to know for sure whether your messages were delivered is to check the inboxes yourself. Manual follow-up can be time consuming, but your ESP, as well as specialized third parties can automate the monitoring for you. Periodic audits are the least expensive option; but for those of you who strive for 100 percent delivery, I would recommend that you sign up for a dedicated service that checks your delivery status on a regular basis.

What Else Can Legitimate Emailers Do?

Here are a few more tips to help you get your messages through the gates of your customers' ISPs:

Get added to your recipients' address book: Encourage subscribers to list your email address in their address book and safe lists. You can make the request at the top of each email and on any opt-in and "update profile" pages on your Web site.

Send from a user-friendly address: Email generally displays two pieces of information about the sender: the "from" address and the "from" text. The "from" address is the sender's email address. The "from" text is a short name or phrase used to identify the sender. Some marketing email systems use coded "from" addresses with long strings of numbers and letters (a2n38978@yourcompany.com). Then they put a nice name or phrase in the "from" text (customerservice@yourcompany.com). But certain email clients (AOL, for example) display *only* the "from" address, and the recipient is left looking at a string of unattractive code. You'll have better open rates if you use a friendly "from" address, rather than a coded address.

Use your brand: Make sure your recipients know that the message is from you. Put your brand in the "from" field and the subject line. Even if they don't remember opting-in, if they know and trust your brand, they will opt-out rather than hit "spam."

Always use the same email address: Once you've been added to your recipients' personal address books, you don't want to reduce your deliverability odds by throwing a new address into the mix. Beware that some EMSs use special codes in the "from" address to attach a reply message to a particular campaign. Although this technique makes the EMS's job easier, because it continually changes the "from" address, you'll find it impossible to get that chameleon-like address added to your customers' address book. Also, because challenge-response filters send out a separate challenge to each code, your messages will never have a chance of reaching users that use this type of filter.

Clearly state your intentions: The more information you give your customers, the better the chance that they'll remember they wanted to hear from you. Include a text message at the top of each email that clearly identifies you as the sender and states the purpose of your message.

Remind them where they opted in: You'll definitely help your case if you remind the recipient where and when they originally subscribed to receive your message (e.g., "You are receiving this message after opting-into www.yoursite.com on 6/22/03").

Make it easy to opt-out: Recipients will be less likely to hit the "spam" button if they can easily opt-out instead.

Deliverability Services

If all else fails, you can try turning to one of several companies that market innovative solutions to deliverability problems. IronPort,

Habeas, and Goodmail Systems are just a few of the deliverability solutions providers out there.

IronPort has designed a reputation-based system called BondedSender. Senders put up a financial bond, against which money is deducted if too many complaints are received against them. ISPs and corporations can also use the BondedSender list as a white list, knowing that participating senders will have to pay real money if they allow spam to be delivered from their IP addresses. Habeas embeds copyrighted text in its message headers, a sort of code that enables legitimate messages to pass through spam filters. But if spammers try to use the same text, Habeas sues them for copyright infringement. Finally, Goodmail Systems sells their accredited high-volume senders encrypted "stamps." By adding a cost to each delivered message, Goodmail essentially erases the profitability of high-volume spamming.

Deliverability services offers great promise, but it is a still-emerging field. As of this writing, no provider has even come close to solving the problem.

The Importance of Having a Good ESP

Deliverability is an ever-changing art. Tackling all of the issues I've outlined in this chapter is not as simple as picking up the phone and calling your ISP—it requires a significant time and resource commitment.

Don't assume that you can handle your deliverability issues without any help. Most of the high-end email service providers out there will monitor and fine-tune your message delivery for you, letting you focus on what you do best—building relationships with your customers. Think of it this way: Deliverability is just a tiny part of your company's business. ESPs, on the other hand, live or die by it. Their personnel, equipment, and software are designed to spot any changes, no matter how subtle, to filtering patterns almost as soon as they occur. Because they monitor deliverability for hundreds of customers, ESPs not only substantially lower the cost of monitoring, but they are also able to spot trends much faster than an individual monitoring email for a single company.

When selecting your vendor, consider the following issues:

Separate IP addresses: Ask your ESP whether your company will have a unique IP address. Sharing an address could confuse your emails with those of other senders (especially disreputable ones). Having a unique IP address is especially critical when your send volumes number in the hundreds of thousands per month, the point at which most spam filters start paying attention to incoming mail.

Expertise: Look for an ESP with extensive experience working with ISPs and spam filtering companies. Vendors who have established relationships with ISPs can help you quickly resolve any problems you might encounter.

Client list: Find out what other clients your ESP represents. Even if your company is assigned a unique IP address, a few questionable clients could influence your provider's credibility should they ever need to convince an ISP that the blip with *your* message was just a mistake.

Dedicated personnel: Vendors who are on top of deliverability issues should have a dedicated staff that maintains ISP relationships and keeps abreast of changes within the industry.

Deliverability consulting: The best vendors will be able to review your current email procedures, list management, address collection, message content, and permission strategies and recommend improvements.

Bounce handling and abuse response: Experienced ESPs should quickly and efficiently handle bounces and respond to incoming customer complaints.

Success rates: Ask whether your prospective ESP has the numbers to prove their delivery rates. If they do, find out whether their reports break out delivery and performance by domain, or whether their numbers are just overall averages.

Black list status: Finally, do a bit of detective work. Visit a few black list Web sites and see how often your prospective ESP's IP addresses are listed. Don't get alarmed if you see the ESP mentioned here and there—most high-volume ESPs will be listed from time to time. But if an ESP is listed on a major black list for an extended period of time, I would recommend that you start investigating another vendor.

When making your final decision on an ESP, beware of hollow promises. If a company "guarantees" deliverability, they either have no clue what they're talking about, or they are using questionable techniques (such as blasting through huge numbers of IP addresses) to get their clients' messages delivered. There is no way to achieve 100 percent deliverability. That said, you can increase your odds by adopting cutting-edge techniques, using great software, hiring top experts, and, above all else, being a responsible sender.

RENDERABLITY 101

Once your messages fight their way through all of the spam filters and arrive in your recipients' inboxes, your troubles are over, right? Far from it.

One of the most significant—and most overlooked—causes of reduced response rates is broken or unreadable messages. Nearly half of all emails sent by Fortune 500 companies contain missing graphics, raw HTML code, or other readability errors, according to a study performed by my company, Silverpop. Thirteen percent of messages are completely unreadable.[9] If your customers can't *read* your messages, there's no way they're going to *respond* to them.

As I mentioned in Chapter 7, Multipurpose Internet Mail Extensions (MIME) standardizes the use of different formats within an email message. But MIME does not ensure 100 percent interoperability. Not all browsers and email programs are created equal. Literally hundreds of different combinations of email vendors, product versions, ISP systems, operating systems, security systems, and browsers exist. These ever-changing combinations dramatically affect the way your HTML messages look in a recipient's inbox. Just because a message views correctly in your version of Microsoft Outlook, does not mean that it will appear the same (or appear at all) to your customers.

Standard HTML email won't display correctly on AOL versions 4.0 and 5.0, for example, because these browsers require a special kind of MIME body type for Rich Text Format (RTF). In 2002, an estimated 7.5 million subscribers were using AOL 4.0 and 5.0. Even in 2004, as many as 70 million people were using Lotus Notes, which interprets MIME and HTML a bit differently than most other email clients. The Silverpop study discovered that 90 percent of HTML emails sent to the two AOL versions and Lotus Notes contained disruptive errors. That means that as many as 70 million recipients may be unable to see some, or even all, messages sent by Fortune 500 companies if they were not encoded with Notes and AOL in mind.[10]

In the wild world of email, simply following the standards is not enough to ensure that your messages are delivered and readable. As your technology team constructs your campaigns, they—and your tools—must be able to accommodate the huge variety of nuances and incompatibilities that still exist across the Internet.

The following five primary problems cause rendering issues:

1. Idiosyncratic email clients: Each email client comes complete with its own set of quirks. Some clients will chop off the last character of a message; others will place an unattractive line between side-by-side graphics. Although these minor annoyances reach only a small number of recipients, they can affect those recipients' perceptions of your company.

2. MIME: As I mentioned earlier, not all MIME bodies display the same. Much of the problem has stemmed from AOL versions 4.0 and 5.0. Though these versions still have a large subscriber base, more and more people are beginning to upgrade to newer AOL versions, so we should soon see the problem diminish.

3. Advanced HTML: JavaScript, style sheets, "DIVS" (advanced HTML used for complex message layout), and other advanced forms of HTML will undoubtedly jazz up your messages and make them more visually appealing, but support for these formats is inconsistent. The more effects you use, the greater the risk that your messages won't render properly in some email clients.

4. Rich media and active content: Video, audio, and Macromedia Flash add dimension to an otherwise flat message, but rich media can present significant renderability issues. Users' security settings often disable Flash or video players. Some messages may "fail gracefully" and not show broken HTML. But in the hands of less technical marketers, media-rich messages may wind up with a broken or frozen image where your video should have been.

5. Link and image suppression: As I mentioned earlier, many sophisticated email clients use image and link suppression to thwart spammers. Although image suppression software might stop a few spammers, it will definitely ruin the layout and usability of your message.

What Can You Do?

How well you handle your renderability issues hinges on one thing: how much you know. You need to know which email clients have renderability issues and how to work around them. You also need to know how much fancy text and rich media you can put into your messages to make them visually appealing yet still renderable.

Most of my clients deal with renderability in one of three ways: they stick to a simple HTML structure, they design their messages however they like and let a few customers suffer poor quality, or they employ experts who have the know-how to create advanced messages that work across the widest range of email clients. Technology can help, too. For example, Silverpop has a built-in expert system called SmartView that does much of the fine-tuning automatically. Though it lacks the subtlety of a real live human specialist, it does a great job formatting most messages for a fraction of the cost of hiring an expert.

■　■　■　■

Sadly, spam isn't going away anytime soon. While spam exists, spam filtering and the problem of false positives will also exist. Hopefully within a few years, filtering and deliverability technologies will have matured to the point where they will provide real solutions for legitimate emailers.

Until that time, ESPs are in a unique position to help marketers improve their deliverability. When picking a service provider, make sure you're familiar with all of the issues first. And remember, no matter how competent the ESP you choose, there are no magicians out there who can wave a magic wand and make all your messages float effortlessly into your customers' inboxes. At best, your ESP will have the relationships, the technology, and the expertise to help you noticeably improve your delivery rates.

If you try to handle your own deliverability issues, use the information I've discussed in this chapter to learn to spot problems before they occur. Once you're armed with the right tools, at least you won't have to sit around waiting for that call from an ISP warning that they have blocked your messages. Trust me, it will never come.

Chapter 20

ADVANCED TECHNIQUES

Half the money I spend on advertising is wasted; the trouble
is I don't know which half.
—John Wanamaker, nineteenth-century retail magnate

Not all email marketers are created equal. What truly separates the serious Level 2 and Level 3 emailers from the blasters are the techniques they use to segment and deliver their messages. Level 1 senders load up their campaigns and fire away at the largest lists they can build. Sophisticated emailers, on the other hand, test, target, and gather preferences to aim the maximum relevancy at each customer.

Tailoring message to audience involves a variety of techniques. Some, such as segmenting and testing, have been around since the old days of advertising and direct marketing. Others, such as dynamic content and life cycle automation, are more recent innovations.

Segmenting and testing were initially slow to catch on among email marketers, simply because blasting was a much faster and cheaper way of getting messages to their destination. But in our new reality of overflowing inboxes and rampant blocking and filtering, blasting may no longer be a viable option in many cases. So email marketers have picked up on the established testing and targeting methods, but they've given them a new twist. Whereas direct mailers test and target simply to manage costs, email marketers are learning to use these techniques to deepen customer loyalty and preserve EBV.

Although dynamic content and life cycle automation similarly have roots in the offline world, they have been relegated to niche applications because they drive labor and production costs sky high when attempted by nonelectronic distribution systems. But with email, these techniques suddenly become economically viable and increasingly available, even to nontechnical marketers.

SEGMENTING

Segmenting (as we mentioned in Chapter 6) is all about improving relevancy—sifting through your master list until you find the subset (or subsets) of your audience that will find your message most compelling and relevant. The trouble is, segmenting takes a great deal more effort than the old "batch and blast" technique of sending out as many messages as possible to the widest audience. Some marketers can't help but see segmenting as a lose-lose proposition: It *costs more and requires more effort* than blasting and it *receives fewer responses.*

As my friend, Matt Leonard, who manages customer information privacy and policy worldwide for IBM, puts it: "One of the biggest reasons why marketers don't segment and target their email campaigns is that they fear the three questions their boss will inevitably ask when he or she reviews the campaign results:

- If the results fall below expectations: 'So, if you had mailed to the whole list you might have received more orders?'
- If the results meet expectations: 'So, if you had mailed more segments you could have received more orders?'
- And if the results exceed expectations: 'So, if you had mailed to more segments, you could have really cleaned up?'"[1]

To senior management, segmenting email can seem like an unnecessary luxury. Unfortunately, if you continue to send every message to every customer, you threaten your customer relationships and your EBV.

List segmentation can take a variety of forms. A few years ago, the Direct Marketing Association asked marketers which criteria they used for segmenting both email and postal mail. Figure 20.1 shows the results for email.

Figure 20.1 Segmentation Techniques US Direct Marketers Use for Housefile List Selection for Email vs. Postal Mail (as a percentage of respondents) Source: Direct Marketing Association[2]

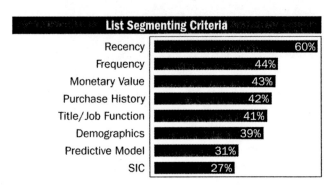

Email marketers can choose from a wide variety of segmentation options. The option you pick will depend on the richness of your customer data and the extent of your technical sophistication. The following are just a few of the more commonly used email segmentation methods:

- Demographics: Quantifiable customer characteristics, including age, gender, education, and income level
- Geographic location: The customer's city, state, and distance from your nearest retail outlet
- Customer preferences: The frequency and types of messages that most interest them
- Analytic scoring: Behavioral or demographic analysis to identify the customer characteristics that will most likely result in a particular behavior (e.g., a purchase)
- Online behavior: A customer's email use, past opens or click-throughs, Web page visits, and conversions
- Customer type: Whether the customer is a repeat buyer, inactive, or a new customer
- Customer satisfaction: A customer's past experience(s) with your company

- Timing or event based: A customer's recent action or an upcoming event, such as a purchase or a subscription renewal

Using dynamic content, you can target multiple segments simultaneously with the same message. JupiterResearch polled a number of email marketers in July 2002 and found that they were using a widely ranging number of segments per mailing:

Figure 20.2 Number of segments email marketers used per mailing
Source: JupiterResearch[3]

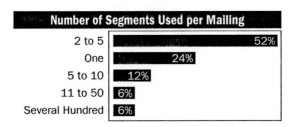

One of the most novel forms of email segmentation is *timing*, which can segment customers by their *past behaviors* and even respond to those behaviors *in real time*. My favorite case study on timing-based segmentation was done a few years ago at eBags. Larry Martine, eBags's then director of Retention Marketing, and his team set out to identify the day and time that would generate the highest response rates and online sales. After conducting a variety of tests, they found that sending their weekly promotions at 2:00 a.m. PST every Tuesday morning garnered the most responses. This one timing exercise would have been enough for most companies, but Martine and his team wanted to take it even further.

Rather than using a one-size-fits-all approach for optimal timing, they wanted to find the optimum time and day for *each individual customer*. Martine and his team hypothesized that the best time to reach each customer would be the same day and time that the customer *opted-in*. If the customer's schedule afforded them time to opt-in, they surmised, it might also be the best time for them to consider an offer and make an online purchase.

Using their 2 a.m. Tuesday segment as a control group, Martine's team staggered their weekly promotion to the remaining recipients over a seven-day period. Each recipient received the message on the same day of the week and time of day as they had originally opted-in. The results of this segmentation were nothing short of astonishing. Compared with the control group, click-throughs in the test group climbed 20 percent; conversion rates jumped 65 percent; and the average order size increased by 45 percent. The *average revenue per recipient climbed 187 percent relative to the control group.* "Our approach helped get our messages through the clutter, and we were able to reach people when they had more time to shop," says Martine.[4] Using insight, targeting, and execution, eBags was able to nearly triple their revenue without changing their list or increasing the number of mailings.

Many segmentation tools and techniques don't differ all that much between email and direct mail. However, when coupled with testing, email offers a richer and much more appealing set of options than direct mail. Email testing is more cost effective than its offline counterpart. It's also faster. Segmenting and testing cycles that take weeks in direct marketing can be done in a matter of hours online. For the same amount of effort, email marketers can achieve a much finer degree of targeting than their offline colleagues.

TESTING

Email intrinsically offers a greater wealth of customer information faster and more cost-effectively than direct mail, yet many marketers fail to take advantage of its potential.

Email is by design fast, inexpensive, easy to use, and exceptionally measurable. It's easy to find out which elements of your message work and which are flops. You simply need to test them. With the right tools, setting up tests can be almost as easy as sending regular campaigns. And email tests generate so much data that they can not only identify customer actions (conversions), but also brand affinity (opens) and content relevancy (click-throughs) to provide far deeper insights than traditional offline marketing tests.

You can test just about any aspect of a message. Which population groups are responding to your emails? Which offer drives the greatest conversions? Which subject line generates the most opens? Do your customers prefer text or HTML? Do they respond to a catchy subject line, or are they more responsive to a straightforward promotion? Which of your customers are most likely to make a purchase?

MarketingSherpa asked more than two thousand marketers which tests were worth the investment. As you can see from Figure 20.3, landing pages, subject lines, and HTML versus text were among the most popular tests.

Figure 20.3 Most worthwhile tests, according to more than two thousand survey respondents
Source: MarketingSherpa[5]

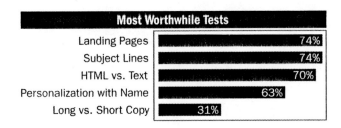

The greatest benefit of testing and segmenting, according to Kaenan Hertz of Sallie Mae, is that it prevents customer tune out. "If you carpet bomb everyone, you will get the maximum number of responders per campaign, but you run the risk of damaging your brand equity pretty quickly. Over time, your overall response rate will drop dramatically and your opt outs will increase. *The fact is, people will eventually tune you out if you don't do a good job of testing and segmenting.*"[6] Once again, it's all about relevancy.

Testing does not end once you've gathered your email response data. For your tests to be worthwhile, you must link responses back to your customer source data. Analyze demographics and purchase history together with response information, and you'll uncover the real high-value segments that will most likely respond to your campaign. Although this process may sound involved, it can actually be turned around quite rapidly. Sallie Mae is able to run its tests and execute a full mailing within twenty-four hours.

A Few Simple Testing Guidelines

Here are a few questions to consider when setting up your tests:

What do I want to test? You can test an almost unlimited number of message characteristics and permutations, from offer to creative design to subject line. The beauty of relationship-based email communications (as opposed to advertising) is that you don't have to test everything at once. Roll out your tests gradually over a period of months or quarters, analyzing each characteristic individually or in related groups. You could try out different subject lines in the first mailing, for example, but test optimal day of week over a period of several months.

How do I execute the test? Let's assume you are sending a newsletter to a large audience, and you want to find out which elements work and which are better left out. You could test your newsletter via one of three methods:

1. Vary different message elements over several mailings. Try out different article lengths or send out the newsletter at different times of the day to identify which characteristics generate the highest response rates.

2. Split your list. Divide your list into two or more groups (sometimes called an A/B split) and change one characteristic (e.g., subject line) for each group. Assuming that you divide your groups randomly so that each represents an accurate cross-section of your overall recipient base, and everything else about your message remains the same, your results should clearly reveal the best-performing characteristic(s).

3. Test to a list subset. The most advanced testing method is the equivalent of an email dress rehearsal. You pick a small subset of your recipient list, against which you try out various message characteristics. That way, you can identify the optimal message characteristics, and the potential trouble spots, *before*

you send the newsletter to your entire list. Each list subset is often referred to as a *test cell*. (For more on testing, refer back to Chapter 6.)

How many recipients should be included in the test to yield the most meaningful results? Unless you are a statistician, there are no easy answers on how many recipients you should use when running tests. The idea is to pick a test cell size that contains the smallest number of recipients, but one that will still be indicative of overall customer behavior. Sallie Mae, whose customer count is in the millions, tries to build its tests around cell sizes of at least twenty-five thousand addresses. But the real purpose isn't necessarily to pick the right number of recipients. The point is more about generating the optimum number of responses from the test. The most meaningful tests will generate response counts in the hundreds. The size of your original recipient list will depend upon your anticipated response rates and the number of responses you want to generate.

Also keep in mind that email lists are already somewhat biased toward online users. Active emailers do not necessarily share the same demographics and characteristics as the general population or your overall customer base. Make sure you don't mistakenly use email response data as a proxy for your overall customer behaviors and response expectations—especially if a large portion of your customer base is not online.

What can I learn from tests? With testing, your goal is not just to get the highest response rates that drive conversions *for a single mailing*. Your goal is also to learn as much as possible about your recipients and apply what you've learned to future campaigns.

Response data becomes truly significant when it helps build the marketer's entire customer knowledge base. Only when integrated with preferences, demographics, purchase history, and other customer traits will testing start to reveal not only which message characteristics most appeal to recipients, but which recipient characteristics best align with various message elements.

Whereas testing message characteristics will help your response rates and, to some extent, increase relevancy, understanding individual preferences within your recipient base will directly *drive* relevancy. With testing, you're not simply evaluating which offer is best for your overall customer base; you're determining which groups of customers prefer specific offers. This last step will take you fully into Level 2 territory, and possibly even inch you closer to Level 3 status.

I must point out that the options I've outlined barely scratch the surface of all the email testing possibilities available. Understanding campaign responses and their implications to future customer behavior can get into incredibly complex statistics, analytics, and modeling. Fortunately, those of us without a PhD can still use the basic testing methods to enrich our ongoing customer relationships.

I should also caution that although segmentation and testing are undeniably beneficial, past a certain point (which has yet to be determined) the effort of testing exceeds its value. If you segment so rigorously that many of your customers simply don't hear from you anymore, you no longer risk damaging your EBV, instead, you risk having your brand forgotten altogether.

The fundamental testing methods I've discussed should serve you well. But if you find that you want to dive into more advanced testing, I would recommend that you consult your agency and your ESP, as well as the Internet and your local library.

DYNAMIC CONTENT

Dynamic content is the ultimate form of personalization. Beyond simply merging an email with a recipient's first name or account number, dynamic content allows you to build messages, piece by piece, based on specific recipient characteristics. David Daniels, Research Director at Jupiter, defines dynamic content as, "automatic assembly of an email based on predefined content, rules, and templates."[7]

Because dynamic content is such a broad term, its terminology varies from one ESP to another. For the sake of clarity, we'll stick with the following definitions:

- Each changeable area of a message is called a *content block*.

- Each content piece that can be inserted into a particular content block is called a *content element.*
- Individual content elements are placed in each content block based on a set of *rules.* A rule is a simple (or complex) criterion similar to a segment (e.g., gender = male).

Mark Twain once said, "To a man with a hammer, everything looks like a nail." To a marketer with dynamic content, everything looks like a potential content block. Dynamic content is such a powerful tool that it is often used in situations for which it is not best suited. I recall one client who was trying to create dozens and dozens of rules for a dynamic content block. It seemed like overkill to her, so she asked for help. After a quick review, her account manager told her that by simply changing the way she imported her data, she could get the same result with some simple personalization (field replacements).

With two or more content blocks per message, you get into more complex assemblage. For example, a hotel newsletter might contain three content blocks:

1. Geographically targeted: The first block includes one of ten hotel photos, selected by its proximity to the recipient's home state.
2. Past stays: The second block is a promotion that varies based on whether the recipient has stayed at one of the chain's hotels.
3. Travel habits: The third and final block is a travel tip that varies by the recipient's level of travel (infrequent or regular traveler).

As you can imagine, the number of possible permutations can get so high (in this case, forty) that trying to manually build individual message versions would be impossible. This is where dynamic content really shines. *With dynamic content, you can automatically target your messages into dozens—even hundreds or thousands—of individual segments within a single campaign.*

How Dynamic Content Works

"Most of the heavy lifting with dynamic content is in the setup phase—defining the rules, identifying the content, and tying it all together," says Daniels. "After that, the work is in place and the system takes care of the rest."[8]

Because dynamic content is a relatively new concept and is not yet widely used, there is no single established method for setting it up. Different ESPs have different user interfaces for accessing this feature. But the fundamental approaches to dynamic content can be broken into two categories:

1. Multiple rules sets per message: This is the most intuitive approach for many marketers. Each content block is assigned its own elements (images, promotions, etc.) and set of rules. The following diagrams illustrate how two content blocks and their associated rules would work in the "multiple rules sets" approach.

Figure 20.4 An example of two possible content blocks with three different rules each, resulting in nine different messages (3 elements in block 1 multiplied by 3 elements in block 2)

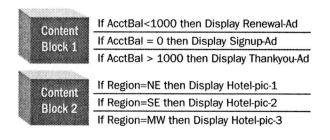

Even though the multiple rules approach is intuitive, it can lead to challenges. As soon as the number of content blocks gets above two, the permutations start to multiply faster than a supercomputer. Three content blocks, each with ten elements, can easily spawn one thousand different permutations, or one thousand possible messages (e.g., 10 x 10 x 10 = 1,000).

The vast number of potential permutations can lead to several complications. Testing every possible combination of elements to ensure the HTML renders properly can be onerous or impossible. Confirming that every combination of offers and targets actually makes sense can lead to very complex rules. Or, keeping track of every single unique message can be cumbersome in industries (such as financial services) that have to audit every email sent.

2. Single rule set per message: The second approach to dynamic content creates a single set of rules for all content blocks and elements in a message. If the rule is true (e.g., gender = male), then an individual element (an offer for discounted ties) is placed in each content block. Many single rule sets are defined as a table or matrix:

Figure 20.5 An example of a single rule set with three rules that define two content blocks, resulting in three different messages

Region	AccountBalance	Content Block 1	Content Block 2
NE	<1000	ContentA2	ContentB7
SE	<1000	ContentA1	ContentB3
MW	All	ContentA2	ContentB1

Even though many marketers find this approach less intuitive than multiple rules per message, it does limit the number of potential permutations. Each possible combination is listed explicitly in the table, making testing and reporting easier and allowing marketers to eliminate combinations that will obviously not work.

Dynamic Content Features to Look For

As I was writing this book, few solutions let marketers choose which of the two dynamic content approaches they wanted to use. But over time, I expect that the ESPs will evolve their service to give marketers the option of choosing from multiple approaches based on the dynamic content needs of their particular campaign or industry.

In the meantime, when you are evaluating your EMS for dynamic content, look beyond the content and rule-creation interfaces. Find out how they support the testing and reporting of dynamic content. Is the testing easy? Does the system intuitively register individual permutations? Will reporting sort results by dynamic content element—i.e., will you be able to see which click-throughs and opens occurred in each block and each element?

The great benefit to dynamic content is that "you can send fewer campaigns and get better responses," says Daniels.[9] Without having to dramatically increase your email program sophistication, you can improve targeting, control frequency, and drive relevancy all at the same time. I've also seen marketers use dynamic content to solve problems that have nothing to do with relevancy. For example, a friend of mine works at a Fortune 500 retailer. Because approvals at his company are slow and onerous, he squeezes multiple campaigns into a single mailing with dynamic content so he has to request approval only once.

Dynamic content distinguishes email from other marketing mediums, and it provides compelling proof that its value will only continue to grow over time.

LIFE CYCLE AUTOMATION

Life cycle automation (also known as automated sequencing and campaign automation) is the most drastic departure from the blast mentality that once pervaded our industry. Life cycle automation adds another dimension to targeting—time. Rather than assuming that every recipient wants to receive a communication at the same time, life cycle automation times each message so that each recipient gets a message when most appropriate for them. As Stephen Diorio says, "timing is targeting."[10] As you'll see, timing may be the most powerful form of targeting that exists.

How Life Cycle Automation Works

Life cycle automation can be accomplished in the offline world, but it is much easier and less expensive to carry out with email. The primary difference between life cycle automation and traditional segmentation techniques is the element of time. Timing can be executed in several ways:

External event: Your EMS receives notice of some kind of external event and in response triggers a series of messages. The event can be as simple as a customer opt-in, or as complex as a recipient's failure to open several messages in a row. When a customer opts-in to your message, you could send an immediate thank-you, followed by a survey thirty days later to assess their experiences with your company. If the recipient does not open your messages, your EMS might initiate a specific follow-up with a heavily promotional subject line. The defining characteristic of life cycle automation is that the triggers generate a *sequence* of messages, not just a single response.

Threshold: Your EMS monitors certain customer characteristics and sends a message when a customer reaches a particular threshold. A simple threshold could be a congratulatory email sent to a frequent flyer when he has flown a certain number of miles. This approach generally requires a high level of integration with your marketing and operational databases. (See Chapter 16 on Email Data Integration and the synchronized approach.)

Time and date: The classic example of time and date is the birthday or subscription reminder. Sending a customer a happy birthday message is an easy and highly targeted (not to mention thoughtful) way to use life cycle automation.

A more advanced example is a set of reminder notices sent four weeks, two weeks, and two days prior to a customer's subscription termination. Of course, the trigger logic must be set up to stop messages once the customer does renew.

As triggers and life cycle automation begin to see widespread use, I expect that many marketers will raise the issue of frequency. In a world of Level 1 blast-away promotions, frequency limits are a blunt but useful approach to help marketers avoid overwhelming their customers with messages. But fear of upsetting their carefully crafted frequency policies may deter many companies from evolving to the next sophistication level with life cycle automation.

In the absence of more sophisticated techniques, frequency is, at best, a mediocre proxy for relevancy. Consider this scenario: A customer of a home DIY retailer purchases materials for a new backyard deck on week one and contracts a kitchen remodeling project on week two. The purchases trigger the retailer to send two or more life cycle messages within the same month. Although the extra messages may cause the retailer to exceed its frequency policy, will the customer mind? Probably not, because the messages are relevant to him, especially if their promotional aspects are balanced with helpful deck construction and kitchen remodeling tips. When weighing relevancy against frequency, the former is by far the more important consideration. Armed with the Level 3 approaches described in this chapter, marketers should see their relevancy skyrocket, making many, if not all, of their frequency concerns moot.

On its own, time is a powerful segmentation tool. But when combined with traditional segmentation techniques (e.g., demographics and customer behavior), it delivers even greater targeting ability.

Yet, according to a JupiterResearch study, the majority of marketers still stick with the traditional campaign cycles. Only a pioneering 3 percent have adopted more advanced techniques. Although the data in Figure 20.6 are a bit dated, my experience is that most marketers have still not incorporated individual timing into their email campaigns. The opportunity for marketers to gain a competitive advantage by initiating specifically timed campaigns is still wide open.

Figure 20.6 Frequency of retention campaigns
Source: JupiterResearch[11]

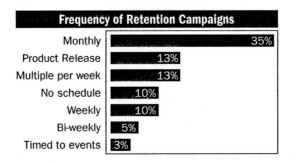

Life Cycle Automation in the Real World

Staples is the largest office products retailer in the world, and it was one of the first office supply stores to jump into the e-commerce business. A few years ago, Staples launched an initiative to improve the overall relevancy of its email marketing and customer communications. One of the most significant outcomes of the exercise was that the company began to focus on life cycle automation.

"Staples's products are uniquely suited to automated life cycle emails," explains John Giusti, director of customer sales and marketing at Staples. "Customers don't just buy them once; they buy them over and over again."[12]

Giusti's team has used several different approaches to life cycle automation as they fine-tune their efforts. One approach analyzes the average use time of a product, then uses the data to anticipate when a customer will run out of the product and sends the customer a reminder to repurchase. Another approach Giusti has used with great success is the cross-sell. A customer who buys an inkjet printer will almost certainly need paper and replacement ink. Computer purchasers will eventually want extra storage disks and/or drives. Giusti and his team have set up multiple automated campaigns that can vary follow-up timing by purchase date to maximize response rates.

Staples' response rates are proof that customization and automated follow-up work. The company doesn't need to rely solely on promotions to drive increased conversion. Its highly targeted and timed life cycle messages alone have driven strong incremental sales.

Life cycle automation is one of the most effective ways for retention marketers to communicate with, and sell to, their existing customers. It combines customer knowledge and past purchase behavior to let marketers achieve a degree of relevancy that is practically unheard of with any other medium. With life cycle automation, open rates can climb to 70 percent or more, and click-throughs can get well into the double digits—even in today's world of overflowing inboxes. But possibly the greatest benefit to life cycle automation is its ease. Once set up, it will automate many of your formerly manual marketing and communications efforts. You can sit back and watch your systems automatically send countless messages every day. Your job will evolve from hands-on campaign execution to monitoring and fine-tuning ongoing campaigns.

■　■　■　■

When used individually, each of the four advanced techniques can dramatically improve your EBV and land you squarely within the realm of Level 2 and 3 emailers. But to achieve the real promise of our medium, these techniques must work in tandem. The combination of segmenting, testing, dynamic content, and life cycle automation drives email so far beyond other communications tools that even the most ardent skeptics must admit that it will forever change the world of customer communications.

Chapter 21

THE BEGINNING OF THE MIDDLE

It is a mistake to try to look too far ahead. The chain of
destiny can only be grasped one link at a time.
—Sir Winston Churchill

No matter where you go, there you are.
—Peter Weller as Buckaroo Banzai
in the movie *The Adventures of Buckaroo Banzai*

CUSTOMER COMMUNICATION MANAGEMENT IN REVIEW

In a world where the economics of marketing have turned 180 degrees, companies of all sizes need to rethink the old rules. Budgets and expertise are no longer effective governors for determining how often, to whom, and with what message companies should communicate to their customers. A new level of active management is now required. That active management, which I call Customer Communication Management, ensures that brands are protected and laws are followed; it also provides a clear way for companies to substantially deepen customer loyalty and improve cross-channel revenue through email.

The foundation of CCM is relevancy. CCM helps marketers shift their approach from what *they want to say* to what their *customers want to hear.*

Types, preferences, and channels together increase your relevancy and help drive your Email Brand Value. *Types* differentiate email communications based on their value to the sender versus their value to the recipient along the Campaign Value Exchange. The less a communication benefits the recipient, the more permission is required.

Preferences and channels put your customers in the driver's seat. When customers have the authority to define what messages they want to receive, their perception of your email program rises significantly.

But no matter how relevant a campaign is to its recipients, it becomes ineffective when managed in isolation. Multisender organizations need to establish governance models, governing bodies, and, for day-to-day management, insightful and actionable email policies to align all email efforts across the organization. The combination of infrastructure, technology, and allocation processes enable companies to simultaneously act locally and think globally.

With the right enterprise infrastructure and campaign-level architecture in place, organizations are ready to begin execution. The most basic email implementation starts with list building and delivery management. As organizations find early success, their tools and techniques will grow in sophistication. They will add the technology and expertise to implement dynamic content and life cycle automation. At Levels 2 and 3, as they add timing, targeting, and customized content to their repertoire, email marketers will find that their increasingly relevant messages are opening the door for unprecedented communication opportunities. At this final level, organizations are ready to move past the operational phase and enter the forward-thinking stage, in which they explore new ways to improve the loyalty, response, and lifetime value of their online and offline customers.

TRENDS DRIVING EMAIL MARKETING

One of my favorite hobbies is collecting old predictions of the future. I find the practice much like going to Disney World and seeing Tomorrowland: You think to yourself, "did we really believe the future was supposed to look like this?"

So before I jump into prognosticating the future of email, I need to share a few quotes to remind us that visioning the future is a dicey game at best. The most memorable predictions of the future are the ones that foretell the failure of something innovative and exciting.

- *I think there is a world market for maybe five computers.*—Thomas Watson, chairman of IBM, 1943.

- *Everything that can be invented has been invented.*—Charles H. Duell, Commissioner, U.S. Patent Office, 1899.

- *This "telephone" has too many shortcomings to be seriously considered as a means of communication. The device is inherently of no value to us.*—Western Union internal memo, 1876.

- *Who the hell wants to hear actors talk?*—H. M. Warner, Warner Brothers, 1927.

- *With over 50 foreign cars already on sale here, the Japanese auto industry isn't likely to carve out a big slice of the U.S. market.*—*Business Week*, August 2, 1968.

Mark Twain once said, "Rumors of my death are greatly exaggerated." As you'll see from the experts with whom I spoke about the future of our medium, rumors of email's demise are greatly exaggerated as well.

Social Trends

As a starting point to predicting the future of my favorite medium, let's look at two social trends that are influencing email today.

Inbox Overflow: Technology is leading the charge to save the inbox with address book white lists, Internet-wide reputation databases, and authentication schemes. Consumers are also adapting to spam and other irrelevant email by intelligently changing their behavior. They are learning about filtering. They have taught themselves to quickly assess what they want to read and ignore the rest. Consumers are not going to stop reading marketing messages, but marketers need to understand how technology and consumer behavior are changing the way their messages are received.

Marketing Expertise: Back in 1995, not many companies could set up a Web site (and few wanted to). When the Internet boomed in the late 90s, however, Web sites flourished and the demand to build them exceeded the supply of people skilled enough to create them. The result was a short-term gap in expertise. But today, Web sites are ubiquitous and most companies "get" why they should have one. Whether they build their site in-house or outsource the work, much of the mystery has dissipated. Email marketing is likely to follow the same course. When email is no longer a mystery, email marketers will once again be able to focus on the "marketing" part of their title.

Navigating the Email Roadmap

Whatever the future of email, most analysts and marketers agree that it will be significant. When people ask me, "how significant?" I am reminded of a conversation from the movie *Ghostbusters*:

Dr. Egon Spengler: "…all my recent data points to something big on the horizon."

Winston Zeddemore: "What do you mean, big?"

Dr. Egon Spengler: "Well, let's say this Twinkie represents the normal amount of psychokinetic energy in the New York area. Based on this morning's reading, it would be a Twinkie thirty-five feet long, weighing approximately six hundred pounds."

Winston Zeddemore: "That's a big Twinkie."

Email is a big Twinkie. JupiterResearch found that companies spent *$2.1 billion* on email marketing in 2003, and their annual email spending is expected to grow at a compound rate of 24 percent per year, reaching *more than $6 billion by 2008.*[1] To put these figures in perspective, many analysts estimate that Web analytics, marketing automation, and online webinars *combined* didn't account for $2 billion in spending in 2003. Email is a REALLY BIG Twinkie.

No one can argue that email will have a significant impact on business communications. But when anyone, especially people outside our industry, are asked to peer into the crystal ball, their predictions for the medium are diverse and not always optimistic. Many see email usage and effectiveness declining in the face of rising spam. Others see email losing its standalone identity and blending into other, more important categories, such as CRM solutions, or dissipating into yet another channel in our multichannel marketing world.

Before we can really decipher what we see in our crystal ball, though, we need to understand that email is more than just email. Like the proverb of the blind men who run into an elephant—one thinks it is a tree, another thinks it is a wall, and yet another believes it is a snake—email is a many-faceted animal. What it is and what it will become depends upon which part of it you are looking at.

Although there are countless ways to look at email, most marketers start by dividing it into acquisition and retention. Since this book is really just about retention, let's dig in a bit deeper and see what the proverbial retention elephant really looks like.

In my view, retention-based email marketing and email customer communications can be divided into three separate buckets: direct marketing, life cycle automation, and administrative.

Direct Marketing: Building and segmenting customer databases, executing campaigns, and analyzing responses are the fundamentals of direct marketing. Although email marketers will continue to build on and improve these traditional approaches, the decades-old techniques will provide them with a solid foundation.

Life Cycle Automation: Probably the most exciting, and potentially highest-impact aspect of online retention marketing, life cycle automation does for customers what no other marketing medium has been able to effectively do—reach them with just the right communication at just the right time in a highly cost-effective manner. I put this kind of email communication into its own bucket because its techniques (reporting, analysis, etc.) and technology differ from almost anything that has come before it in the online world. In a sense, life cycle automation follows the dictionary definition of classic Customer Relationship Management, and can borrow much from the last five years of online CRM innovation. But when applied to email, life cycle automation breaks new ground. Whereas CRM is used primarily for inbound management (call centers and Web sites), life cycle automation is both inbound and outbound—it is really about dialogs driven by customer events. Issues such as frequency, permission, and user preferences take on entirely new levels of importance when life cycle automation or CRM is handled via the email medium. Additionally, new technologies such as Short Message Service (SMS),

Multimedia Message Service (MMS), Instant Messaging (IM), and Really Simple Syndication (RSS) have particular application to life cycle automation and will undoubtedly move its functionality beyond email into the broader world of messaging.

Administrative: Every day, countless trees sacrifice their lives for the "noble" cause of delivering bills and other customer notices. Fortunately for the trees, consumers increasingly want to interact with their vendors online. And businesses are realizing that saving a few trees translates into a lot of cost savings. Over time, email will become a vital route for communicating the periodic and somewhat monotonous information that regularly passes between companies and their customers. But, just as with any new approach, companies face a myriad of challenges as they try to move beyond paper. There are back-office systems to integrate and cultural and regulatory issues to consider. Administration gets its own bucket because of the unique obligations it places on businesses as they move from paper into the digital world.

THE FUTURE OF EMAIL MARKETING

My friend Stephen Diorio has a colorful way of looking at the world. When I asked him about the challenges marketers face as they look to the future of their enterprise email programs, Stephen found an interesting metaphor for the evolutionary process:

"In the early days, email in large corporations was like my backyard. There was green grass here and there, but what really stood out were the weeds. Each departmental email effort was like a weed and they were popping up everywhere and growing out of control.

"So in came senior management, determined to get the yard under control. They took out the lawn mower and just mowed down all the weeds, trying to clean up all of the uncoordinated email efforts. Although mowing was a necessary process, the lawnmower got stuck in the mud of corporate bureaucracy, leaving a lot of unfortunate side effects like paralysis, lotteries, meaningless policies, brute-force access control, legal control, and dictatorships. If companies are unable to get their lawn mowers out of the mud, the weeds will pop up again and they'll be right back where they started. Getting out of the mud is tough and it's something most companies haven't been able to accomplish yet. However, when they do, they will reach a state I call 'enlightenment.' No matter how difficult and unintuitive its evolution, in the end, email becomes organic—an instinctive part of what every marketer does. It's like learning baseball: 'If you focus on the mechanics, everything becomes natural.' You become enlightened.

"Marketers know they've reached the enlightened state when the conversation shifts from frequency and bulk campaigns to architecting 'dialog streams' for each customer. That's when you know you've figured it out."[2]

Multichannel

Jim Nail has a thoughtful view on the subject of multichannel marketing. As Forrester Research's top email analyst, Jim probably spends as much time thinking about the future of email and marketing as anyone.

"Everyone asks me, 'What is the future of email?' What they really need to ask is, 'What is the future of marketing?'" he says.

Jim is a big believer in multichannel marketing and the increasingly vital role email will play in it. "You still need advertising—you need a way to get that brief introduction," he says. "But by itself, advertising can no longer convince someone to buy something. At best, it says, 'my company has something you might find valuable.'" In Jim's mind, advertising is only the first step to an integrated marketing strategy. You use it to engage a consumer's emotions and deliver an initial brand impression. After that, you need to involve the consumer in an ongoing relationship. "Email is one of, if not the most, powerful tools for creating that ongoing relationship," Jim says.

Jim believes that "Email will become deeply woven into the fabric of the overall marketing mix. It becomes the lynchpin in the ongoing relationship you are trying to build. It becomes the one delivery channel that can personalize communications at a cost well below the phone, postal mail, and even TV commercials of the future."[3]

Where email becomes most valuable is in its ability to help you build and use knowledge about your customers. If you retain email as a single channel, that ability is limited. But if you act on your customer knowledge with a channel agnostic strategy, email will transform your customer communications.

Spam

For every underfunded get-rich-quick scheme, there will be spam. For every half-rate techie who is willing to skirt the law to make a buck, there will be spam. I don't have to predict the future of spam—it is as inevitable as death and taxes. But although the scourge will never be eradicated, it can be tamed. An increasing number of consumers have rolled up their sleeves and decided to do something about it. They've educated themselves, purchased filters, set up their own white lists, changed their primary email address, adopted disposable email addresses, and become wary about handing out their email addresses to strangers. For many people, these efforts have been successful in reducing spam from a debilitating problem to a minor annoyance.

Unfortunately, the release from spam might take a little longer for people who rely on corporate and ISP anti-spam solutions. By relying on centralized technology, these recipients are often left with little or no access to filtering at a personal level. ISPs use customer-wide voting mechanisms so the majority (or the vocal minority) defines for every customer what level and kinds of messages are spam. Employees of large corporations have even less control over their own filtering systems. The majority of companies tend to follow the same spam-avoidance approach. One person, usually someone in the lower echelons of the company, is crowned spam czar. He becomes the sole arbiter of spam control for the entire company. This person is often overworked, underresourced, and underpaid. More often than not, the spam czar just throws up his hands and turns the filters so high that nothing commercial gets through. Nobody wins.

The technology to reduce spam already exists, and it is improving every day. It's only a matter of time before it becomes widespread enough to have a real impact.

Legislation

Consumers are mad as hell and they're not going to take spam anymore. Like air pollution, spam can never be eradicated entirely, even when regulated. Just as emissions regulations will never stop every stinky car, CAN-SPAM will never stop every bulk emailer. However, it will make our inboxes more livable if it can take down the worst offenders. And with continuing pressure from international governments (see Chapter 8) and American citizens, CAN-SPAM may not be the final word in U.S. spam legislation. State laws, FTC rulings, and further federal legislation should continue to put pressure on spammers, chipping away at their incentives and increasing the punishments for their illegal behavior.

Delivery

Email marketers often claim that deliverability is their greatest challenge. It causes more headaches, more late nights, and more heated discussions than any other aspect of email marketing. Unfortunately, as long as there is spam, there will be filters. And, as long as there are filters, there will be deliverability issues. The real question is: Will deliverability ever improve?

Before I answer this question, let me make one important point. Email is no longer free. For spammers, the costs are still relatively low. But even if they don't realize it, legitimate marketers are already spending real money on their email programs. The costs come in the forms of sophisticated commercial software, cost-per-message (CPM)-based delivery fees, and monitoring of inboxes and bounce rates. The costs may also be indirect. Every time customers contact a call center to complain that they didn't receive a critical email, the company pays a premium to deliver the message verbally (not to mention having to apologize and suffer the brand impact). Every customer who doesn't receive a promotion is a missed revenue opportunity. One way or another, large enterprises are paying for email.

If email already costs money, wouldn't buying "email stamps" be the next logical step as many experts are predicting? Personally, I think an Internet-wide email delivery fee is a silly idea. How in the world would Hotmail collect money from the millions of people who use its service? Even if Hotmail could collect a fee from every user, wouldn't the extra charge just drive senders to another webmail solution that didn't charge fees? A universal, consumer-level pay-for-delivery service is simply not realistic.

If there's no place for a universal fee, is there some version of pay for delivery that makes sense? The answer is: yes and no. Most ISPs won't knowingly let pornographic spam through their system, for example, even if senders are willing to pay to get it delivered. On the other hand, ISPs very much want to deliver the local Cub Scout newsletter for free, even if they perceive it to be "bulk mail." In my mind, the solution is not about paying for delivery but *paying for better delivery*. The more you pay, the more spam filters you bypass and the higher the complaint threshold before the ISP cuts off your messages.

Even if senders don't directly pay ISPs, they will end up paying subscriptions to various delivery assistance providers. Bonded senders have to post a bond. Reputation databases have a sign up and maintenance fee. The owners of copyrighted text need to be reimbursed to cover their legal fees (see Chapter 19). Pay for delivery is inescapable as long as spam and spam filters exist.

The ultimate solution to this mess is simple, and it has worked in the offline world for years. When businesses want to be absolutely sure their packages reach their destination, they spend the extra money to overnight them using UPS or FedEx. Just like the price distinction between third-class mail, first-class mail, and UPS or FedEx, the cost of email delivery will be scaled—the higher the cost, the more assurance that your messages will get through. That's it. Whether you purchase a bond, hire a delivery expert from your ESP, or even pay the ISP directly, the expense will balance out over time—greater investment is rewarded with better delivery.

Outsource Versus Insource

In the insource versus outsource deliberation, marketers will always seek the least-expensive solution, but only if they do not have to sacrifice creativity, flexibility, and responsiveness to new opportunities.

Ultimately, the decision hinges not only on cost, but on expertise, security, integration, and deliverability.

From a cost perspective, the benefits of doing email internally are not universal. Some companies have existing infrastructure and cost-accounting methods that make it more cost effective to host and run their email programs internally. Other companies have less internal support, and they find that outsourcing enables them to tap into the tremendous economies of scale achieved by large ESPs (bandwidth, shared servers, and shared expertise).

On the services front, the need for external expertise depends on the type of email program. Simple newsletters don't require much email expertise beyond deliverability. But email campaigns that require constant innovation can always benefit from an expert partner.

Security is an important consideration when companies use email for highly sensitive communications. Integration becomes an issue when the email program needs to be closely tied to an ever-changing set of customer events and triggers. Whether to insource or outsource these functions depends upon the needs of the individual company.

The final determinant of insourcing versus outsourcing is deliverability. More than any other consideration, deliverability has pushed marketers to seek help from outside parties. The issues are changing every day, and very few companies have the resources or the depth to keep up. Most industry experts agree that the challenge of deliverability will never go away. But as the industry matures, the expertise for it should become more widespread. As this happens, companies that have the infrastructure to run their email internally, or that prefer to insource their data handling for security reasons, will have the know-how to handle email on their own.

Jim Nail best sums up the bottom line on the outsourcing debate: "In the world of marketing, there will never be a single best answer for whether companies should outsource their email or do it internally. Each company's needs are different—they should look hard at their email road map, their culture, and their cost structure to determine which approach is best for them."[4] I hate to end this section without putting the issue to rest, but I have to agree with Jim. There will never be a single-best approach to insource versus outsource that works for all companies.

Technology

My background is more technology than marketing. I've been involved in a variety of technology businesses for most of my career. Over that time, software, hardware, and bandwidth technologies have advanced rapidly, just as their costs have plummeted. In 1988, a mere half dozen Britney Spears MP3s would have filled up the hard drive on my PC. Today my hard drive could hold ten thousand of her songs (just imagine). Improved technology and lower costs lead to greater accessibility. Greater accessibility means easier access for marketers with less reliance on IT. Having watched technology for the last twenty years, I can tell you one thing with confidence: Current email marketing systems (including the ones my company offers), are in their infancy compared to the technology available in other aspects of business. The degree of sophistication and ease of use available to emailers today leaves a great deal of room for improvement. The advancements that get me most excited about the future include:

Intelligent content: For recurring content such as promotions and newsletters, the EMS will be able to automatically control frequency by consolidating multiple articles/offers into the exact number of messages that fits each recipient's frequency preferences. The entire process will become dynamic—each element of a campaign will be inserted and managed autonomously as your EMS builds its database of content and customer information.

Multichannel: The EMS systems of the future will not only manage traditional email, but they will also seamlessly incorporate such new technologies as SMS, RSS, IM, and even voice. Customers will have total control over the channels used to reach them and the circumstances under which they may be contacted.

Automated campaign tuning: By watching campaigns in progress, especially ongoing life cycle campaigns, future EMS systems will learn which kinds of recipients respond best to certain messages. The EMS will then vary day of week, time of day, and even subject lines and offers to improve response rates and customer satisfaction in real time.

Acxiom helped introduce the marketing world to technology years ago, when computers were just becoming the foundational tools for direct marketing. As Acxiom's head of e-products, John Ripa watches traditional marketers readying themselves for the next age of digital marketing, the age of email, "I see more and more sophistication creeping in," he says. "New tools are making email more sensible and approachable to marketers. Email marketing is starting to be treated as a business—just like any other part of the marketing department."[5]

Other Kinds of Messaging

The distinction between wireless and wired, handheld and desktop, and multimedia and text blurs more and more every day. Wireless messaging capabilities such as SMS and MMS are converging with traditional email service on PDAs and other handhelds. Wireless messaging will introduce a new form of targeting—location. Whereas standard email systems can only target based on a recipient's home or work address, location-based services can determine exactly where a customer is standing at a precise moment in time and communicate information based on that location. Other forms of nonwireless, non-email messaging are also enriching communication opportunities. IM and chat are augmenting, and, in some instances, even replacing traditional email.

Even newer is RSS, whose letters stand for either Really Simple Syndication or Rich Site Summary, depending on whom you ask. RSS is a new and unique form of messaging. Similar to email, an RSS browser "subscribes" to a message provider (such as CNN, ESPN, and the *New York Times*). RSS users see a list of messages that can be opened and read. Each message has a short description, from which the user can link to an HTML page for the full article or newsletter. What makes RSS so different from email is that the RSS software polls the sender's site and asks for the latest messages. If the user wants to unsubscribe, he or she simply stops polling the sender. Without the ability to reach out to the user, the sender is unable to send unsolicited messages. Presto—no more spam. RSS will likely prove to be an ideal tool for marketers who want to distribute a single piece of content, such as a news article, product update, or newsletter, to a wide audience.

David Daniels, research director at JupiterResearch, believes that tools like RSS will ultimately eclipse email for certain kinds of communications. "RSS browsers are becoming increasingly available, and may even be built into Internet browsers and other popular desktop tools in the future. As their availability widens, I expect to see increased awareness of and then demand from consumers for their vendors to deliver certain kinds of communications through that new medium. I can easily see common things like newsletters and product updates being delivered through solutions like RSS instead of through traditional email channels."[6]

Over the next few years, messaging will no longer be synonymous with email. Communications technologies will become so diverse that successful marketers will be hard pressed to keep up. Marketers will need the technical expertise to ensure that their messages are delivered seamlessly without requiring their customers to be technical experts themselves.

CONCLUSION

Email promises to drive some of the most profound changes in customer communications since the dawn of direct marketing. Its early misuse as a mass-advertising tool has fizzled and will never recover. Like the ill-tempered child who grows into a well-mannered adult, email is evolving from a crude mass advertising medium into a sophisticated retention tool. But, unlike any other retention tool or medium, email promises the sort of cost benefits, measurability, and targeting that have never before been possible.

Adopting CCM is no longer an option for most companies. Whether your motive is brand protection, revenue maximization, or pure legal compliance, your company must begin to manage email communications at an enterprise level. If none of those motivations drive you, consider this. A mid-2004 Forrester Research study indicates that consumers no longer trust TV, newspapers, and magazines like they used to. Next to word of mouth, consumers ranked branded web sites and permission email as their most trusted sources of information for making buying decisions.[7] Traditional offline mediums now trail online for customers' trust, and the world is unlikely to ever go back. Email is not only the most cost-effective and measurable communications medium available to your company, but it is also *what your customers prefer.*

I truly hope that you have found this book helpful. The process of writing it has introduced me to some of the brightest minds in my industry, and inspired thought-provoking discussions with old friends and colleagues. All have generously shared their insights on using email as a strategic enterprise communications tool. My goal in writing this book was to pass that advice on to marketers as they transform their own email programs. As I type these last few words, I feel as if I have made a good start on that goal.

That said, the ideas here are by no means complete. There are many email marketing lessons yet to be learned. If you have new lessons or feedback on the ideas I have presented, I encourage you to visit the book's Web site at http://www.QuietRevolutionInEmail.com and share them with me.

The quiet revolution in email is already under way. The most important question you must answer is whether you are going to be part of that revolution or just another bystander watching from the sidelines. As you consider your answer, I will leave you with a slight adaptation of Mr. Churchill's opening quote: *On to the beginning of the middle…*

Appendices

GLOSSARY OF TERMS

A/B Split A form of segmentation that divides an email list randomly into two parts to compare various message elements.

Administrative Email A message that communicates account status updates, billing information, policy updates, or other requisite administrative information between customers and vendors.

Affirmative Consent As defined by CAN-SPAM, any situation in which the recipient grants express permission to receive messages in response to a clearly stated request.

Analytics A set of computational tools used to analyze huge volumes of data and produce meaningful insights about customers, prospects, and their behaviors.

Append The process of adding a customer's email addresses to an existing postal address record.

Application Programming Interface (API) The mechanism by which two computer systems communicate data and commands to each other.

Application Service Provider (ASP) A software company that provides their products online rather than installing them in their customers' data centers.

Authentication Schemes A spam-filtering technique that enables an ISP to confirm that the origin of a message is what it appears to be.

Auto Responders See Triggered Messages.

Batching A technique used by spammers, in which they put large numbers of related addresses in the message To: or Bcc: line.

Bayesian Filters Spam filters that use probabilities to predict whether incoming messages are spam.

Black Lists Lists maintained by watchdog groups and corporations containing the addresses of email servers that are believed to be used to send spam.

Blasting A technique made popular in the early days of email, in which marketers send out the same message at the same time to their entire list.

Bounce The return of a message to its sender as a result of a server error, spam filtering, or invalid email address.

Campaign Automation See Life Cycle Automation.

Campaign Value Exchange (CVE) A concept that enables marketers to determine whether a specific campaign provides more value for the sender or for the recipient.

Centralized Governance (see also Governance) An enterprise email governance approach in which all email execution falls under a single point of control.

Challenge-response A method of filtering which stops and holds a message until the sender performs some authenticating action (e.g., typing in a code and hitting "submit").

Channel A similar set of emails or campaigns that can be grouped together for the purpose of policies and management.

Click-through The action by which a recipient clicks on a link in a message and arrives at a Web page on the sender's Web site. Also called Response.

Click-through Rate (CTR) The percentage of recipients that clicked on a message (number of click-throughs divided by number of recipients).

Co-branded List As opposed to rented lists, which often appear to come from the company renting the list and whose product or service is being promoted, co-branded lists appear to come from both the list owner and the advertiser.

Commercial Electronic Email Message (CEMM) As defined under CAN-SPAM, any email message whose primary intent is to promote a commercial product or service.

Confirmed Opt-in An opt-in process in which the recipient gets a follow-up message confirming that permission has been obtained.

Content Blocks See Dynamic Content.

Controlling the Assault of Non-Solicited Pornography and Marketing Act of 2003 (CAN-SPAM) Federal legislation, passed in 2003, that regulates the use of email to send commercial messages.

Conversion The realization of a desired recipient action (e.g., a sale) from a promotional email.

Cookie A tiny piece of information sent by a Web server to a user's browser to track the user's movements across a Web site.

Co-registration "Renting" space on a heavily trafficked Web site to encourage additional opt-ins.

Cost-per-acquisition (CPA) A method of list rental in which the marketer pays the list owner for each recipient that responds (as opposed to paying for every recipient that receives the promotion).

Cost-per-click (CPC) A method of list rental in which the marketer pays the list owner for each recipient that clicks on the link in the message.

Cost-per-message (CPM) A method of list rental in which the marketer pays the list owner for each address to which the message is sent.

Customer Communication Management (CCM) A new strategy for email marketers, which moves email from a mass advertising tool to a customer relationship tool.

Customer Lifetime Value The long-term worth of a company's relationship with a customer.

Customer Permission Assumed (CPA) An approach to permission confirmation that assumes the recipient has granted permission unless the recipient takes specific action to opt-out.

Customer Permission Request (CPR) An approach to permission confirmation that requires a specific action on the part of the recipient (e.g., a reply or click).

Customer Relationship Management (CRM) A popular class of software application that tracks, analyzes, and manages customer actions across a variety of touch points, including call centers, Web sites, and sales calls.

Data Warehouse A database, used primarily by the marketing department, that pulls together data from various business systems.

Decentralized Governance (see also Governance) An email program executed locally, within each department or division, with little or no intervention at the enterprise level.

Deliverability Issues (e.g., bounces and filters) that determine whether a message reaches its intended destination.

Dictionary Attacks Spammer technique that automatically generates sequential addresses, such as lisa@aol.com, lisaa@aol.com, lisab@aol.com, in the recipient's "to" field.

Direct Marketing Association (DMA) The trade organization that oversees all direct marketing, including email marketing.

Domain Name System (DNS) A Web directory that converts domain names into IP addresses.

Double Opt-in An opt-in process in which the recipient must not only grant permission, but must also actively respond to a confirmation message.

Drip Campaign Any form of sequenced messages, but most often refers to the process of sending follow-up messages to customers who did not respond to an earlier campaign.

Dynamic Content Varying individual pieces of content to deliver a unique message to each recipient based on her profile.

Dynamic Message Assembly See Dynamic Content.

Email Brand Value (EBV) The measure of a company's brand as it relates to the customers who receive its email messages.

Email Client A software program that enables its user to send and receive email.

Email Marketing System (EMS) A complex software program that helps email marketers handle targeting, high-volume delivery, content management, reporting, and analytics.

Email Service Provider (ESP) A company that provides services and technology to assist marketers with their email initiatives.

Enterprise Email Assessment (EEA) The process by which companies review their current email program to gain an enterprise view of their overall email marketing initiatives.

Event Triggered Messages See Triggered Messages.

False Positive Legitimate emails that are mistakenly blocked by spam filters.

Federated Governance (see also Governance) A governance model that runs underneath a strong central policy, yet still allows a certain amount of autonomy at the departmental level.

Filter A technology used by email systems and service providers to weed out incoming messages that the recipient does not want.

Forward The action by which a recipient sends a message she has received to other people.

Frequency The rate (e.g., daily, weekly) at which messages are sent to a particular customer.

Full-Service Provider A company that offers total email marketing solutions, from creative design to results analysis.

Global Opt-out Honoring a recipient's opt-out across an organization.

Governance (see also Decentralized Governance, Centralized Governance, and Federated Governance) A term that refers to managing email efforts across an entire organization or enterprise.

Harvesting The illegal practice of compiling email addresses from public Web sites and message boards.

Header The section of an email message that contains information that the outgoing and incoming email servers use to process and deliver the message (e.g., sender's address and recipient's address).

House List A list of email addresses owned by a company, consisting primarily of opted-in prospects and customers.

Hyptertext Markup Language (HTML) The code that tells Web browsers how to display Web pages and email messages.

Image and Link Suppression A filtering method in which the ISP or email program disables all images and links in messages originating from an unknown sender.

Image Hosting A third party, usually an Email Service Provider (ESP), that holds message images on their server and delivers them only when a recipient opens the message.

Impression See open.

Informational Email A message that transfers knowledge from company to customer (a newsletter, for example).

Initiate A CAN-SPAM term meaning to send or transmit a message (not to be confused with Sender).

Internet Message Access Protocol (IMAP) A standard by which the recipient's client retrieves a message (see also Post Office Protocol (POP3)).

Interpersonal Email A message sent from one person to another person or small group (between two friends, for example).

Interruption Marketing As termed by Seth Goden, an approach by which marketers try to get consumers' attention by interrupting them with an advertisement. Examples include television, radio, magazines, and billboards.

Internet Service Provider (ISP) A company that provides its subscribers with access to the Internet and email.

Internet Protocol (IP) Address A unique set of numbers assigned to each computer on the Internet that can be used to identify that computer.

Life Cycle Automation A technique that enables marketers to automatically send a message at the most appropriate time for each recipient.

List Aggregators Companies that compile email addresses from several sources (for example, sweepstakes) and rent those lists.

List Brokers Companies that provide advice, service, and sourcing around list rentals.

Mailto link An HTML link that automatically opens a new email message with the "to" field already filled in.

Masterfile A master list of email addresses pulled from several sources. Generally used by list aggregators.

Message Body The main section of the email, which the recipient sees when she opens the message.

Message Transfer Agent (MTA) A specialized server that transfers messages between the email clients of senders and recipients.

Multipurpose Internet Mail Extensions (MIME) A standard, defined by the Internet Engineering Task Force, which divides the simple text message body into multiple sections, each capable of containing a different message element (e.g., attachments).

Nthing A form of segmentation, which pulls every nth (every tenth or twentieth, for example) record from an email list to create a near-random set of subgroups.

Open The act by which a recipient clicks on a message subject and her email client opens a window to display the message.

Opt-in The act of adding one's name to a company's email list to receive messages (also called Subscribe).

Opt-out The act of removing one's name from a company's email list (also called Unsubscribe or Remove).

Permission The act by which a customer grants a marketer consent to contact him.

Permission Marketing A technique by which marketers learn about their customers, earn their trust, and then get their approval to send them messages.

Personalization Adding unique information to a message for each recipient.

Point of Sale The event and location at which a customer purchases a product, generally in a retail store setting.

Policy A set of rules or guiding principals that define how a company uses email for the purposes of marketing and communications.

Post Office Protocol (POP3) (see also Internet Message Access Protocol (IMAP)) A standard by which the recipient's email client retrieves a message from his email server.

Preferences The method by which recipients indicate the kinds of messages they wish to receive, as well as the frequency at which they wish to receive them.

Profile A term used to describe the information a marketer collects about a customer (e.g., gender, address, and date of birth).

Promotional Email A permissioned message sent to an existing customer with the purpose of eliciting a purchase.

Prospecting Email A nonpermissioned message sent to a noncustomer with the purpose of eliciting a purchase.

Redirect A Web technology that routes the user through the sender's email marketing system, records the recipient's click-through and message, then redirects the recipient's Web browser to the final Web site destination.

Registration The process by which new customers fill in personal information on a company's Web site. This process often includes email sign-ups.

Relevancy The appropriateness of a message to its recipient.

Remove See Opt-out

Renderability The ability of a recipient to view a message in his email client in a form visually similar to what the marketer originally intended.

Reply A customer response to a message (e.g., a question, follow up, or opt-out request).

Reporting Engine The technology that translates recipient clicks, opens, and forwards into the behavioral and response data that marketers need to measure campaign success.

Rich Media Video, audio, and animation used to add depth to an email message.

Rich Text A format that includes more advanced fonts, colors, sizes, and spacing than plain text.

Routine Conveyance As defined by CAN-SPAM, the transmission, routing, relaying, handling, or storing of an email message.

Rule of 24 A rule created by marketers to dictate email frequency. The rule suggests that twenty-four is the maximum number of emails to send each customer per year.

Scalability The ability of any technology system to handle large-volume transactions. In the case of email marketing systems, scalability refers to the volume of messages that can be sent in a given period of time, as well as the number of responses, (e.g., click-throughs) that the system can handle at once.

Segmenting Dividing an email list into specific groups to increase the message relevancy to each group. Random segments can also be created to enable testing of different message elements.

Select Creating a segment or subset of an email list.

Self-Service Email Service Provider (ESP) An email marketing company that provides software and technical support only.

Sender A CAN-SPAM term defining the person (or persons) who initiates an email message, and whose product or service is promoted by that message.

Sequenced Messaging See Life Cycle Automation

Service Bureau ESP An email service provider that provides account management, various professional services (e.g., best practices), and on-demand fulfillment, while still enabling marketers to utilize the self-service approach.

Simple Message Transfer Protocol (SMTP) An Internet standard that ensures that the text files containing the message reach their destination intact.

Spam A term for unsolicited "junk" email (once referred to as Unsolicited Commercial Email (UCE) or Unsolicited Bulk Email (UBE)).

Spam Trap An email address posted publicly for the sole purpose of snagging harvesters.

Subscribe See Opt-in.

Targeting Tailoring a message to the interests of a specific recipient or groups of recipients on a company's list.

Test Cell A set of list segments whose primary purpose is to test various elements of a campaign.

Testing A standard marketing technique, which helps senders identify the most effective elements of a campaign.

Timing A form of email segmentation that segments customers based on the time and date they should receive specific messages.

Third-party list A list of email addresses that are available for rental by marketers.

Transactional or Relationship Messages (TRMs) As defined under CAN-SPAM, any message sent within the context of an existing business relationship or transaction (e.g., an electronic receipt).

Triggered Messages (see also Event Triggered Messages or Auto Responders) A form of email automation that automatically sends a message in response to a customer action (e.g., an opt-in) or some other external event.

Types A way to differentiate between categories of email messages so that marketers can appropriately handle each message category.

Unique Opens The total number of recipients that have opened a message (rather than the number of times each recipient opened the message).

Unknown Senders A method of filtering messages by determining whether the sender's address is in the recipient's address book.

Unsubscribe (see also Opt-out) The act of removing one's name from a company's email list.

User Interface Any interface or computer screen that marketers or their full-service vendors use to set up, execute, and report on campaigns.

Viral When an individual forwards a message to friends, family, or co-workers.

Web Beacon A small, invisible image placed in an HTML email message that automatically tracks when the recipient opens the message (also called a Web bug).

White Lists Lists of legitimate senders that ISPs will allow through some of their spam filters.

BIBLIOGRAPHY

Chapter 1

1. Swartz, Jon. "Is the Future of Email Under Cyberattack?" *USA Today*, June 14, 2004.
   http://www.usatoday.com/tech/news/2004-06-14-email_x.htm

2. Associated Press. "Enthusiasts Call Web Feed Next Big Thing." *New York Times*, March 3, 2004.
   http://www.nytimes.com/aponline/technology/AP-Deliver-Me-Web.html

3. Salkever, Alex. "Email: Killer App—Or Just a Killer?" *Business Week Online*, March 1, 2002.
   http://www.businessweek.com/technology/content/mar2002/tc2002031_3760.htm

4. Gartner, Inc. "Gartner Says Marketers Must Differentiate Email Marketing from Spam." Press release, September 29, 2003.

5. "Individual Consumers to Receive More Than 3,900 'Spam' Messages Annually by 2007, Predicts JupiterResearch." JupiterResearch Press Release, September 18, 2002.
   http://www.jupitermedia.com/corporate/releases/02.09.04-spamreport.html

6. Fallows, Deborah. "Spam: How It Is Hurting Email and Degrading Life on the Internet." Pew Research Center, October 22, 2003.

7. "Preferred Method of Communication Among Businesses Worldwide." eMarketer, April 2003.
   http://www.emarketer.com/products/chart.php?30326

8. Susan White, interview by the author, Santa Monica, California, March 25, 2004.

9. "Worldwide Email Usage Forecast, 2002—2006: Know What's Coming Your Way." IDG, September 18, 2002.
   http://www.marketresearch.com/researchindex/823422.html

10. "Teenage Life Online: The Rise of the Instant-Message Generation and the Internet's Impact on Friendships and Family Relationships." Pew Research Center, June 20, 2001.
    http://www.pewinternet.org/reports/toc.asp?Report=36

11. "Email at Work." Pew Research Center, December 8, 2002.
    http://www.pewinternet.org/reports/toc.asp?Report=79

12. "G2 Report", Gartner Inc., March 2002.

13. John Ripa, phone interview by the author, Atlanta, Georgia, March 23, 2004.

Chapter 2

1. Godin, Seth. *Permission Marketing: Turning Strangers into Friends, and Friends into Customers.* New York: Simon & Schuster, 1999.

2. "Enterprise Permission Marketing: Best Practices for Managing Targeted Email Programs Across the Organization." IMT Strategies, 2001.

3. "DoubleClick 2003 Consumer Email Survey." DoubleClick, October 2003.
   http://www.doubleclick.com/us/knowledge_central/documents/research/dc_consumeremailstudy_0310.pdf

Chapter 3

1. "The State of Postal and Email Marketing." Direct Marketing Association, 2002.

2. "The Power of Email Personalization." YesMail, 2002.

3. "Evaluating Email Marketing Effectiveness (Or Not)." e-Dialog, July 30, 2002.
   http://www.emarketer.com/news/article.php?1001421&ref=ed

4. Direct Marketing Association, 2002.

5. "New Study Finds Marketers Investing More This Year in Digital Marketing to Stay Competitive." *USA Today*, CMO Council, and *B2B Magazine*, January 19, 2004.
http://www.responsys.com/corporate/about/news_latest.asp

Chapter 4

1. "eMail Landscape." eMarketer, November 9, 2000.

2. "Email at Work," Pew Research Center.

3. "How Customers Can Enter and Remain in the Customer Email Inner Circle." Quris, September 2003.
http://www.quris.com/resources/pdfs/QurisViewFromInboxInner Circle.pdf

4. Godin, *Permission Marketing*.

5. DoubleClick, October 2003.

Chapter 5

1. Interbrand. "The 100 Top Brands." *BusinessWeek*. August 2003.

2. "Building Brand Loyalty with Email." Quris, October 2002.
http://www.quris.com/resources/pdfs/Quris.BuildingBrandLoyalty WithEmail.pdf

3. "How to Ensure Your Email Practices Win and Not Lose Long-Term Business." Quris, October 2003.
http://www.quris.com/who/release102803.html

4. Elaine O'Gorman, interview by the author, Atlanta, Georgia, January 28, 2004.

5. "Permission Email Marketing: The View from the Inbox." Quris, May 2002.
http://www.executivesummary.com/about/samples/quris.pdf

6. Reichheld, Frederick F. *The Loyalty Effect*. Cambridge, Massachusetts: Harvard Business School Press, 1996.

Chapter 6

1. IMT Strategies, 2001.

2. "First Half 2003 Blocking and Filtering Report," Return Path, 2003. http://www.returnpath.biz/pdf/Blocking_Filtering_Report.pdf

3. "Target Marketing: Using Dynamic Content to Improve Results." JupiterResearch, 2003.

Chapter 7

1. "Q2 Email Trend Report," DoubleClick, 2002. http://www.doubleclick.com/us/knowledge_central/documents/trend_reports/dc_Q2emailtrends_0209.pdf

2. Beth Fisher, phone interview by the author, Atlanta, Georgia, January 16, 2004.

Chapter 8

1. "'Spam and the Law' Experts Offer Hope, Criticism for U.S. Anti-Spam Measures." Institute for Spam and Internet Public Policy, January 26, 2004. http://isipp.org/news20040126.php

2. "Spam: How It Is Hurting Email and Degrading Life on the Internet." Pew Internet and American Life Project, October 22, 2003. http://www.pewinternet.org/reports/pdfs/PIP_Spam_Report.pdf

3. "Spam Driving Away 25% of Emailers." Clickz.com, November 21, 2003. http://www.clickz.com/emailstrategies/rept/article.php/3112291

4. Senator Conrad Burns, interview by the author, Atlanta, Georgia, January 28, 2004.

5. Ibid.

6. CAN-SPAM Act of 2003, 108th Congress, 1st sess., November 25, 2003. http://www.spamlaws.com/federal/108s877.html

7. Ibid.

8. Ibid.

9. Ibid.

10. Ibid

11. John Ripa, phone interview by the author.

12. John Delaney, interview by the author, Atlanta, Georgia, March 16, 2004.

Chapter 10

1. eMarketer, November 9, 2000.

2. "Email Marketing Permission Level Desired by U.S. Consumers, August 2002." NFO WorldGroup, October 15, 2002.

3. Anne Holland, phone interview by the author, Atlanta, Georgia. February 13, 2004.

4. "Executive Summary: Email Marketing Metrics Survey Results—1,711 Marketers Reveal Data." MarketingSherpa, August 21, 2002. http://www.marketingsherpa.com/sample.cfm?contentID=2137

5. Isaacson, Ben. "The Confirmation Quandary." Clickz.com, August 4, 2003. http://www.clickz.com/experts/em_mkt/em_mkt/article.php/2243611

6. "U.S. Consumer Attitudes Toward Legitimate Email Marketing and Spam, November 6—9, 2003." Harris Interactive commissioned by Digital Impact, December 2003.

Chapter 11

1. Brondmo, Hans Peter. *The Engaged Customer.* New York: HarperBusiness, 2000.

2. "U.S. Email User Personalization Preferences, 2001." IMT Strategies, September 2001.

3. DoubleClick, October 2003.

4. Ibid.

5. Godin, *Permission Marketing.*

6. "Sales Lead Generation Email Test—Do Short Forms Really Work Better Than Long Forms?" MarketingSherpa, July 10, 2002.

7. Stephen Newman, phone interview by the author, Atlanta, Georgia, February 20, 2004.

Chapter 12

1. "Overcoming the Spam Effect: Maximizing Email Marketing Message Delivery." JupiterResearch, 2003.

Chapter 13

1. "Function that Owns Email Policy Enforcement," *IMT Strategies interviews with best-in-class marketers*, 2001.

2. Stephen Diorio, phone interview by the author, Atlanta, Georgia, April 4, 2004.

3. Elaine O'Gorman, interview by the author.

4. The Federal Trade Commission. "Privacy Online: Fair Information Practices in the Electronic Marketplace: A Federal Trade Commission Report to Congress," May 2000. http://www.ftc.gov/reports/privacy2000/privacy2000text.pdf

Chapter 15

1. "Number of Separate Email Databases Per Enterprise," *IMT Strategies interviews with best-in-class marketers*, 2001.

2. "Best-in-Class Permission Policy Enforcement Methods," *IMT Strategies interviews with best-in-class marketers*, 2001.

3. "Email Marketing Frequency Used by Retailers in the U.S., 2003," the e-tailing group, April 2003.

4. "Frequency with Which Online Consumers in North America Would Like to Receive Permission Email Promotions and Advertisements, 2002," Forrester Research, April 2002.

5. Sam Fay, phone interview by the author, Atlanta, Georgia, March 15, 2004.

Chapter 17

1. Kaenan Hertz, phone interview by the author, Atlanta, Georgia, May 28, 2004.

2. "Email Marketing Vendor Selection," JupiterResearch, 2004.

Chapter 18

1. MarketingSherpa, August, 21, 2002.
   http://www.marketingsherpa.com/sample.cfm?contentID=2137

2. "Annual Email Address Churn Rate Among U.S. Consumers for Work and Personal Addresses, August 2002." eMarketer, 2002.

3. MarketingSherpa, August 21, 2002.

4. Jay Freshwater, interview by the author, May 10, 2004.

5. Matt Corey, interview by the author, March 3, 2004.

6. Elizabeth Leahy, phone interview by the author, March 3, 2004.

Chapter 19

1. Zolli, Andrew. "How 2.0," *Popular Science*, 87, April 2004.

2. "The State of Email Marketing," JupiterResearch, 2003.

3. Stone, Brad. "Soaking in Spam," *Newsweek*, 66, November 24, 2003.

4. ReturnPath, Inc. "Email Blocking and Filtering Report," March 2004.

5. Daniels, David. "The State of Email Marketing: Perfecting the Appropriate Mix of Art and Science," JupiterResearch, August 25, 2003.

6. DiGuido, Al. "The Delivery RFP," Clickz.com, April 8, 2004. http://www.clickz.com/experts/em_mkt/opt/article.php/3336901

7. Asaravala, Amit. "Yahoo Spam Filter Thwarts FTC," *Wired News*, June 28, 2003. http://www.wired.com/news/politics/0,1283,59427,00.html

8. "House File Deliverability Rates," JupiterResearch Email Marketing Survey, January 2004.

9. "The Broken Link: What Do Recipients *Really* See?" Silverpop, November 2002.

10. Silverpop, November 2002.

Chapter 20

1. Matt Leonard, email interview by the author, Atlanta, Georgia, April 19, 2004.

2. "Segmentation Techniques US Direct Marketers Use for Housefile List Selection for Email vs. Postal Mail, 2002," Direct Marketing Association, October 2002.

3. Jupiter executive survey, JupiterResearch, July 2002.

4. Larry Martine, phone interview by the author, June 11, 2004.

5. MarketingSherpa Email Metrics Survey, MarketingSherpa, 2003.

6. Kaenan Hertz, interview by the author.

7. David Daniels, phone interview by the author, Atlanta, Georgia, May 26, 2004.

8. Ibid.

9. Ibid.

10. Stephen Diorio, phone interview by the author.

11. "Jupiter Executive Survey," July 2002.

12. John Giusti, phone interview by the author, Atlanta, Georgia, May 13, 2004.

Chapter 21

1. "Marketing and Branding Forecast," JupiterResearch, February 12, 2004.

2. Stephen Diorio, phone interview by the author.

3. Jim Nail, phone interview by the author, Atlanta, Georgia, May 21, 2004.

4. Ibid.

5. John Ripa, interview by the author.

6. David Daniels, interview by the author.

7. Nail, Jim. "The Consumer Advertising Backlash," Forrester Research, May 28, 2004.

ACKNOWLEDGEMENTS

I cannot even begin to thank all of the people who have helped both directly and indirectly with this tremendous effort. First and foremost, I'd like to thank my colleagues, my clients, and my family who have been so generous with their support and encouragement. A great deal of credit for this project goes to my friends and clients throughout the industry who have spent hundreds of hours with me to help develop the thinking behind CCM. Many of these people have generously contributed the case studies and quotes you have seen throughout the book.

There are a few individuals I specifically want to recognize because they played key roles in bringing this book to completion. I want to thank Diane Stuckey, who thought I should try my hand at writing, and Stephen Diorio, whose nonstop mind helped me form many of the core ideas in this book. Thanks to Elaine O'Gorman, who is the only Level 4 emailer I know. Thanks to Jennifer Harrison, who helped produce this whole project from beginning to end. Thanks to Pete Nelson who designed the beautiful cover art and page design. But most of all, I want to thank Stephanie Watson, who helped me write this book, word for word. Stephanie helped me transform hundreds of pages of notes, interviews, and case studies into something readable, fun and, hopefully, educational.

Last but not least, I want to recognize the wit and wisdom of Sir Winston Churchill. His quotes inspired many of the chapters in this book. One of my favorites describes the journey of an author, "Writing a book is an adventure. To begin with, it is a toy and an amusement; then it becomes a mistress, and then it becomes a master, and then a tyrant. The last phase is that just as you are about to be reconciled to your servitude, you kill the monster, and fling him out to the public."

INDEX

A

A/B split, 69, 288
Access control, 200
Acxiom, 20, *See* Ripa, John
Administrative emails. *See* Message Types
Advertising, 305
Affirmative consent, 68, 101, 133, 257
Agencies, 76, 237
American Airlines, 63, 124, 144
    opt-out strategy, 162
    preference page, 144
Animation. *See* Rich media
AOL, 83, 145, 273, 278
APIs, 88, 235
Appends, 69, 246, 252
Application Service Provider. *See* ASP
ASP, 76
Audio. *See* Rich media
Authentication, 109, 273
Auto responders, 80

B

Bayesian filters, 270
Behavior targeting, 79
Beyond-E, 11
Black lists, 263, 266, 277
Bombay. *See* Corey, Matt
BondedSender, 276
Bounces, 69, 73, 89, 268-269
British Sky Broadcasting. *See* Sky
Brondmo, Hans Peter, 142
BSkyB. *See* Sky
Burns, Senator Conrad, 98, 122

C

California spam law, 97
CallerID. *See* Authentication
Campaign automation. *See* Life cycle
    automation
Campaign Value Exchange, 118, 299
CAN-SPAM, 21, 94, 195, 307
    adult content label, 108
    bounty system, 109
    deliverability, 264
    governance, 174
    interpersonal email, 122, 159
    opt-outs, 106, 126, 154, 190, 209
    penalties, 103
    physical address, 106
    subject label, 109
    viral, 75, 122
CCM, 8, 11, 13, 22, 43, 48, 160, 174,
    184, 299
CEMM, 100, 117, 140
Challenge response, 271
Channels, 192
Click to view, 77
Click-throughs, 75
    tracking, 92
CNN, 231
Co-branded list rentals, 248
Commerical electronic email message.
    See CEMM
Confirmations, 138
Confirmed opt-in permission. *See* Levels
    of permission
Content block, 290
Content element, 291
Content rules, 291-292
Control group, 70, 286

341

Expertise, 301
Expertise, types of, 226
Expertise, validation of, 227

F

False positives, 78, 263
Fay, Sam, 205
Federal Trade Commission. *See* FTC
Filters. *See* Spam filters
Flash (Macromedia), 77
Forward to a friend. *See* Viral
Frequency, 32, 39, 63, 147, 187, 189,
    198, 200, 202
From field, 33, 37, 61, 190, 251
FTC, 98, 122, 155, 263, *See* Goodman,
    Michael

G

Global opt-out. *See* Opt-outs, global
Godin, Seth, 30, 54, 74, 149
Goodman, Michael, 107
Governance, 188
    centralized, 180, 199
    decentralized, 179, 200
    federated, 180, 200
GSG Entertainment. *See* Leahy,
    Elizabeth
Guiding principles. *See* Policy

H

Hard bounce, 73
Hertz, Kaenan, 232, 287
Holland, Anne, 136
House list, 68, 175, 245
HTML email, 82, 84, 278

I

IBM, 155, 283
Image hosting, 85, 250
Image suppression, 139, 272, 280
Images suppression, 92
IMAP, 84
Inbox overflow, 301
Initiate, 102
Insource, 224, 308
Instant Messaging, 311
Integration, 156, 191, 207, 228, 295
Interpersonal email. *See* Message types
Interruption marketers, 30
IronPort. *See* BondedSender
ISPs, 10, 79, 90, 103, 131, 229, 262,
    264, 266, 273, 306
IT department, 42, 86, 207, 215, 217,
    224, 228, 231, 308

J

Jupiter Research. *See* Daniels, David

L

Lands' End, 39
Leahy, Elizabeth, 259
Legislation. *See* CAN-SPAM and Data
    Protection Directive
Leonard, Matt, 283
Level of emailer, 36, 228, 236, 241, 290
    level 1, 36, 282
    Level 2, 38
    Level 3, 40, 211, 214, 231
Levels of permission, 68, 131
    confirmed opt-in, 135
    customer permission assumed, 140,
        252
    customer permission requested, 140
    double opt-in, 136
    opt-in, 134
    opt-out, 132

ABOUT THE AUTHOR

Bill Nussey's long history with email began with his role as CEO of Da Vinci Systems, a pioneer in personal computer electronic mail. Over its ten-year history, Da Vinci sold more than 3 million licenses in 45 countries. In 1994, Nussey sold Da Vinci to Boston-based ON Technology. Nussey then spent several years in venture capital with Greylock Managementwhere he was involved with the funding of DoubleClick, MediaMetrix and several other early leaders in online marketing. Nussey left Greylock to become President and, later, CEO of one of Greylock's portfolio companies, iXL. During Nussey's 3-year tenure, iXL executed its initial public offering, grew revenues 10-fold, added several thousand employees and provided consulting services to hundreds of Global 1000 organizations. While at iXL, Nussey was named "The Most Influential Consultant" in the world by Consulting Magazine. In 2000, Nussey left iXL and returned to the email marketing industry as the CEO of Silverpop. Mr. Nussey lives with his family in Atlanta, Georgia. Nussey earned a bachelors degree in Electrical Engineering from North Carolina State University and an MBA from Harvard Business School.

ABOUT SILVERPOP

Silverpop is a leading provider of permission-based email marketing solutions, strategy and services, helping marketers cultivate and maintain long-term strategic relationships with customers and partners. The company has had the privilege to partner with over 150 clients including The American Management Association, The Bombay Company, British Sky Broadcasting, CheckFree, Museum of Modern Art, The Principal Financial Group, Sallie Mae, Mazda, Volvo, and The Weather Channel. In 2004, JupiterResearch ranked Silverpop as offering the "highest overall business value" in the ESP industry.

The revolution in online direct marketing is changing how companies acquire and utilize technology-driven services like email marketing. Silverpop differentiates itself through strong technology, strategic services, and the industry's most flexible service model. Visit http://www.silverpop.com/ccmbook for more information.

0-595-33060-6

Printed in the United States
44097LVS00004B/43

9 780595 330607